AUSTRALIAN RESIDENTIAL PROPERTY DEVELOPMENT FOR INVESTORS

REVISED AND UPDATED

AUSTRALIAN RESIDENTIAL PROPERTY DEVELOPMENT FOR INVESTORS

REVISED AND UPDATED

RON FORLEE

WILEY

First published in 2015 by Wrightbooks, an imprint of John Wiley & Sons Australia, Ltd 42 McDougall St, Milton Qld 4064

Reprinted with updates 2022

Office also in Melbourne

Typeset in 11.3/14 pt ITC Berkeley Oldstyle Std

© Sandale Pty Ltd 2015

The moral rights of the author have been asserted

Cover design by Wiley

Cover Image: © Franck Boston/Shutterstock

Disclaimer
The material in this publication is of the nature of general comment only, and does not represent professional advice. It is not intended to provide specific guidance for particular circumstances and it should not be relied on as the basis for any decision to take action or not take action on any matter which it covers. Readers should obtain professional advice where appropriate, before making any such decision. To the maximum extent permitted by law, the author and publisher disclaim all responsibility and liability to any person, arising directly or indirectly from any person taking or not taking action based on the information in this publication.

To my father, Gordon Forlee, who passed away this year, 2014 — your strong cultural beliefs and honesty are embedded in my memory forever.

Contents

About the author

Ron is an architect, property developer and author. He is also the CEO of Phaeton Pty Ltd, a blockchain technology enterprise creating innovative blockchain solutions in real estate development and investment.

Over the past 42 years, Ron has been involved in a range of real estate developments, from housing estates and hotels to shopping centres, which he has managed and financed. As an architect, he has master-planned large-scale communities and infrastructure projects and designed commercial buildings such as shopping centres, office blocks and tourism developments in Australia, South Africa and China.

Ron has hands-on experience in real estate and infrastructure development through undertaking personal real estate developments. As an expert in real estate development, infrastructure, master planning and architecture, Ron has written and published several books on real estate development and building construction. He has also delivered papers at seminars about his primary interest.

In addition to his books, Ron provides online educational courses on real estate development through his website www.ronforlee.com. These courses are based on his experience over four decades as an architect and real estate developer. In providing these programs he aims to educate people to undertake developments properly. Developers make money by taking a significant risk, but this should not be their sole motivating factor. Developers are decision-makers in creating environments for future generations. Their responsibility is therefore to create ecologically sustainable environments that all can enjoy.

Acknowledgements

This book would not have been possible without the support and encouragement of certain people who have contributed to my life in so many ways. I express my special gratitude to:

- my mother, Mabel, for her unwavering support, for encouraging me to live my dreams, and for teaching me to become an ethical and honest person who contributes to society

- my late wife, Cindy, who loved and supported me through good and bad times, and always gave me the space and freedom to further my career and to write my books

- my children, Taryn, Jared and Charisse, who have loved and supported me in every possible way

- my family and close friends who have always believed in me as I have pursued my career endeavours and personal aspirations.

Preface

It has been over eighteen years since my first book *The Intelligent Guide to Property Development in Australia* was published followed by *Australian Residential Property Development* six years later. Since these publications, I have gained additional knowledge and experience. Over this period, I travelled to three continents, Australia, Asia and Africa, working on various projects from housing estates to large scale infrastructure developments for private and listed companies and government Institutions. So, in 2014 I wrote *Australian Residential Property Development for Investors*. This book is an updated version of that 2014 volume.

Although the majority of my work in property development over the last twenty years has been in the commercial and infrastructure sector, I have found that there is still a strong interest in Australia in the residential sector as shown by the numerous emails I received over the years. It is for this reason that I decided to write another book on residential development with new information and new concepts. Although this book is similar to *Australian Residential Property Development*, this book is more advanced and sheds new light on how modern technology can facilitate the development process with additional chapters such as 'Utilising modern technology' and 'Development economics', a subject that is vital to any property developer.

The book describes the fundamentals of residential property development in Australia and then covers specific asset types from residential land developments to apartment developments with case studies. Examining these asset types individually shows that while the development principles are similar, each type has its own peculiarities. It does not discuss additions and alterations or single home speculation, subjects that are well covered by other authors.

This book is a prequel to my new book *Real Estate Development Strategy for Investors* which covers various strategies, including forming syndicates and joint ventures, developing with minimal cash, creative financing, securing low-cost development sites and creating a real estate portfolio with passive income. It also covers the new technology movements of Proptech, Fintech and Contech and how Blockchain Technology is disrupting the real estate industry. If you want to advance your career in property development, it is worthwhile reading this new book.

Ron Forlee B.Arch
info@ronforlee.com
February 2022

CHAPTER 1
An overview of property development

As the global population continues to increase, so does the demand for food and shelter. Our survival depends directly on how we use and manage our land and resources. As humans have evolved, so have our uses of land—for agriculture and shelter, but also for recreation, shopping, education, transport, business activities and entertainment. In our homes we live, eat and sleep; commercial buildings provide space for social and business interaction, and retail centres for selling of goods and services. As our communities expand, the demand for all these facilities increase, and this is where property developers are needed. The population of Australia, currently around 26.8 million, is projected to rise to 40 million by 2060; much more housing and facilities will have to be provided to accommodate this growth.

In simple terms, property development can be described as providing solutions to the demands for real estate in our society by designing, financing and constructing facilities that satisfy this demand. It is a profession that requires meticulous and thorough research together with a firm understanding of the property industry, and current and future market conditions. Some consider property development a skill, but in reality it is the analytical process of aligning the current and projected market with the associated risks and financial rewards in relation to a specific development project. Successful developers understand these fundamentals and are therefore able to sustain their reputation in a highly volatile industry in which others have failed through bad strategies or timing or simple greed.

The role of a property developer

A property developer is a disciplined professional with an entrepreneurial flair who specialises in creating new developments and successfully marketing and selling them. Depending on the type and scale of the development, some developers work with partners in order to share the risk and workload. Developers come from a wide variety of backgrounds. Some work for companies that undertake large-scale developments while others work on their own, focusing on smaller residential projects. Some hold university degrees in commerce or have a background as a real estate agent, property valuer, builder, engineer or architect. It is regrettable that only a few universities offer degrees in property development, as property developers are people who ultimately control our urban fabric, influencing the social outcome of communities.

Property development is a risky business with many challenges, but at the same time it can be very exciting and financially rewarding. Before taking on a project, developers need to assess a wide variety of potential sites to determine which will be financially feasible and marketable. A seasoned or visionary developer can look at a vacant site and conceive a potential opportunity or analyse an older building and envisage its transformation for an alternative use. In either case, the developer will embark on the development only if the demand exists. Experience in the property market is important: a developer must understand the market well in order to establish whether or not a project will be viable. Developers also need a business network and contacts in local government who can assist them in accomplishing projects. These contacts may range from people in the planning department who can provide recommendations to help push a project through to councillors who can assist in promoting their projects or real estate agents who can source potential development sites.

A reputable property developer is the leader and visionary of a development team. They work with architects, engineers, contractors, politicians, real estate agents and numerous other professionals to see a project through from inception to completion. Developers have to select good teams, organise them well and manage them effectively, meeting the needs of the project and the team members while maintaining control of the overall development. They can select a particular area of specialty, such as land subdivision, residential apartments, low-income housing, commercial offices, retail shopping centres or hotels. They may choose to work in a specific geographical location or across a wider region where their skills gives them an edge over local developers.

Types of property developers

There are many different types of developments in the property industry, and by the same token there are many different types of property developers. They can be part-time investors or full-time professionals. Whatever category they fall into, the underlying development principles and strategies remain the same. Listed below are definitions of some typical developers.

Part-time developers

This group consists of novice developers, investors who hold a full-time job, or small syndicates of friends or business associates. These developers often aim to hold onto the development as a long-term investment. They may purchase a single lot and build a small residential building or a small shopping centre, or they may buy an existing building and then add value through renovation and by negotiating new leases with existing or new tenants. Most will pursue a long-term investment but a small percentage will seek to sell at a profit. Their developments are characterised by a frequent number of transactions, a small number of holdings, low equity, the importance placed on long-term capital gain and a positive rental income.

Full-time professionals

This group consists mainly of individuals or partners who have decided to pursue property development as a career. They may be accountants, quantity surveyors, construction managers, project managers, builders, architects, engineers, real estate agents or other individuals whose first few developments were financially rewarding. These developers are normally highly geared and well aware of the latest financial instruments. They seek to maximise taxation benefits and capital gains from their developments. The majority of this group focus on small to medium projects, from strata residential buildings to smaller commercial retail developments. They concentrate their efforts in locations with good infrastructure, including convenient access to transport.

Corporations

This group includes property development companies and major financial institutions. They could be privately owned corporations, public companies listed on the stock exchange, large insurance groups, superannuation funds or trade unions. Generally, these groups develop larger commercial properties such as regional shopping centres with a view to generating profits for their shareholders through long-term capital gain and good cash flow through positive rental income. These corporations generally have a number of qualified professionals who seek new developments and manage the project from inception to completion. Thereafter the property management division will take over and ensure the smooth running of the building.

Government/institutional

This category consists mainly of state governments, at times assisted by the federal government. Types of developments include government offices, hospitals, police stations, industrial land subdivisions and other public institutions. In some state-run programs they may involve the private sector and either seek a joint venture or tender a developable portion of land to private developers.

Fee developers

Fee developers are professionals with both qualifications and experience who will contract with an owner of land to develop their property for a fee. These developers are experienced in all phases of commercial or residential development. They are familiar with all aspects of developments including finance and feasibility studies. They understand the risks involved and how to mitigate them. These developers may also be part of an investment syndicate, and while they maintain a shareholding they are paid a fee to manage the development process. Fees charged for their professional service can range from 3 to 5 per cent, depending on the complexity of the project. First-time developers and time-poor investors should consider employing such professionals.

Residential versus commercial developments

Before you decide to embark on a career in property development, it is important to a gain a good understanding of the difference between residential and commercial property development. Residential is a lot easier to understand and to start out with, while commercial requires more experience and is associated with greater returns and higher risks.

The key difference between residential and commercial developments is the assessment of their value as an asset in dollar terms. With residential, the value is based mainly on supply and demand, whereas the value of commercial properties is based on the income stream or annual rent of the property known as the 'annual yield' from the property. This means that no matter how architecturally attractive the commercial building may be or how much it cost to build, its value will ultimately depend on the leases and the net income stream the building produces. Other differences between these assets are described later and summarised in table 1.1.

Table 1.1: residential versus commercial developments

Residential	Commercial
Market research localised	Market research based on macro or regional level
Valuation based on supply and demand	Valuation based on the net income of the property
Improving value a lot easier	Limitations to adding value
Less sensitive to competition for rental growth	Sensitive to competition from similar building types
More opportunities for building improvements	Fewer opportunities for building improvements
Larger purchaser base	Smaller purchaser base
Easier finance	More complex financing
More flexibility in exiting	Limited exit strategies
Less sophisticated purchasers — shorter negotiations	Sophisticated purchasers — longer negotiations
Greater capital growth in boom times	Less capital growth in boom times
Shorter vacancy periods	Longer vacancy periods

Research

In analysing the property market for a potential development, one would need to undertake more intensive market research with commercial property than with residential. While residential supply and demand is localised, the demand for commercial properties is based on a macro or regional area as commercial properties require greater market audience to make a development viable.

Long-term values

The long-term value of any property, whether residential or commercial, is subject to a range of variables, which can include neighbourhood characteristics, demographic shifts, level of development activity, community facilities, schools, transport services and the status of the local economy. A well-selected residential property in the right location allows for the most effective management and control of these variables. By contrast, commercial property can depreciate as a result of a single unforeseen event, such as the closure of a road or construction of new outlets close by. Commercial property can also benefit from a monopoly, however, especially if there is no further development that would create competition.

Value adding

Developers in residential property can potentially add value to their properties, for example by constructing a second storey or garage or by renovating the kitchen or bathroom. On the other hand, with commercial properties these opportunities are relatively limited even in prime locations, where the established street frontages and local government regulations can prohibit large-scale renovation works. On the positive side, the owner of commercial property can improve the returns and capital value of their building by undertaking a cosmetic makeover to improve the look of building or by changing the lease to offer more favourable terms.

Rental growth

Although rental growth will vary according to location, commercial property offers greater opportunities for growth when compared with residential. Rental yields, which are based on supply and demand for accommodation, are generally lower in residential properties than in commercial. Annual rental increases on commercial leases are generally in line with the consumer price index (CPI) or 4 per cent, whichever is the greater. This is not always achievable with residential property. Commercial property leases tend to be much longer as well—from three to twenty years—and are quite often secured by bank guarantees, which make them a secure investment.

Market size

Depending on its location, a residential development can cater for a broader market than a commercial property. It is also easier to market and sell a residential development, such as an apartment block, as it can be broken down into smaller units that can be divided into strata sections and sold to a number of purchasers. A commercial building with similar floor area, such as small office block or shopping centre, would look to a single purchaser.

Initial investment

Based on the scale of the development, most residential projects require a smaller amount of capital to get started. In addition, lending institutions have the infrastructure and systems to make it easier for the consumer to apply for a home loan. With more banks and new mortgage companies entering the market, finance for a home is a lot easier to secure than for a commercial development. As commercial developments require larger capital, the application for funding is more complex and takes longer to gain approval.

Liquidity

With residential finance more readily available for end-purchasers, housing developments are a lot easier to sell than commercial developments. This allows residential developers to exit their development earlier. In addition, there are generally not as many conditions attached to the purchase of a residential property, making settlement and the sales procedure a lot quicker. With commercial developments, finding an end-buyer can be complicated as these buyers, being more sophisticated, will impose more stringent conditions. A commercial project will also generally take longer to construct, thereby incurring more interest.

Purchasers

Purchasers of residential property are not as sophisticated as seasoned investors interested in commercial properties. Commercial property investors will generally negotiate strongly on a number of issues thereby delaying the settlement, which in turns affects the developer's profit. A residential property generally is sold based on a standard offer and acceptance executed by a real estate agent, whereas for larger commercial properties a solicitor is required to formalise the purchase.

Capital growth

During the boom period of a property cycle, residential properties have a far greater capital growth than commercial. A shortage of residential properties on the market will drive prices up, whereas the value of commercial properties is tied to the term of a lease with only a CPI-related increase in value. However, most commercial properties have a rent review over an agreed period to make up the loss of capital growth during the boom period.

Leasing

Commercial properties can be harder to lease owing to the specific requirements of commercial tenants. In some instances, owners who are pressed to find a commercial tenant will offer generous lease terms to make sure the property is not vacant. These terms can take the form of rent-free periods or heavy expenditure to meet the tenant's specific needs. They could also delay a project as a certain percentage of leases could be a precondition for construction finance. With residential, the developer has the flexibility to sell part of the development to individual purchasers and rent out the balance — if, of course, the residential developer has selected to develop in a location where there is good infrastructure.

From the foregoing assessment it may seem that commercial properties involve greater risks. In general this is true, but for the knowledgeable and experienced there are greater profits to be made for the same investment of time and personal engagement in the commercial sector than in residential developments. Remember, the higher the risk the more profitable the investment.

Types of residential developments

Residential developments can be categorised into the following areas.

Renovations

Some older suburbs in capital cities offer exceptional opportunities for renovating older homes and the developer can be rewarded with good returns within a short period. These renovations may require structural alterations or additional rooms or involve no more than adding some paint to bring the building to present market standards.

Speculative homes

The speculative new home is usually built on a single lot in a new land subdivision or on an older block that has been subdivided to create smaller lots, as normally found in older suburbs. Developers can also market 'house and land' packages, subdividing the land into smaller lots and then selling two contracts, one for the land and the other with a selected building contractor.

Small units

These smaller unit developments of two to six single- or double-storey units are commonly found in suburban areas of both new and old subdivisions and may be defined as villas or townhouses. They can be developed as strata-type units or small green title lots. This scale of development is ideal for the novice developer as they sit in the lower risk category, subject to the developer selecting the right location and undertaking a comprehensive market research and analysis.

Group housing

Under this category one would find a group of eight or more units, which can include townhouses, villas or retirement villages. Each development will have its own architectural theme defined by similar use of materials, scale and building style. Larger projects of 20 or more units are best built in phases in order to mitigate risk and improve cash flow.

Apartments

These buildings are found mainly in the inner-city areas of capital cities. They are defined as dwellings in a group of more than one where any part of a dwelling is built vertically above part of any other. As urban populations grow and infrastructure costs in sprawling cities increase, suburbs close to the central business districts (CBD) with good services and transport systems are allowing increasing densities, which encourages apartment developments.

Government housing

Also known as public or social housing, these developments are provided by the government for members of the community who cannot afford either to purchase their own home or to cover the higher rents demanded in the marketplace. Given their own limited resources, governments cannot provide all the social housing required and will enter into joint ventures with developers or provide tax incentives to developers in providing such housing.

Residential land

These developments can vary in scale from small backyard subdivisions to larger scale suburban community land developments. The latter require intensive town planning in conjunction with the local council's planning department and various other government authorities. While these developments carry less construction risk, the developer will require enough cash to endure the lengthy and protracted approval process.

Niche residential developments

In addition to the foregoing residential developments, we can consider a number of developments as niche markets. These include:

- holiday homes
- timeshare apartments

- cooperative housing
- student accommodation
- lifestyle villages
- caravan parks.

Types of commercial developments

Commercial properties can be categorised into the following areas.

Office buildings

Office buildings are rented to non-retail commercial users. These structures are designed as low-rise, mid-rise or high-rise buildings and can consist of one to 20 stories or more depending on the zoning and density regulations. Users of the office space sell and administrate a service to the public. Offices do not need a retail location and depending on their quality and finishes can be classified as class A, B or C offices. Following are various types of office accommodation:

- renovated house
- strata title offices
- office parks
- multi-storey office blocks.

Retail centres

While individual investors without any particular expertise frequently own small strip shops and neighbourhood shopping centres, more experienced, knowledgeable and financially able investment groups usually undertake investment in larger retail outlets. The bigger retail developments also involve complicated analysis, planning, financing, leasing and management problems. These retail centres include:

- corner-shop convenience store
- strip shopping
- neighbourhood shopping centre ($1000m^2 - 5000m^2$)

- district shopping centre (5000m² – 20 000m²)

- regional shopping centre (20 000m² plus)

- hyper-centre (20 000m² plus)

- theme centres (size varies)—these are retail centres designed around a common theme, such as a:

  - discount centre

  - factory outlet centre

  - fashion centre

  - car care centre.

Industrial buildings

Buildings that provide rental space to users of bulk storage are defined as industrial buildings. These buildings are designed for users, requiring a small percentage of office space (10 to 20 per cent) with the balance being large warehouses with loading facilities. Industrial properties are broken down into:

- office–warehouse

- service industrial units

- distribution centres

- bulk distribution

- manufacturing facilities

- storage facilities.

Tourist accommodation

Tourist buildings include varied facilities common to different types of short stay or destinations such as accommodation, restaurants, eateries, entertainment, leisure and relaxation. They can be further defined as:

- hotels

- serviced apartments

- motels
- casinos
- entertainment centres
- resort golf course estates
- marina developments
- waterfront developments
- theme parks
- conference centres.

Educational centres

Educational facilities can vary from private primary schools to tertiary centres such as colleges and universities with adjacent science technology parks. Categories include:

- child-care centres
- primary to high schools
- colleges
- universities
- science and technology parks.

Medical buildings

The development of medical facilities can be lucrative if well-located sites are found. Facilities can vary from small doctor's rooms to operating theatres in larger buildings. The buildings can be categorised into:

- clinics
- suburban medical centres
- neighbourhood medical centres
- private hospitals
- regional hospitals.

Mixed-use developments

A mixed-use development can vary with different asset classes, with a mix of residential and commercial buildings. This type of development is found closer to the central business district or transport nodes.

Niche markets

These specialised developments are not normally available to the average investor or developer and can include:

- petrol outlets
- sports stadiums
- parking lots and garages.

Benefits and risks in property development

Development, whether of a residential or a commercial property, can be a very exciting and financially rewarding exercise. However, it is a business where the stakes are high and where fortunes are made and lost. It is therefore not for the faint-hearted but rather for bold entrepreneurs who are willing to test their abilities, vision and smart decision making. These decisions can shape our environment and communities or win immortality for the developer who creates a striking architectural building or complex.

When calculating the risk–reward equation, developers should weigh up all the positives against the negatives. A common analogy is that higher potential returns call for higher degrees of risk, and conversely lower returns require less potential risk. Although there are a number of risks associated property developments, the following lists include the most universal.

Rewards in property developments

Despite economic changes, property development and real estate in general retain many unique benefits compared with other investments. Real estate offers tax and leverage advantages that are not easy to obtain with routine stock and bond investments. The following are a range of possible benefits with property development that should be balanced against the potential risks.

Entrepreneurial opportunities

Compared with other investments such as shares, property development can offer a number of entrepreneurial business opportunities. By providing their own labour and limited capital input, developers can realise a vision to improve or renovate existing buildings, or rezone and subdivide land, resulting in healthy profits. Many real estate millionaires started with small-scale residential or renovation developments. Today these entrepreneurs are building our cities and creating job opportunities.

Cash flow

Cash flow can be generated by sales of residential units or strata commercial office or industrial units that have been completed or sold off plan. Alternatively, units can be rented at market value, thereby generating cash flow and further capital growth. The rental income should exceed the interest cost to ensure a positive cash flow.

Financial leveraging

Most property developments are made using borrowed funds from financial institutions, otherwise known as *leveraging* (or *gearing*). A small amount of personal equity is used to borrow the total capital cost of the development in order to realise a larger return than the initial deposit invested.

Tax benefits

To assist the various housing and infrastructure needs of our increasing population, governments offer a number of tax incentives for the private sector to invest in property development. In addition to depreciation, a number of other expenditures involving property development can also be deducted as expenses. It is often possible to deduct the development costs, property rates and taxes and any payable interest as expenses, ultimately reducing taxable income.

Creative financing

Yields from property development can be greatly improved by creative financing techniques and clever negotiating strategies. Astute developers with a strong understanding of financing have launched developments with minimal personal financial input. Some creative developers have managed to secure 100 per cent financing without any security excepting the property they are developing.

Manufactured equity

Instead of buying a newly completed building at market value, a property developer can develop a similar building at 15 to 20 per cent below market value. This is generally known as the developer's margin, with the agent's commission, marketing and other costs usually included in the price of the sale. By holding property as an investment the developer has automatically created a manufactured equity. This means the rental yields will be higher than for someone who bought their property at market value.

Equity build-up

Apart from the manufactured equity, developers can hold properties as long-term investments to improve their equity position as inflation is constantly increasing the value of their equity. This equity can be used to provide a deposit for another development or sold and leveraged for a larger project.

Pooled equity

Developers working on larger projects can establish a syndicate of investors to provide additional equity. This pooled equity allows access to investment in larger development opportunities, markets and diversity that might not be available to individual investors. A developer can also enter a joint venture or partnership with landowners to share the required equity for a new development.

Easier refinance

Once the development is complete, the developer can approach lenders to refinance their property. If an 80 per cent loan can be secured based on the retail value when completed, then the 20 per cent is close to the manufactured equity, which allows the developer to take out their initial equity. Banks are usually comfortable with this as they are not financing development risk and the loan will always be underpinned by the security of real estate.

All these benefits allow the developer to grow their property portfolio faster than by investing in established properties. Developers can be owners of high-growth properties that cost them less to own and at the same time provide generous returns on the initial equity plus tax benefits.

Risks in property developments

All investments are subject to risks. They may go down in value as well as up, and investors can experience investment losses as well as gains. Different types of investments perform differently at different times, having different risk characteristics and volatility.

There are many risks (of varying degrees) associated with property development, including market risk, leasing risk and construction risk. It is imperative that a developer understand all these elements and mitigate the risks by applying certain strategies and targeting a return relative to such risks.

General risks

General risks that can affect a development include:

- *Economic risk:* Returns are affected by a range of economic factors, such as changes in interest rates, exchange rates, inflation, general share market conditions or government policies, fluctuations in general market prices for property, and the general state of the domestic and world economies.

- *Taxation risk:* Tax returns from any development may be influenced by changes in taxation laws or their interpretation.

- *Terrorism risk:* The unpredictable nature and social and physical destructiveness of terrorist events may affect the earnings and attractiveness of investments, resulting in losses.

Global risk

World events such as the recent pandemic affected many businesses including real estate. The lockdowns affected supply chains and lead to worker shortages to a point where many building companies collapsed.

Market risk

Any change in property market sentiment during the construction of a project may influence the price and the targeted return. This can affect the profitability of the project and/or the developer's ability to repay the construction loan. To mitigate this risk the developer should undertake thorough market research and analysis into the type of property and the market needs in the area.

Development risk

Risks associated with any property development may include:

- *Planning approval risk:* Planning approvals for a project may be delayed or denied for a variety of reasons. This can affect the time it takes to commence or complete a project.

- *Interest rate risk:* Upward movement in interest rates may affect the profitability of projects.

- *Legal and regulatory risk:* A project may be affected by changes in government policy and/or legislation.

As part of a project's due diligence, the developer should review the project feasibility report prepared by experienced consultants in the planning and approval process. Depending on the risk profile of the project, these risks may be mitigated by fixing interest rates, imposing pre-sale requirements or investing only after development approval has been obtained.

Liquidity risk

Unlike other commodities such as shares or bonds, property cannot be traded on a daily basis. A developer may plan to develop a property for a quick sale but may be stuck with the property if the market is in a downward trend. Property is generally sold with conditions and these could delay the flow of funds and hence the developer's cash flow. To mitigate this risk, it is advisable that the developer has a contingency cash reserve for this eventuality.

Borrowing risk

Borrowings will magnify gains or losses and increase the volatility of returns. Volatility will result from fluctuations in interest rates and risks associated with refinancing loans once the terms expire. A way of mitigating this risk is for the developer not to leverage or gear too highly. Depending on the project's risk profile, the developer should aim not to exceed debt levels of 65 per cent of the final asset value or 70 per cent of the total development cost.

Risk of bad purchase

A developer will always face the risk of paying too much for a development site, buying in the wrong location or failing to obtain the development approval (DA) for the type of building they envisaged. This can happen if the developer is impatient and does not obtain the correct market information or is influenced by an overzealous real estate sales consultant. The risk of a bad purchase can be reduced by better negotiating skills, more extensive market research and making settlement conditional on securing a DA.

Construction risk

During the construction phase of a development potential risks can include the following:

- The construction costs for a project may exceed the budget, which will reduce the potential profit from the project.

- The construction period may exceed the projected building schedule, delaying settlement of sales and/or leasing of the building.

- The builder may run into financial problems and may not be able to complete the building, requiring the developer to employ another builder, which could ultimately increase costs.

To reduce these potential risks, the developer should appoint reputable and experienced contractors who have adequate insurance cover and sufficient financial resources for the type of works for which they are engaged.

Business failure

All types of business are subject to the risk of business failure and property development is no different. It can be a result of bad management, a decline in the local economy, change in consumer tastes or bad timing, for example. Good management, careful market research and creative marketing can help to reduce this type of failure.

Minimising risk

The aim of the developer is to minimise these risks as far as possible. Some additional strategies that can be applied are listed here.

- *Allow for contingencies*: To protect against financial risk during the purchasing stage, prepare for various contingencies in the contract.

- *Diversify investments*: Diversification of development and investment activity into different building types as well as localities will assist in the mitigation of risk.

- *Limit ownership liability*: Property developers should select a special purpose vehicle (SPV) for each project to protect themselves from personal liability in relation to tenants, consultants, contractors and the general public.

- *Limit financial liability*: Developers should aim to effect non-recourse financing for all loans and use an SPV to shield their personal assets. Another approach is to find financial equity partners who will help to carry any financial losses.

Summary

This chapter provides an overview of property development and the risks and rewards in both residential and commercial development. You must decide whether you have the motivation and personality to take up this profession or whether the industry carries too much risk for you personally. If you conclude that it is worth your while you need to understand that success will not be achieved overnight. It will take several years of learning and experience, and some hard knocks, to build up a full understanding of what it means to be a property developer. The following chapter offers some key insights into being a successful practitioner.

CHAPTER 2

Characteristics of a successful developer

The property development industry offers boundless opportunities for those who are prepared to take the time to acquire the knowledge that most buyers and sellers of established real estate do not have. It is *not* a business that will reward those who act quickly or spontaneously or who operate purely on gut feeling. Only a few who depend for success on luck alone will profit by it. It is a risky business, in which the stakes are often high when compared with other ventures. But with high risks come potentially higher returns. The successful developers I know work on strategies to reduce the risks associated with their projects as well as their personal financial exposure.

What makes a successful developer

Property development is an innovative and rewarding entrepreneurial activity that attracts a diverse range of people with various backgrounds and skills. In a development project of any size, a team of people with different skill sets is required from start to finish, and for the project to succeed there must be a leader, a highly motivated visionary and entrepreneur who drives the team. As in all businesses, there are good, principled entrepreneurs and unethical ones. Consistently successful developers take a professional and ethical approach to their business.

The successful property developer has a full understanding of the development process from the inception of the project to the final operation of the building(s) and understands the roles of the various participants in the process. As leader, he or she must have the ability to analyse, conduct and test the feasibility and financial aspects of the project. Other prerequisites for success are good management skills in development planning, development management and project management and a good understanding of construction methods. As with all entrepreneurs, the property developer must have the ability to read the market. Last but not least the developer has to understand the various risks involved in the project and develop strategies to mitigate these risks. In summary, successful property development requires the following interacting components.

Passion

Successful developers are passionate about property and thrive on all aspects of this stimulating industry. They talk about property constantly and read voraciously to build on their knowledge and skills. They relish the challenges that property development offers and are prepared to take risks. These developers have a passion for excellence and an eye for detail. A failed project or new building with poor quality standards reflects a developer who does not possess these qualities. In addition, the successful developer follows a very simple formula, which is to listen carefully to the needs of the market and deliver a product suitable for that market.

Experience and knowledge

It takes years of hard work and hands-on experience before you can lay claim to being a developer. Successful developers build their knowledge through reading and attending various courses. They undertake their own development through hands-on experience. This experience can be gained either by working with a seasoned developer or by employing a professional development or project manager. Once you have a full understanding of the development process and the risks involved you can embark confidently on your own projects.

Planning

A well-conceived, comprehensive plan is a key component of a successful development. Planning the project, from initial concept until final operation, should be thoroughly considered, analysed and managed.

The planning should cover not only the design of the building but also the various development strategies to be applied. Very few businesses can operate successfully by means of crisis management, but there will always be situations in which the developer must make quick decisions, whether in negotiations or to keep the project on schedule. With proper planning these determinations are in effect not crisis decisions but are the result of the developer's selecting from a number of considered options.

Financial management

Property developments can take longer than expected so the developer should carry enough cash reserves to navigate any slumps or unforeseen circumstances. It is good practice to allow for a contingency cash amount in your feasibility study. The successful developer keeps an eye on lesser items, such as minor overheads and additional professional advice, that may be required. A good financial package can add to the profitability of the project. The lower the cost of servicing a loan, the more profit will end up in the developer's hands. Good knowledge of finance and how banks operate places the developer in a strong position to negotiate a cost-effective financial package. The structure of the financing will play an important part in the evaluation of risks and how to react if the project fails to perform.

Budget and program control

In most developments construction costs and schedules have a nasty habit of not keeping within the projected limits. Careful monitoring of budgets and time schedules is an essential element of a profitable development. Projects can exceed their budget as a result of unforeseen costs such as poor soil or rock conditions or the increasing cost or poor estimation of building materials needed. Each cost element should be thoroughly analysed before construction starts. Wherever possible, fixed prices or fixed rates should be negotiated with the contractor. In addition to budget controls, time and program schedules should be strictly adhered to. The longer the construction takes the less profit the developer will make because of the delay in leasing or selling the project. The extra time will also cost additional interest on money borrowed. At the time of negotiating the contract with the building contractor, the developer should ensure that there are strict penalties for any delays. Conversely, the contractor can be financially rewarded for completion ahead of schedule.

Management

Developing property is undoubtedly one of the most complex businesses around. The key to a successful development is effective and responsible management—more specifically, management of the people involved. Every day the developer must deal with a diverse range of people, from professionals to government bureaucrats to contractors to building materials suppliers. Experienced developers understand that it is virtually impossible for one person to handle all of these people at the same time, so among the good management and leadership skills they learn is the art of delegation.

Skilled negotiations

Successful property developers work on the basis that the real profit is made when a site or parcel of land is first purchased. Paying too much for the land would means reducing building costs at the expense of quality in order to make a profit. Only by having extensive knowledge of the area and market, together with the skills to negotiate a realistic deal, will the developer be able build a quality project. Negotiations can be complex, difficult and acrimonious, but there are various helpful negotiating tactics that experienced developers keep in mind throughout the process.

Reputation

The building industry is riddled with stories of bad workmanship and poor service. We often hear of developers selling inferior products. Remember the old adage: you can fool some of the people some of the time, but not all of the people all of the time. It is very easy to spend a great deal of money in marketing your development, but if you do not deliver the goods as promised, people will eventually catch on and you may lose more money in the long term. If you want to make money out of property development there are no short cuts. Like any other successful business, superior service and products are of the utmost importance.

Deliver these and you will enhance your reputation as a credible and trustworthy developer.

Due diligence

Before launching a new development, successful developers always undertake a thorough due diligence process on the project. This process will identify the potential risks and determine what strategies may need to be adopted in order to mitigate these risks. The successful developer will evaluate the development by preparing a detailed feasibility study to determine if the project has the ability to meet the targeted return. They will perform a sensitivity analysis by testing a number of possible scenarios to determine their impact on the profitability of the project. The developer should also understand other influencing factors, such as local government regulations and restrictions, local tax issues, and planning and environmental issues, and be satisfied they can be effectively managed.

Luck or persistence

In property development, luck has little or nothing to do with long-term success. Of the developers I know, very few believe that luck plays more than a very minor role in their success. One novice developer I spoke with recognised after reading my two earlier books that even though he had made money on his first project, he would lose money on his next if he followed the same principles. Opportunities present themselves to us all from time to time; some we grasp but others we overlook. Successful developers are no different. They have lucky breaks and disappointments just like everyone else. The difference is that more often than not they are working consistently and conscientiously towards a defined goal. Their 'lucky breaks' are more likely to be opportunities that they have engineered in one way or another. In climbing the ladder of financial success, all developers have made mistakes and had setbacks along the way, but they keep going. Persistence is one of the key qualities shared by these developers.

Location and timing

The successful developer also has a very good understanding and knowledge of (a) location and (b) timing.

Location

We have all heard it many times: 'Location, Location, Location' or 'Position, Position, Position'. Of course, what is a good location for one type of property use may be entirely unsuitable for another. For example, a high traffic area may be ideal for a commercial property that would benefit from the marketing exposure but much less attractive for housing. A good location is part of a cohesive structure that takes into account a combination of amenities and services such as shopping, recreation, quality housing, efficient traffic network, education facilities and efficient council services.

Timing

Another critical factor is 'Timing, Timing, Timing'. Most failed developments have not been in tune with the economic cycle. The developer has not read the market correctly and has introduced the product when there is an oversupply and demand has waned, creating a drop in prices and resulting in a severe financial loss for the developer. Supply and demand together with price fluctuations affect all investment markets. Poor developers tend to believe that when markets are buoyant and prices are rising, these conditions will go on forever. Unfortunately this is not the case, and many developers come unstuck by failing to understand the property market cycle, explained later in this chapter.

Setting goals

At the start of a new project successful property developers establish their objectives, including both short- and long-term goals. These objectives fall into the two broad categories of *financial* and *social*. They consider any significant challenges and related risks they may encounter in pursuing these objectives. Each project type, whether residential or commercial development, has its own set of unique requirements for operational and financial success. For example, developing and managing a shopping centre is different from developing an apartment block.

Financial goals

The successful developer determines how much profit should be made relative to the risk of the development. Both long- and short-term financial goals should be analysed. This analysis is based on the developer's current financial position — that is, their current cash flow and net worth — and the targeted long-term profit. A developer in need of cash may want to take a quick profit and move on to the next development. If a particular project is likely to have an extended pre-development stage owing to complicated zoning, environmental or community issues, it is best to recognise that money will be tied up in legal and consultants' services. If a lending institution does not finance speculative projects, then other ventures should be considered. When an objective has been selected, the developer should review their position once more and consider alternative options before making financial commitments.

Social goals

Social goals relate to the local area and the surrounding community in general. Before starting the development, the unique challenges associated with a particular location should be considered carefully. If the developer is selfish and believes only in taking from, but not contributing to the community, the environment and community will suffer. In the long term, this may contribute to the destruction of what was a strong market, which in turn will affect the developer's objectives and reputation negatively. Developers should always consider contributing to the community and environment. These social objectives mean designing a project that blends into the social and historical setting of the community. They include being sensitive to surrounding neighbourhoods, well-planned traffic flows, and retaining or replacing any trees or vegetation destroyed during construction. They also involve using building materials and designs that are sympathetic to the surrounding area and local customs and are environmentally friendly.

Understanding the market

For a property developer, understanding the market is vital for good decision making. With the significant capital involved in a project and the long development process any error of judgement could lead to financial ruin. From the inception of the project through the site selection, planning, building design, financing and construction, the developer should be considering every aspect of the market requirements. By understanding the following points, a developer will be better placed for the market being targeted.

Supply and demand

History has shown that property markets are cyclical in nature. When compared with the erratic performance of the stock market, property trends are more predictable, which makes the forecasting of property supply and demand conditions a lot easier. However, property cycles differ between property types and locations. For example, housing markets tend to relate more closely to the overall growth of the economy and of the local population, while the office market relates more closely to business activity.

Property markets are often considered in terms of the balance between supply and demand, also known as a state of *equilibrium*, in which the volume of buildings under construction should equal the volume of buildings in demand. Unfortunately, markets cannot maintain stability for any period of time owing to their cyclical nature. It is therefore important to understand where a market stands in relation to its equilibrium state in order to assess future demand. An awareness of these variations in property cycles can be a valuable guide for developers. Reading business articles and talking to people in the real estate industry are ways of maintaining awareness of where the market is sitting.

Evaluation of future demand

As mentioned, demand factors can vary from one property type to another. For example, the level of employment in the area is of primary importance for office and industrial properties, whereas residential demand relies on population growth. An analysis of the office space vacancy rate, employment distribution (as derived from government forecasts and data collected by the Australian Bureau of Statistics), building approvals, buildings under construction and the quantity of similar types of projects in the planning stages can all assist in determining demand.

Key supply and demand ratios at both the urban and regional market levels can provide a good guide on how markets are moving. On the demand side, the net absorption of building space or demand for rental properties gives an indication of the strength of demand in relation to the market's capacity. On the supply side, building approvals indicate the pace of development in terms of the market's size. Comparing these two ratios in the context of the market's current position in the cycle is a step towards understanding the historical and expected changes in market.

Analysing the market demand for specific developments

Gathering market information is vital for narrowing down the general performance to the potential performance of a specific new development. Analysing a group of comparable and competitive properties in a specific location will provide an aggregate of the sales and rents that a new development could potentially command.

Researching trends in new home building starts or absorption of commercial building space over time and upward movements in asking rents helps determine how competitive properties have performed in the past. Combining this research information with the building type will assist developers to judge the appropriateness of a particular product type and building for a particular market.

Developments currently under construction and projects on the drawing board are good indicators of short-term supply. The scale of projects in the planning phase can differ greatly from what ultimately comes out of the ground. But if you know your market and the development environment, accurate planning information can serve as a guide to supply activity over the longer term.

The effect of the economy on new developments

With property development the risks at the micro level of a particular project are influenced by what is happening at the macro level of the economy. Any market movement in the broader economy can provide important information for understanding the micro market and how to formulate strategies in the specific location. Armed with this information the developer is in a better position to take advantage of opportunities or limit the impact of the changing property market on a proposed project. This is achieved by identifying the vital and relevant levels of risk in both sales and rental.

In conclusion, an understanding of these points is essential in the development process. An in-depth study not only provides information of what the market is looking for but can fine-tune a project to achieve greater success within the targeted market. Reading business and property newspapers or bulletins on the internet, speaking to people in the industry and attending seminars and conferences help to build this market understanding.

The importance of research

Market research is invaluable but is largely ignored by some developers I have come across in my career. Since the 1960s we have observed many changes that have affected marketing and business enormously. The tradition of single-salaried families has been increasingly superseded by twin-salaried households in which 'housewives' have become career-oriented executives. Technological advances have brought us into an information age that is moving at an incredible pace. These changes have increased competition, decreased profit margins and, in most cases, increased costs of new buildings and developments. All of these and other obvious shifts have forced developers to re-evaluate their products and target markets, making good research even more necessary and important.

All property developers need a great deal of information to keep ahead of the competition, understand the needs of their target market and provide products to suit it. To be competitive, developers need to develop and market innovative products more quickly and effectively than their competitors. Producing a new product is hugely expensive, and any mistake can have disastrous consequences. How often have you been annoyed by a sales person who assumes certain things about you when trying to sell you a product you don't want? Good developers research their target market and customer base thoroughly so their marketing messages are pertinent to it and their understanding of it is evident.

When starting a new development project you need to know the following:

- Is there a need in the market that you can meet?
- Is there a need for your product or service?

- Who would benefit most from your product?

- What would they expect to pay for it and why?

- How should it be packaged?

- What is the potential size of this market?

- What support services are required for this product?

Success in selling or leasing a new development depends on the developer's awareness of his competition. An evaluation of properties of a similar type to the one being proposed will help the developer in planning strategies for a successful approach. For any proposed development and any specific market, the market feasibility study is designed to answer two basic questions:

1   What is the current condition of the market?

2   How will the market respond to the proposed project?

A field survey is the most important component of any market study. The first step in any market study is to define the market area. There are several basic approaches to this problem. One common method is radial analysis. A series of concentric circles are drawn around the site at, for example, distances of three, five and ten kilometres. The areas within these circles are then analysed.

A second method is to base market areas on boundaries between local governments. In this method, regional, township or city boundaries become the boundaries of the market area. This is a simple solution as most secondary data are reported by political demarcations.

A third method is to analyse and research the smallest geographical area from which a project can expect to generate 60 to 70 per cent of its support. It is not as simple but it gives a better reading of the true market area for a project. When undertaking such a study for a specific site, the researcher should look at a range of factors, including geography, demographic analysis, mobility patterns and area perceptions.

Geographical factors

Rivers, major rail routes, hills and major freeways often define neighbourhood boundaries. These factors influence where people move. In fact, geographical factors are often more important than local government boundaries, as market areas often cross regional, township or city borders.

Demographic factors

Population and household trends, housing and income characteristics, differences in the socioeconomic makeup of individual neighbourhoods and growth figures are all analysed. Radial analysis cannot take all these characteristics into account and often can slant a report by including neighbourhoods of vastly differing socioeconomic makeup.

Mobility factors

Interviews with local real estate professionals and planning officials will help to identify mobility patterns. These patterns within an area are predictable, and while individuals occasionally act counter to prevailing trends, mobility analysis for a particular project can help pinpoint where most people are the most likely to come from.

Area perceptions

Interviews with council planning officials, project managers and real estate professionals will help to determine area perceptions and how they relate to the other factors discussed. These perceptions will help to determine mobility patterns, a key component of any market feasibility study.

Build a business network

Seasoned professional developers know that business will not just fall into their lap. Developing contacts that generate opportunities takes time, dedication and a lot of legwork. For any chance of success many hours must be spent networking with business contacts, community members, past clients and people in the property industry. One of the best ways of minimising risk in any business is to develop a strong business network. This is particularly important in property development where the stakes are high. Relationships are built on continual networking, which means developers should communicate regularly with their business network.

How networks develop

Not many businesses today can survive without the assistance and patronage of other businesses. For example, a retailer extends credit because of an expectation of an increase in future business. If things go well and the parties regard each other as reliable and good to work with, a business relationship is created. Over time this network will generate effective business contacts, partnerships and friendships.

Similarly, developers have to plan and create essential networks in order for their business to prosper. Business relationships do not develop automatically. Every developer must seek out real estate agents to offer them potential development sites, investors to provide equity, financiers to provide construction funding, professional advisers and marketing specialists, and then develop successful and mutually profitable relationships.

Why networks are created

When creating a network, property developers should first identify the most important business contacts that will underpin their business and growth strategy. Other networks that need to be developed can provide:

- investment advice, finance, seed capital, taxation advice and development feasibility studies

- information on competitors, new concepts, new products, market movements, potential associates and any other information that might affect a development

- introductions to public sector departments, local council members and politicians, and advice on lobbying and any other public contacts

- general assistance with contacts, advice, referrals, personnel selection and other property development specialists.

Creating a network

When creating a business network, the first consideration is to develop a consistent, disciplined procedure for converting a contact into a strategic component of your network. A contact is not the same as a close friend; rather, it is someone you will call on as required from time to time. You need to have a rapport with your contacts, to be remembered by them as someone for whom a favour is worth doing. Assess potential contacts on the following basis:

- Are they important to you?

- Do they have the skills, relationships or know-how you may need to draw on?

- Do they belong to an organisation that could be useful to you?

- Are they key decision makers in the organisation (or their assistants)?

- What can you contribute to them in return?

Building a network becomes easy if you have a disciplined procedure and adopt the following basic guidelines:

- Create an impression whenever you meet someone new by being courteous and talking about their interest. Remember their name and you will more likely be remembered.

- When you meet someone for the first time, always keep in mind that they may be a future contact. You may not get a chance to meet them again so use your meeting productively.

- Distinguish clearly between a genuine contact and a social encounter. Good networks are built on sincerity, integrity and lasting associations.

When setting up your network, write down a list of the people and organisations you need to form relationships with. As a guide, note:

- the categories of organisations you need to connect with

- the organisations you should contact within each category

- the key players to contact in each organisation

- a list of people who can assist in making the contact.

Reading property market cycles

Property markets are cyclical because of the equilibrium sway between supply and demand for building accommodation. The market cycle can be broken into four phases (as illustrated in figure 2.1). Advances in technology and electronic media have affected the property industry as momentously as they have wider society. Instant information on the internet and new software has greatly increased the efficiency of property markets. Developers can often tap into all the information they need from their desktop rather than having to call in experts or wait for published reports. Comprehensive information, for example on current prices, property listings or past sales within a certain location, is readily available.

Figure 2.1: the property market cycle

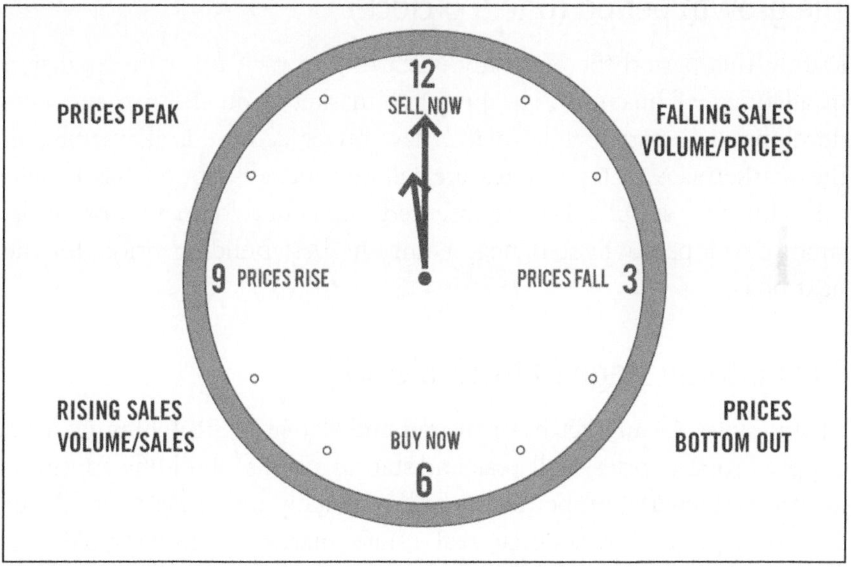

PRICES PEAK

12 SELL NOW

FALLING SALES VOLUME/PRICES

9 PRICES RISE

PRICES FALL 3

RISING SALES VOLUME/SALES

BUY NOW 6

PRICES BOTTOM OUT

The market cycle can be further described as follows.

The market in decline (12 to 3 o'clock)

During this phase the property market becomes oversupplied with new buildings. Prices start to fall with concessions offered to the buyer, interest rates are increasing, properties are taking a longer time to sell, finance becomes more difficult to obtain, liquidations are increasing, unemployment is increasing, businesses are defaulting, investor confidence is decreasing and business bankruptcies are increasing. Smart developers are looking for promising sites and buying them at bargain prices.

The bottom of the market (3 to 6 o'clock)

During this stage the market is at its worst. No new developments are being built, little activity is happening in the market, interest rates have peaked, investment is at its highest level and very little economic activity is taking place. The smart developer will start the design and planning of new developments and begin to obtain approvals.

The growth period (6 to 9 o'clock)

During this period the economy is starting to pick up with expansion in all types of business. The property market is on the rise and new developments start to take place, new buyer activity is happening in the marketplace, interest rates are falling, and absorption has caught up with the supply. Having secured their development approvals, smart developers will start negotiating the best building prices for the next phase.

The maturity stage (9 to 12 o'clock)

At this stage the market has matured and demand is catching up with supply. Property prices will peak and start to stabilise, building approvals are on the increase, properties are selling quickly, investment confidence is very high and residential real estate market is growing. Market demand for all types of products is increasing, excessive prices are paid for properties, unemployment is falling and businesses are expanding. During this period the smart developer sells.

Opportunities in development

To a certain extent, earnings in property development can be as predictable as profits in any established business where the operator has taken the time to develop skills for which the public is willing to pay. Car manufacturers, furniture makers and wine producers all make profits in ways the general public understands. They create a product and sell it to retail outlets, who sell it on to the public at a higher retail price. These earnings, however, are only as good as the strategies employed. Following are some opportunities and strategies exploited by successful property developers.

Adding value, improving net worth

Adding value is what property development is all about. In today's economic climate of low inflation and relatively modest property growth rates in the established property sector, many investors have taken a more proactive approach and become small-time developers, adding value to their properties by refurbishing, rezoning or just building new. By adding value the developer will build up equity or net worth a lot quicker than conservative investors who are content to buy a property and wait until the market and economic forces provide them with capital appreciation.

Generating cash flows

Developing a property will increase your equity faster than purchasing an established property. The smart developer building, say, a block of apartments would sell most of the units but retain a few for rental. This strategy will give the developer a stable positive cash flow where the rental income is greater than the mortgage on the property. In addition, with the equity and positive cash flow the developer is in a position to tackle another development and repeat the strategy.

Generating fees

Most seasoned developers generate fees in the site procurement, management and construction phases of a development. These fees are used primarily to pay overheads and running costs while the balance will provide profit for the developer. Fees that can be charged can vary and will depend on the role of the developer. Fees can include a project procurement fee, development management fee, project management fee, construction management fee, marketing fee, leasing fee or property management fee.

Land conversion

Assembling and rezoning a group of residential lots to commercial, or residential to a higher density such as apartments, can bring healthy financial rewards to those who identify such potential. These opportunities occur, for example, where traffic volumes are increasing or new highways are planned for older suburbs. Often these busy roads cut through older residential areas, where the associated noise and danger are not attractive to many residents but where commercially viable buildings will benefit from the marketing exposure.

Subdividing, strata title

Purchasing large tracts of land, subdividing them, providing the necessary infrastructure and then selling them on can be financially rewarding. Subdividing land, or strata titling an apartment block, allows the developer to sell off segments of a larger piece of real estate, thereby reducing the debt on the property. This approach generally cannot be applied to a retail shopping centre or a large industrial warehouse.

Subleasing

Leasing land or a building and then subleasing it is not new in property. Often government-owned land is leased at fairly low rates to developers who add improvements and then sublease to tenants. These opportunities are not always easy to find, as prime government-owned land is normally offered by tender, which increases the lease repayments because of the higher demand.

Syndicates

Most residential apartment buildings and commercial developments are larger in scale, but a developer does not necessarily have to take on all the risks alone. Sponsoring a syndicate offer developers opportunities greater than those they might be able to handle individually. Syndicate developers pool the resources of several investors to acquire a more expensive property, diversifying the risk of ownership. As an added benefit, sponsors maintain control of properties that otherwise could not be controlled through contractual agreements with buyers or sellers.

Summary

A career in property development can be both satisfying and financially rewarding. It offers many opportunities for those who are prepared to invest time in researching and studying the markets. Successful developers take on projects that are financially viable, that suit their financial goals and that are sensitive to the environment by offering long-term sustainability so both they and the community at large will benefit — a win–win situation. If you are new to the game or just starting a new development on your own, it is recommended that you bring an experienced development and/or project manager into your development team. It is important to educate yourself thoroughly before taking on significant financial risk.

Summary

CHAPTER 3

The development process and participants

The property development process can be compared to a manufacturing process that involves a combination of inputs by various parties in order to achieve a usable product. For a small residential project the process is simple; for larger developments such as commercial buildings it can be complex and it can take a considerable time for a project to come to fruition. Each development is unique in terms of location, site conditions and design and the public scrutiny it will generate. In this chapter the broad development process is set out. Later, in chapters 8 and 9, the process is explained in depth.

A number of people and organisations will be involved at various stages during the development process. All these players will contribute in different ways to bringing the development to fruition, although they may have different motivations and expectations for the final outcome. It is the responsibility of the developer to ensure that each player is working towards the common goal and to influence those who are obstructing it.

The process

The development process can be broken into the following main stages:

1 inception

2 assessment

3 due diligence

4 commitment

5 planning and cost estimates

6 planning approval

7 marketing

8 working drawings

9 construction

10 hold or sell.

The sequence explained in the following pages represents a typical property development. Some stages may overlap or may be tackled in a different order. For example, if the project is pre-sold or pre-let then stage 10 will precede stages 2 to 7.

Stage 1: Inception

A development is initiated when a potential site is offered for sale or a specific site is considered suitable for a special use because of the demand for that use. The idea, vision or concept may come from any players within the property and construction industries or from professional consultants or business leaders, but ultimately it is the developer who drives the idea. The creation of a new development normally starts when demand for a specific facility is created as a result of changing demographics, economic movement, social changes or new transport infrastructure. A developer who recognises the opportunity will undertake market research and seek approvals from local authorities.

Stage 2: Assessment

This stage of the development process is very important as it generates information on which the developer will base key decisions. In the assessment the macro and micro market will be researched and a preliminary prefeasibility study of the project will be undertaken. The assessment process involves the combined advice of the developer's professional team. The research and feasibility studies will be continually worked on until the point at which the developer is persuaded that the potential development is financially viable. The financial evaluation process needs to ensure that the cost of the development is realistic and to establish the potential profit in relation to the risk undertaken. No commitment should be made until this stage has been completed.

Stage 3: Due diligence

If the decision is made to proceed, before acquiring the development site, the developer should undertake further due diligence in the following areas.

Site conditions

A physical site analysis should be undertaken to evaluate whether the site can accommodate the proposed development. This includes investigations of soil conditions, vegetation, access and supply of bulk infrastructure. If there is no available data on the soil conditions it is advisable to appoint an engineer to undertake a geotechnical survey. The availability of bulk infrastructure supply services such as telecommunications, electricity, gas and water should be investigated to evaluate if the capacity of these services is sufficient for the proposed development. A lack of any of these infrastructure services can seriously impact on the financial viability of the project.

Legal and planning conditions

All legal aspects relating to the project should be investigated, including ownership, easements, caveats and zoning. A preliminary design and planning concept should be drafted to ascertain whether the developer's proposal will comply with the current town planning regulations. The same design should be submitted to the planning division of the local council for confirmation that the developer's proposal is compliant and will be supported by the council.

Finance

Before committing to the development, the developer should secure appropriate finance on favourable terms. The three levels of finance required are (a) seed capital for the development approval application, (b) finance to cover development and construction, and (c) long-term finance if the developer intends to hold on to the development as a long-term investment. The developer's credentials and detailed information of the proposed development are essential to the lending institution providing the finance.

Stage 4: Commitment

Before deciding to go ahead with the development, the developer has to ensure that all the preliminary work described in stages 2 and 3 has been carefully assessed. The developer must be satisfied that the assessment is based on the best possible information on the project's viability.

Having made the offer to purchase the site, the developer must keep all costs to a minimum until the land is settled. The main costs include professional fees and staff salaries. Depending on negotiations and whether the site purchase is still conditional, the professional team may be willing to work on a speculative basis or at a reduced fee in order to secure full appointment should the development proceed. In addition, the developer should offer to purchase the land subject to obtaining necessary planning approval, although this might not always be acceptable to the seller. The developer also has to make a commitment to purchase subject to finance but should carefully assess land values in the area to ensure the offer made is in line with the market.

At various stages, contracts will be signed to secure the land, procure finance and appoint the professional team. At each stage the developer must ensure that the decisions around signing the contracts are based on the correct information.

Stage 5: Planning and cost estimates

Once the site due diligence is completed satisfactorily and the site is acquired the initial design concepts will be worked on further. Designing a new building is a continuous process that runs parallel with other stages of the development. The concept sketch plan becomes increasingly detailed as the development increases in certainty. The concept sketch design should have sufficient information that a quantity surveyor or builder can prepare cost estimates. These plans together with the initial cost estimates will enable the developer to prepare the preliminary feasibility study (PFS).

If the concept design proves to be feasible then a full set of drawings showing plans, elevations and sections of the building will be prepared for submission for development or planning approval. The planning and cost estimate stage involves key members of the professional consulting team, and the developer has to ensure all members are aware of the importance of the project's viability and budgets.

Stage 6: Planning approval

Across most of Australia any change of use or building operation, unless of a minor nature, requires planning or development approval from the local council authority. The developer submits preliminary plans showing the plans and elevations of the proposed development and seeks approval from the council for the project to proceed. If the local community is affected then the development is advertised for members of the public to comment on before the approval is granted. This process can lead to delays if the development is controversial.

For some projects the approval process can be complex, requiring a thorough knowledge of the appropriate legislation and policies, and a good understanding of how the local council in the area operates. Using experienced consultants for this process will be important, especially where problems are encountered. Depending on the scale of the project the developer, in addition to local council approval, may need approval from other authorities such as environmental or state planning bodies before planning approval can be granted.

Stage 7: Marketing

If the project's success depends on pre-leasing or pre-sales, the developer will appoint a marketing team to undertake this exercise. In most cases, bank funding for the construction phase is conditional on pre-leasing or pre-sales. For example, if the developer is building an apartment block, most banks will provide finance only once there are enough sales of units to cover the bank's loan.

Even if the developer has sufficient funds and a good track record where pre-leasing or pre-sales may not be a condition for finance, it is good practice to ensure there is a market for the facilities being developed and a pre-commitment from potential tenants or buyers.

Stage 8: Working drawings

Once planning approval is granted and the marketing of the project has been successful the developer's professional team may proceed with the working drawings, taking into account any conditions imposed by the council. These plans should also comply with the Building Code of Australia (BCA), local by-laws and any conditions imposed by other governing authorities. The drawings together with specifications are used either to negotiate costs with a builder or to tender out the project to several builders. The same drawings will be used by the appointed builder to obtain a building licence.

The quality of the information available on the working drawings and specifications correlates directly to the outcome of a tender and future construction on site. Poor drawings and documentation often lead to mistakes that can prove expensive for the project.

Stage 9: Construction

Construction starts when the contract with the building contractor is signed and finance is approved. The flexibility that was possible during the earlier stages is now limited and any variations during construction, while still possible, can be costly. The goal at this stage is to ensure that the construction is completed on time and on budget without compromising the quality of the build.

Although several types of building contracts are available through institutions such as the Royal Australian Institute of Architects, the Master Builders Association, the Property Council of Australia and the Housing Industries Association (HIA), most developers negotiate a lump-sum, fixed-price contract.

Depending on the size and complexity of the project and the developer's own experience, a seasoned project manager should probably be appointed to supervise the construction process. To minimise delays and extra costs, decisions should be made promptly when problems occur during this stage.

Stage 10: Hold or sell

The decision to hold or sell the development is normally made at the start of the project. Some developers, known as traders, plan on developing and selling while others will develop a property as a longer term investment. Those who sell will rely on their motivation and strategy and the prevailing property market conditions at the time.

If the development is held as an investment, the developer must consider whether the property should be managed by a third party or by in-house staff. The latter course would impose more responsibility on the developer. Employing a third party to manage the property would cost additional fees but would allow the developer to focus on other developments. In choosing a third-party agent, care should be taken in evaluating the agent's track record and experience in the specific type of property.

The participants

As already noted, a number of parties are actively involved in the development process. Each party's role can have an impact on the development in terms of both time and cost. In the following list these parties are placed in the order in which they appear in the development process. In many cases they will overlap and their involvement will vary depending on the scope of the project, and in some instances they may not be involved at all. The players involved can include:

- landowners
- property developers
- real estate agents
- government authorities
- financial institutions
- property valuers
- professional consultants

- building contractors
- buyers
- tenants.

Landowners

In most cases a landowner will initiate a development purely out of a desire to improve the value of their land. In some instances the developer will approach a landowner to determine whether they are willing to sell or participate in a project. If a landowner is not willing to sell or to participate in a development, then there is no development. Landowners can be private individuals, companies, government authorities, associations or charities. They can be categorised as follows.

Public landowners

This category includes government authorities (state, federal and local) and public bodies (churches and associations, for example). Their main motive is to provide a service and the land is incidental. In addition, they may be constrained by legal status and will not always be seeking to maximise their return on the land if this is seen as contrary to their main purpose. These owners may be motivated to sell their land because of relocation, expansion or a rezoning within their area.

Private landowners

Owners in this category have financial motives and would be informed of the market values of the land in their area. This group includes individuals, companies and financial institutions that may own large tracts of land through ongoing investment. They may also act directly as developers or in a joint venture with a developer.

Property developers

In chapter 1 various property developers were described, but in simple terms property developers were placed into two main categories — private and public. Private sector developers range from sole operators to multinational companies. Like any other private sector business, their goal is to maximise their profit from the development project. These developers can be further described as either traders (who sell their developments) or investors (who hold on to their developments as investments). Most small development companies tend to trade rather than invest, as they do not have the capital reserves needed to retain the completed projects.

Public sector developers are listed on the stock exchange as property trusts. These developers, who focus on commercial developments, tend not to hold on to their developments in order to build up their asset base, whereas those primarily involved in residential development operate solely as traders because of the market bias towards owner-occupiers.

Real estate agents

Real estate agents can also be instrumental in initiating a development either by finding a suitable site for a developer or by recommending that a landowner sell a particular site because of its development potential. They will generally introduce sites to developers they consider have the appropriate expertise and resources both to acquire the site and to complete the development. They will assist in the negotiations between the landowner and developer. They can also advise the developer on all matters relating to the assessment stage.

With their local real estate knowledge, agents can play a very important role in the development process. They perform this role based on their detailed knowledge of both the property market, in terms of both demand and current prices and rentals for a specific use. For the service they provide, agents receives a fee, generally a percentage of the value of the transaction, which is paid only when the transaction is successful. They may also secure an appointment as the letting or selling agent for the development.

Government authorities

Government involvement in the process will depend on how much they wish to encourage development or to regulate and restrict it. Many local and state authorities embrace economic activities to promote development and investment in their area. Proactive authorities act as a catalyst in the development process where private market forces fail to bring forward development, particularly in areas targeted for economic development. They can assist developers with land assembly, site reclamation, the provision of infrastructure, financial grants and even the relaxation of taxation rules. These authorities will often retain the freehold of their development sites, granting a long-term lease to the developer and sharing in rental growth through the ground rent.

Planning authorities are responsible for approving the plans submitted by a developer in accordance with the policy laid down by government. They are also responsible for determining whether applications for development proposals should be approved or refused. The main purposes of planning are to encourage development and to prevent undesirable development. The basis for screening planning applications is laid down by statute and in a variety of central government policy guidance documents. Local government must adhere to these guidelines and will determine its own local policy through the main medium of development plans.

Planning authorities differ widely in their policies towards development. Typically, those in areas of low economic activity are keen to encourage development activity, putting only minimal restrictions on proposals, particularly those that will provide employment. Authorities in areas of high economic activity see their role mainly in terms of imposing higher quality standards, slowing down development in order to achieve a better balance of uses and improved building design. Increasing conflict between developers and planners has led to greater use of the appeals system, especially in areas of high economic activity.

Financial institutions

Unless the development is being financed entirely with a developer's own capital, financial institutions have a very important role in the process. The great variety of methods for obtaining finance from the banks for both short- and medium-term finance are discussed in detail in chapter 6.

Banks, of course, aim to make a financial profit from the business of lending money. Bank lending may take the form of corporate lending to the development company or lending against a particular development project. The bank will use the property assets of the company or the property itself as security for the loan. Property offers attractive security as it is an identifiable asset with an assessable resale value.

The bank will wish to ensure that the proposed development is viable and well located and that the developer has the ability to complete the project. With corporate lending, the bank is concerned with the strength of the company, its assets, profits and cash flow. In some cases, depending on the size of the loan and in particular where the bank is exposed to above-normal risk, the bank may secure an equity stake in the scheme.

Property valuers

Developers, landowners, tenants, financiers and property investors may at some stage in the development process employ a suitably experienced, qualified property valuer to undertake professional work that will assist their decision-making process. Property valuers are employed by the vast majority of financial institutions and developers to help them determine the current value of a property or of a development on completion.

Developers either love or loathe valuers, who can make or break a development. Banks require an independent valuation to check whether the proposed development has value both in the land itself and when completed. Independent and in-house valuers are also used by some financial institutions and banks for properties for which they are considering making a loan or granting a mortgage.

Professional consultants

Most developers do not have all the skills and expertise needed to carry out a complex development, so they employ a professional team to advise them at various stages of the process. Depending on the scale of the project the team will include all or some of the following professionals.

Development managers

Development managers, normally employed on larger or more complex projects, may be confused with project managers. The role of the development manager is to act on behalf of the developer or investment group and to direct the development to ensure its viability so it can be financed and so the projected returns are achieved.

While the development manager analyses the development's potential and then forms a strategic policy framework, the project manager ensures that these policies are delivered by managing the project from financial close to practical completion. A development manager's fees are normally based on a percentage of the total development cost and paid as a monthly retainer. Besides having excellent contacts in the development industry, a good development manager has the following attributes:

- a full understanding of the development process and the associated risks

- knowledge and understanding of various asset classes of the property market

- an understanding of the legal processes and knowledge of various legal contracts

- sound knowledge and experience in development finance and negotiating skills

- contacts with professional consultants and an understanding of how to direct them

- contacts with building contractors and an understanding of how to direct them.

Project managers

Project managers are employed to manage the professional team and the building contract on behalf of the developer or development manager. They should be appointed before any of the other professional team members so they are in a position to advise the developer or development manager on the best professional team for the project. Their fees are normally based on a percentage of the building contract sum. The role of the project manager is to assist the developer or development manager with:

- negotiation and appointment of consultants and execution of consultant contracts

- organisation of the design team to optimise the design by analysing various options in technical and economic terms

- arranging for supervision and construction of the works and execution of the building contractor contract

- preparation of cash flows, handling of construction claims and payment settlement upon completion

- organisation of completion acceptance and transfer of as-built files to the owner.

Planning consultants

Town or urban planning consultants are employed to negotiate with local planning authorities to obtain permission for a development, particularly on large or sensitive schemes. On smaller development schemes applications can be handled by an architect. Consultants can also advise landowners to ensure their sites are allocated within the town planning scheme or structure plan to their most appropriate or valuable use. This may involve negotiations with the local planning authority at plan preparation stage or subsequent representations at an enquiry into the development plan. Planners normally submit a quoted fee based on the complexity of the project and the time required for the planning approval.

Market researchers

Market research consultants are engaged at the most important assessment stage to provide a detailed analysis of the characteristics of the market in terms of the underlying demand and competitive supply. Many financiers, particularly financial institutions, insist on market analysis when considering a development funding proposal. Market research companies will provide a quoted fee, depending on the complexity of the research, before undertaking the work.

Architects

It is important to employ the architect at the earliest possible stage in the development process to provide a number of design options. Architects are trained to design and plan buildings and may also administer the building contract on behalf of the developer and certify completion of the building work. They are normally responsible for obtaining planning permission when a planning consultant is not employed. They are paid a fee, usually based on a percentage of the total building contract sum.

Some architectural practices offer a comprehensive service including project management, engineering and interior design work. This may be effective on some development schemes, but most developers tend to prefer to assemble their own professional teams to achieve the best outcome. Some development companies, particularly those that specialise, employ in-house architects and design professionals.

Quantity surveyors

In simple terms, quantity surveyors can be defined as the accountants of the building and construction industry. They advise developers on the possible costs of the total building project and other associated costs. Their role includes costing the designs produced by the architect, administering the building contract tender, advising on the most appropriate form of building contract, monitoring the construction and approving stage payments to the contractor. A quantity surveyor should be able to provide the developer with cost-effective ideas as alternatives to those proposed by the architect. Like architects, their fee is based on a percentage of the final contract sum.

Engineers

Engineers are employed to work with the architect and quantity surveyor to provide advice on the design of the engineering elements of the building. They can also participate in the supervision of the construction. Engineers are usually paid a percentage fee based on the value of their element of the building contract. Depending on the scale of a development, some or all of the following engineers may be employed:

- Structural engineers are used wherever structural information is required. They generally work under the architect's direction. The architect normally consults a structural engineer during preparation of the working drawings or at times when the design is more complex during the preparation of the sketch plans.

- Civil engineers are responsible for the design, construction and management of transport systems, gas and water supply, and sewerage systems. A civil engineer will work from an architect's drawings to provide recommendations on the floor levels and advice on stormwater and drainage layouts.

- Electrical and mechanical engineers are normally used on commercial and industrial projects where complex electrical and/or mechanical installations are contemplated.

- Hydraulic engineers are involved with the design of fluid movement systems. They advise on water, sewerage and drainage systems.

- Geotechnical engineers take soil samples from test holes in the substrata of land to be built on. From these test samples they derive significant information about bearing capacities, stability of the soil and sub-surface water tables. These soil tests are often required before the design of buildings on difficult sites can start.

- Traffic engineers evaluate proposals drafted by other consultants and make recommendations on traffic flows and parking. These engineers are generally used during the planning approval process.

- Fire engineers are multidisciplinary, with an understanding of building services, and mechanical, electrical, electronics, chemical, structural and civil engineering, ensuring that all these elements are protected from fire dangers. They will review the architectural plans and make recommendations to ensure that the building complies with fire and safety building codes.

- Acoustic engineers are responsible for monitoring and controlling noise levels. Their duties include rating noise levels, creating noise barriers, using buffer zones and planning walls around highways or high-traffic areas. Their primary role is to find solutions to reducing unwanted sound in populated areas. In buildings such as apartments or offices, they help to design the architectural acoustics to control the noise level affecting such buildings.

- Environmental engineers use engineering and science principles to design solutions that help with environmental problems. With so many older buildings or sites being redeveloped for new uses such as apartments, contamination by toxic elements such as oil or asbestos have to be carefully analysed and disposed of. Their services are also required in 'greenfield' sites, especially where a new land development is being proposed in wetlands.

Interior designer

An interior designer enhances the function, safety and aesthetics of interior spaces while taking into account how different colours, textures, furniture, lighting and space work together to meet occupants' or visitors' needs. They work with both private and public spaces, including residences, shopping malls, schools, offices and hospitals. Their fees are based on the size of the project and are generally quoted prior to engagement.

Building certifier

During the design, approvals and construction phases a building certifier can provide a building compliance advice service, ensuring the building being designed and constructed meets all building codes and other regulatory requirements and that it is suitable for occupation and use on completion. Their fees, based on the size and complexity of the development, are quoted prior to their engagement.

Land surveyor

Land surveyors are trained to take accurate measurements and compile topographical information. Before an architect or building designer starts on the design of a new building it is best to obtain as much detailed information of the building site as possible. For this the appointment of a land surveyor is necessary. The fee charged will depend on the size of the site and the work involved. Land surveyors can also assist with the subdivision of land and the strata title documentation of a building.

Accountants

Specialist property accountants may be employed to provide advice on the complexity of tax and GST regulations, which can have a major cost impact on a development. They can also provide advice on the structure of partnership or financing arrangements.

Solicitors

Solicitors are needed at various stages of the development process, starting with the acquisition of the site and continuing through to the completion of leases and contracts of sale. They are often involved with the legal agreements covering any funding arrangements entered into by the developer. If the developer has to lodge an appeal on a planning application then both solicitors and barristers may be involved in presenting the developer's case at an inquiry.

This list of professionals and specialists employed during the development process is not intended to be exhaustive. Other specialists may be needed, depending on the complexity of the development project, such as landscape architects, public relations consultants, marketing consultants or property managers.

Building contractors

Many small and large building contractors are available, along with a wide variety of contractual systems for the construction process. Some development companies employ their own contractors and in some cases builders take on the role of developer. When a builder is employed as a contractor, their financial profit is related to the building cost and length of contract. Under a design and construct (D & C) contract a builder will take on a design role to provide a cost that aligns with the developer's construction budget. Contractors with the relevant expertise may take on the role of a management contractor, managing all the various subcontracts for the developer in return for a fee.

Basically, building contractors carry out a specialist activity within the development process, commencing at a time of maximum commitment and risk for the developer. The prudent developer will therefore assess the capacity of the contractor to undertake the proposed work, seeking the right balance between the lowest tender and the best performance quality. While the developer seeks the most cost-effective building price, a situation in which the contractor cannot make a reasonable profit or must compromise on quality is not in the contractor's or the developer's interest.

Buyers

In residential developments, buyers can be categorised as either owner-occupiers or investors, whereas in commercial development the buyers are primarily wealthy individuals, investment companies, syndicates or institutional investors.

Most investors are motivated by direct financial gain. Unlike developers they take a long-term view, aiming to achieve capital growth. They seek to minimise risk and maximise future capital gains and income. Buyer investors tend to adopt fairly rigid and conservative policies. They may differ in their individual criteria, but they all tend to seek a balanced portfolio, rather than specialising in one particular use. They will seek properties or developments that fit their specific criteria on location, quality of building and quality of tenants.

Owner-occupiers of residential property have a different motivation. First home buyers are seeking a home based on what they can afford given their income. Second or third home buyers, depending on their age, are looking either to improve their lifestyle or to downsize to a smaller home after the kids have moved out.

Tenants

Most commercial buildings are developed for rental purposes whereas residential buildings are designed to be sold. Residential developers who rent to tenants generally aim for a passive income for the future. Commercial developers who seek tenants know that quality tenants and long-term rental leases will secure them a higher sale price should they decide to sell at a later stage. Similarly, residential developers seek credible tenants who would take care of their property so that if they need to sell they can achieve a higher price than similar residential properties in the area.

Whether you fall into the commercial or residential investment category, quality and credible tenants are vital for income stability. Structuring leases is critical: a longer lease allows the developer to plan future developments without the worry of finding new tenants on short-term leases. If you are a developer investor seeking a long-term passive income it is advisable to find a professional property manager who will take care of the tenants so you can continue with your interest without tenant headaches.

Roles of developer and participants

The role the developer and those of his team members at the various stages of the process are listed in table 3.1 (overleaf), which defines each of the work tasks and indicates the various individuals responsible for those tasks at different stages of the process.

Table 3.1: roles of developer and participants at each stage

Task description	Developer	Financer	Property valuer	Legal/accountant	Real estate agent	Architect/designer	Quantity surveyor	Engineers	Consultants	Contractor	Marketing	Management
Stage 1—Vision												
Determine development concept	•											
Select site	•											
Consult attorney	•			•								
Consult accountant	•			•								
Conduct preliminary market research	•										•	
Meet with council officials	•					•						
Meet with planning department	•					•						
Meet with other relevant authorities	•					•						
Establish property values	•		•		•							
Conduct pre-purchase viability study	•						•					
Arrange finance	•	•										

Task	1	2	3	4	5	6	7	8	9	10	11	12
Purchase the property	•				•							
Complete title search	•				•							
Select list of potential team players	•											
Stage 2 — Concept feasibility												
Create development program	•											
Complete market research											•	
Complete topographic survey									•			
Complete soils test								•				
Complete environmental studies								•				
Complete traffic study								•				
Hold preliminary design meeting	•					•	•	•	•			
Create preliminary sketch plans						•						
Prepare preliminary construction cost							•					
Prepare feasibility study	•			•		•	•				•	•
Submit for planning approval	•					•						
Put together finance package	•	•										

(continued)

Table 3.1: roles of developer and participants at each stage *(cont'd)*

Task description	Developer	Financer	Property valuer	Legal/accountant	Real estate agent	Architect/designer	Quantity surveyor	Engineers	Consultants	Contractor	Marketing	Management
Put together investor package	•											
Prepare legal documents for sale/lease				•								
Draft marketing strategy	•				•						•	
Prepare marketing brochures											•	
Prepare marketing budget	•											
Sign pre-leases/sales					•							
Stage 3 — Technical												
Evaluate the finer details of the design	•											
Revise program of work	•											
Hold and chair regular technical meetings	•											
Complete working drawings						•		•	•			

Task	1	2	3	4	5	6	7	8	9	10	11	12
Prepare structural drawings												
Prepare civil drawings												
Prepare electrical and mechanical drawings												
Complete specifications and addendum				•			•					
Prepare bill of quantities					•	•						
Price out/review construction costs					•	•						
Make final general contractor selection					•		•					•
Prepare tender documents						•	•					
Call for tenders (and closing of tenders)					•		•					•
Prepare contract documents												•
Stage 4 — Construction												
Award and sign building contract			•									•
Obtain all building/development permits			•									
Obtain all builder risk policies			•									
Commence construction			•									
Review construction schedule			•									

(continued)

Table 3.1: roles of developer and participants at each stage *(cont'd)*

Task description	Developer	Financer	Property valuer	Legal/accountant	Real estate agent	Architect/designer	Quantity surveyor	Engineers	Consultants	Contractor	Marketing	Management
Review variation orders	•					•				•		
Supervise builder	•					•						
Construction drawdowns	•		•			•						
Obtain completion certificate										•		
Obtain certificate of occupancy										•		
Complete snag list						•						
Complete all maintenance work										•		
Implement marketing plan					•						•	
Stage 5 — Implementation												
Settlement of sales	•			•								
Owners and tenants move in	•									•		

Task							
Obtain, review and sign leases	•		•	•	•	•	•
Establish accounting controls							
Establish management policies		•			•	•	•
Establish maintenance policies							
Prepare yearly operating budgets							
Prepare yearly capital expenditure budgets							
Prepare yearly tax returns							

Summary

Understanding and experiencing the full development process is important for every developer. The process goes far beyond simply purchasing an existing property with a known income. Although the returns are a lot higher in property development, the developer must determine with confidence that the time and cash investments in the project will pay off. In addition to understanding the development process, it is important that the developer understand the roles of consultants and their related fees. The list of consultants is extensive but those required on a specific project will depend on the scale of the project. The developer's principal — for example, the project manager or architect — should advise which additional consultants may be required on the project.

CHAPTER 4

Development site selection

Over the past decade, advances in technology have brought properties more quickly to the market, thereby increasing competition among developers seeking good development sites. Despite these advances, many fundamentals still apply in selecting a potential development site. To be successful in today's marketplace, property developers have to be sophisticated and demonstrate sound negotiating skills. What has changed, though, is how they gather information and execute development opportunities. While technology has created more competition, developers today can gather site information a lot faster and more accurately than ever before. Generally available property data and sharing of information at lightning speed assist developers to make quicker, more informed decisions.

The ready availability of current demographic and property data is having a tremendous impact on the property industry. Research data from personal observations and market researchers provides developers with the important criteria for the proper selection of a site. Such information assists the developer in understanding present and possible future development trends. It will also give the developer information on the successful and less successful developments in the area, while the demographics will reveal the growth patterns and indicate what criteria to set in the development brief.

Criteria for a residential development site are based on a number of standard factors, whereas for a commercial site another set of rules apply. Because the demographic catchment area of commercial sites is broader compared with residential sites, more emphasis is placed on regional studies. Selection for residential sites is more localised, as is described in this chapter.

Factors that make a good development site

Depending on the complexity of the development and your own level of expertise, you may need the advice of consultants of varied disciplines when selecting a site for development. Site requirements can vary according to the function and operation of the specific development. However, a number of fundamentals will consistently apply, which include the following.

Location

Securing the right location is critical to the success of a development. An experienced developer will have a good idea of the right location for a development and the ability to identify which areas require particular expertise to assist in the site's evaluation. The search will focused on a specific geographical area that demonstrates growth potential, the right demographics, high occupancies and a high demand for the specific development type.

Zoning

A potential development site should be zoned appropriately or have the potential to be rezoned to the developer's requirements. This information can be obtained from the local council planning office under which the site falls. A development's viability can be significantly affected by delays in rezoning or the assessment of a development application (DA). If the land has to be rezoned you must decide if this lengthy process will be rewarding in the end relative to cost. The sooner the application is out of the council, the sooner the project can commence and holding costs can be reduced. In addition, the attitude of the local government and planning officials should be carefully reviewed. If their attitude is generally pro-development, you will receive fewer problems with your applications, while if a no-growth or conservative attitude predominates you can expect lengthy delays.

Size and shape of site

When viewing a potential development site you should verify the total number of square metres of the property to ensure that the area fits the needs of your development proposal together with the density and parking requirements. The zoning of the property can have an effect on the density of the property and can vary from area to area. The higher the density zoning, the more buildings can be constructed, but this can also be affected by the shape of the property. It is imperative that you or your consultant check the zoning regulations with the local planning office. The following regulations should be checked.

Coverage

This relates to the percentage of ground floor area relative to the total site area. For example, if the total site area is 1000 square metres and the allowable coverage is 50 per cent then the maximum area that can be built on the ground floor (or roofed area) is 500 square metres.

Plot ratio

Also known as the bulk or floor space index, this is the percentage of the allowable building area relative to the total site area. Using the above example, if the plot ratio is 0.8, or 80 per cent, then the maximum building area is 800 square metres. Therefore the ground floor can be 500 square metres with a second storey with a floor area of 300 square metres.

Parking

Each building type and each council will have its own set of rules regarding the amount of vehicular parking required. For example, the parking requirements for an apartment development may be 0.75 bays per unit for units under 60 square metres but 1.0 bay per unit for units above 80 square metres, whereas an office may require four car bays for every 100 square metres.

Building setbacks

Also known as building lines, the street setbacks may be different from those to the side or the rear of the site, so it is best to check these with your local council.

Easements

These could be special restrictions pertaining to the specific site such as sewerage easements or stormwater easements. Easements prevent building in areas that might obstruct access by various authorities for maintenance.

Site characteristics

Prior to purchasing a development site, its physical characteristics should be thoroughly reviewed, as they could affect the development and building cost. Areas that should be analysed include the following.

Topography

Flat sites are preferable as significant slopes will add costs. Retaining walls will inevitably be required on steep sites, adding to the building cost.

Soil conditions

The nature and bearing capacity of the subsoil of a site is very important. It is advisable that a geotechnical analysis be undertaken by a qualified engineer as this could have a bearing on the type of foundation required for the project. Clay conditions or underground rock will affect the cost of the project.

Vegetation

Extensive vegetation on the site will increase the cost, but in most cases this cost cannot be avoided. It can also have a positive impact on the development, adding to its character. This can be enhanced by designing the building around the more matured tress. Saving trees on a smaller site can pose a problem, especially if they are located in the best position for the building.

Traffic flow

A study of the street patterns and traffic flow is important to a development, as the success of the development will depend in part on the smooth flow of traffic to and from the site. Any traffic hindrance will affect the marketing of the development to potential tenants or purchasers. Depending on the scale of the project, a traffic engineer could be employed prior to the purchase of the site to analyse the following.

Access and egress

Determine the possibilities of the site's entrances and exits. For a corner site, consider whether entrances on both streets would be of benefit.

Volume of traffic

High traffic volumes are good for retail developments that depend on customers visiting and buying goods, but may not suit residential sites where residents would prefer less traffic and lower noise levels.

Traffic flow

The time and direction of traffic flows should be analysed. Developing a residential site on a highway poses access problems for vehicles approaching on the opposite side of the road. Exiting may also be difficult during peak traffic hours.

Utilities

The supply of telephone, water and sewerage, electricity, gas and internet lines is important for all types of sites. Information can be gathered from the local water, gas and power authorities. Telephone and internet cabling can be obtained from the national carrier Telstra. Ideally, these utilities should already be adjacent to the site. If not, then the developer should analyse the cost implications of bringing the utilities to the site.

Public transport

Proximity to public transport systems benefits both residential and commercial developments. Most local governments now encourage Transport Orientated Developments (TOD) where the density zoning is higher in order to encourage apartment and/or commercial developments.

Real estate tax rates

Property taxes are normally assessed when property changes hands. This includes stamp duty and any other state or local government taxes, such as council rates and taxes or land tax. To determine whether these taxes are in line with the market, the property assessment should run comparisons with similar properties. Information can be obtained from the local tax office and settlement or conveyancing agents.

Developer's contribution

With greater urbanisation creating increased densities in suburbs closer to the CBD, some local councils impose a developer's contribution levy. Councils justify this levy as payment for additional services such as communal facilities, improved roads and public open spaces. The amount to be paid by the developer varies from council to council. It is best that you verify the amount to be contributed as part of your due diligence of the site.

Price of site

Having taken all these factors into consideration you need to determine whether the price of the land is justified for your intended development. The price of land can be broken down into a rate per square metre, but to a developer its true value is how much building can be efficiently constructed on the site. For example, if the price of an apartment development site is $2 million for 5000 square metres then the asking rate is $400 per square metre. However, when analysed against the plot ratio or the number of apartments, the value may be totally different. If the allowable plot ratio is 2.0, or 200 per cent, then the rate is $200 per square metre; an average apartment size of 60 square metres would allow the building of approximately 83 apartments, which equates to $33 333 per apartment.

Environmental issues

Environmentally impacted areas should be evaluated to find out if any problem could affect the value of your development. The local council's building department or local environmental agencies could assist in this regard. You will also need to keep up with ongoing amendments to the legislation. For example, in New South Wales every parcel of land is affected by State Environmental Planning Policies, Regional Environmental Planning Policies, Local Environmental Plans, Development Control Plans, council policies and council resolutions. In addition, the federal government has recently introduced the Biodiversity and Conservation Act and, under the Integrated Development Approval System (IDAS), concurrent approvals are required from affected government departments such as Land and Water Conservation, Roads and Traffic Authority and National Parks. On older sites that have been used, for example, for warehousing or industrial use, the developer should appoint an environmental engineer to check if the site has any contaminants such as oil seepage, asbestos or any toxic elements in the soil, as the remediation of these toxic conditions can be expensive.

Other site considerations

Depending on the type of development, other site considerations may need to be taken into account. For example, a residential development, a site that is close to social infrastructure such as schools, community centres, medical facilities and libraries, has an increased value, whereas commercial developments, especially those involving manufacturing, require access to large labour pools.

At the end of this chapter, table 4.1 provides a land checklist. This table is fairly comprehensive but not all items will be applicable to certain sites. It should be treated as a guide and to prompt you in analysing the variables when selecting a potential development site.

Reviewing established buildings

Development is not all about constructing new buildings on a clean site. For example, for sites close to the CBD, a good return could be made by retaining an existing building, renovating it and then presenting it for sale or lease. Before purchasing an existing building a careful property condition assessment should be undertaken to reveal any faults or features that might make the proposal unviable. By enlisting a knowledgeable team to conduct a building condition and property assessment, you can determine the best way to develop a realistic development strategy.

What is a property assessment?

A basic building and property assessment evaluates the building and site conditions to determine what would be required to bring the property back to an appropriate use level. A detailed assessment is often based on the final use for the property.

With existing properties that require substantial upgrading, the assessment team should look beyond repair and compliance to investigate potential alternative uses and the practicality of making the changes required to support these new functions. The report should include:

- critical repair and maintenance items required to make the building fully operational and limit the more extensive deterioration

- major repairs or restoration, including items that will reach the end of their useful life within five to ten years

- alterations necessary for compliance with building codes and requirements, and local regulations

- upgrades to make a building more marketable or more cost-efficient to operate

- changes necessary to enable a new use, such as converting an office block into apartments.

The assessment team

Depending on the condition of the property and the intended end use, an assessment team usually comprises an architect, a structural engineer, a mechanical engineer and an electrical engineer. The contracts with these consultants should specify the scope of the review.

Heritage assessment

If the potential development site is in a heritage-listed area and if the building itself is heritage listed, a thorough due diligence should be undertaken with a consulting team with both experience and knowledge in heritage building so they can advise on the extent of permissible change to its 'adaptive' use. Of course, heritage buildings have far greater restrictions but if approached correctly they can offer great value. With several layers of approval required, however, it can be a long, drawn-out process.

Visual analysis

The first step in any building assessment is a visual survey in which photographs are taken to record existing conditions and any deficiencies. If team members cannot determine the cause or extent of a deficient item such as structural movement or water leaks during a visual analysis, they may conduct a more in-depth review, such as removing brick, plasterboard or portions of the roof for various tests.

Past documents

In addition to the physical examination of the property, the assessment team can work on information provided by the seller. The team is not responsible for incorrect information provided to them. Past documents, such as initial construction drawings and subsequent renovations and additions, are handy, and the following additional documents can also be useful:

- geotechnical reports
- as-built drawings and specifications of the building, civil and mechanical works
- tenant layouts if applicable
- verification of licences, certificates, approvals, and other evidence of compliance with building codes and authorities
- construction reports prepared by architects and engineers
- any reports on facility or system deficiencies and corrections
- recurring complaints from tenants or occupants
- any capital improvements
- property maintenance program and principal maintenance contracts.

Common defect problems

Every property has its own character and problems, but certain types of problems recur in most buildings. The following list covers some potential areas that should be reviewed.

Paved areas

Annoying to tenants and customers, asphalt problems can have a significant cost impact with large areas of surface parking.

Brick masonry walls

Insufficient detailing or lack of oversight during construction can result in poor fixing of critical components such as flashing, weepholes and waterproofing, causing significant water leaks and expense.

Roofing

Roofing is an important capital item. A thorough report should assess the roofing system's overall condition, including flashings, to assess whether maintenance appears sufficient and to evaluate the roof's remaining life.

Air conditioning

Depending on the type of system in place, increasing the cooling capacity of an existing system can be as nominal as installing additional rooftop units or as significant as upgrading major system components such as condensers, chillers and piping.

Asbestos

Buildings constructed before 1980 will have building products that have been made from asbestos. This can include flooring, internal walls and ceiling panels. An asbestos specialist will need to provide an assessment of the asbestos in the building and the cost of safely removing it and replacing it with a non-asbestos material.

Building regulations and fire safety

The assessment team should have knowledge of the building regulations that were in effect when the building was initially constructed as well as the current ones. When buildings change use or undergo major renovation, most authorities require that the existing buildings be brought up to meet current regulations. Building regulations that could affect any renovations can include fire regulations, building codes and energy ratings.

Analyse the economic characteristics

When assessing the viability of a development site or an existing building, you should not only review the property on a micro market level but also the broader macro market as a regional area. The research should include information on the general economy, comparable properties and future development activities. This analysis should take into consideration the following.

General economic information

In conducting this research, you should obtain the necessary information to make a judgement on the development site.

- What is the general trend of the economy in the region?

- What is the growth rate for the region?

- In which direction is the employment base heading—upward or downward?

- What is the structure of the state and local governments?

- Does the region or city have a pro-development policy?

- Are adequate services provided in the area?

- What is the history of building applications for various types of properties?

Unemployment rates

The local unemployment figures should be evaluated to determine whether the area's rate is rising or declining. A trend towards high unemployment can mean a low demand for sales or rental properties. Information can be obtained from the Department of Labour or the local Chamber of Commerce.

New construction activity and available land

Carefully examine the current and projected commercial and residential construction activity. Is building activity increasing or decreasing? Any new building activity of a similar type to your development will add competition to the market. In addition, the rezoning of any vacant land in the area should be examined, as new land could mean future competition. Information can be collected from the Australian Bureau of Statistics, the local building department, local real estate research firms and local real estate valuers.

Bankruptcy rates

Bankruptcy rates of businesses in the area indicate the health of the market. The higher the rates, the closer the local economy is to a recession or depression. Check and research this information from local banks, legal newspapers, research firms and local accountants.

Local inflation indexes

In preparing your financial forecasts and feasibility study, you will need to know what the past cost of living indexes were and what future trends are predicted. Such information can be obtained from the Australian Bureau of Statistics and or local accounting firms.

Analysing the property market trends

This is one of the most important aspects to investigate before purchasing a potential development site. Analysis of present and predicted market conditions, including rental and occupancy rates, yields, absorption rates and volume of sales of similar types of properties, will determine the viability of your project.

Rental rates

An analysis of local rental rates for the type of property you will be developing will help you to calculate the market rental (the advertised rent) and the net rental (the real rent collected after all landlord costs are figured in). You will then know how your property should fit into the rental rate structure. Such rental information can be found easily through various real estate websites on the internet.

Vacancy levels

As a property developer, you should find out the vacancy history of properties in the market and more importantly evaluate the trend for the future. By talking to local real estate agents, real estate research firms and property valuers you will gain an understanding of the occupancy rate in the area. In addition, you will be able to tell a lot about the health of the real estate market from the rent or sale concessions currently being offered. Carefully review the history of these concessions and analyse where the market is heading. Ensure you research areas that have a similar location, as many properties can be located in areas of low occupancy rates when the market appears to be healthy.

Recent sales

Obtain a listing of the most recent sales of similar type of properties. This list will provide information on what comparable properties have been selling for recently. Evaluate the amount of time these properties have required to find a purchaser and the percentage of the original asking price that they sold for. Also, review the history of appreciation for similar properties over the past few years and estimate the appreciation you may expect in the future. An established local real estate agency can provide both the present and historical sales. Several websites, such as RP Data, can provide you with such information for a small fee.

Absorption rate

Analyse how long a property of a similar type remains vacant before it is either rented or sold. More importantly, if it has been vacant for a period of time find out the exact reasons why. Some properties do not move simply because of location or architectural design.

Avoiding legal pitfalls

Another area of due diligence pertains to the legal limitations imposed on the property. This area includes several key tasks.

Reviewing the title to the property

When reviewing the title, the attorney should determine whether the property could be transferred by the seller or title-holder with a 'clean and marketable title'. A clean and marketable title is one that is free of any liens or other encumbrances. In examining the title the following items need to be reviewed:

- current owner of the property
- mortgage holder
- caveats or liens by third parties
- easements and encroachments
- judgements
- arrear rates and taxes
- poor legal descriptions
- restrictive covenants
- improperly executed deeds or other instruments
- boundary line agreements/party wall agreements.

Assembling several properties for development

With increases in urban population, government planners are under pressure to increase densities in older suburbs closer to the CBD. This presents an exciting opportunity for developers to assemble a group of properties and create a 'super lot' for a new development. However, packaging these sites is often a very testing challenge and the difficulty increases exponentially with increased numbers of landowners.

Careful preparation and research, and experience in dealing with reluctant landowners who do not want to sell, are essential to a successful land assembly. Developers who have a good understanding of this difficult process can appreciate the value of an expert experienced in site acquisition. The site acquisition expert could be a solicitor, an experienced real estate professional or a combination of the two.

Finding suitable sites

When appointing the site acquisition expert you should establish the site selection criteria based on your proposed development policies. All or any of the following issues should be considered:

- What is the proposed development and where would it best be located?

- What is the size of land area required to make the project viable?

- What is the maximum price of each site that the development can accept?

- What is the cost of the additional utilities?

- Is there a developer's contribution due to change or increase of use?

- Are there alternative options, if the first assembly does not work?

With this information, the expert can make a methodical assessment of the market to identify suitable locations and properties. Resources available to assist with completing the assessment include global positioning system mapping tools, online aerial photography from governmental agencies, or local government and planning commissions.

Meeting the landowners

After a list of potential sites has been compiled, communication with landowners will start. Asking landowners the following preliminary questions will help to determine their views towards selling their property:

- Is the landowner interested in selling and if so at what asking price?

- Who owns the land? Is the decision maker a syndicate or a company?

- Do they understand the property sale process?
- Have previous offers to purchase been made?
- What are their key concerns about selling?

In most cases these properties are not on the market and the expert must approach landowners directly. Owners who are reluctant to sell their properties present a big challenge.

Dealing with reluctant owners

When a selected property is not on the market, the landowner must decide whether or not to sell and at what price. Quite often owners either don't know what the property is worth or have unrealistic expectations of its value. The best way to move the process forward is to establish a dialogue and increase the owner's comfort level, find out their real objections and try to overcome them. Although there is no standard procedure to follow, the expert must gain a good understanding of the owner's current and future situation, recognise their motivations and then present a proposal that addresses their concerns.

The most common reasons an owner won't sell are the timing of the offer and unrealistic price expectations. Uncovering these barriers to purchase before the actual assembly process begins saves valuable time. But if it becomes apparent during negotiations that a contract cannot be finalised, you should cease discussions and focus on another site. Sometimes knowing the prospective buyer has moved on will spark interest in a reluctant seller.

Pricing and negotiations

After establishing the landowners' pricing motivations, you can prioritise sites based on which group of properties appears to be in the right price range. The next step is to establish an offer price and terms for each parcel. The final price will range from the offering price to the maximum amount you are willing to pay based on your project's budget, comparable sales and the owner's expectations of market value.

Each sale transaction can take months to complete. Ensure that you allow sufficient time for due diligence in the initial offer and record the progress or delays. Complications multiply as the size and scope of a project increases. In many cases, experts may find themselves in the unfortunate situation of negotiating an extended due diligence period with each owner. A number of issues can delay the project and warrant the need for further extensions. These may involve, for example, development approvals or road widening due to increased traffic.

Another decision in the acquisition process is whether or not to disclose your name and the nature of the project to the landowners. A proposed project plan can be a successful selling tool, but some developers are reluctant to identify themselves for fear that one or more of the landowners will attempt to extract an unreasonable price for their properties.

Concluding a land assembly can be a very rewarding accomplishment. There is no standard procedure for success as the circumstances vary with each site, but with the application of intuition and patience the challenges will be worth the time and effort invested.

Summary

The following summarises some simple but helpful hints, in the form of a list of do's and don'ts, to assist you when selecting a development site. In addition, table 4.1 (overleaf) provides a site checklist to use before entering into any formal contractual relationship with a landowner. Remember, location is one of the basic success fundamentals in real estate, and any poor decision made in site selection could be a source of serious regret.

The do's

- Secure a development site in an established growth area.
- Secure a development site in a high-visibility area.
- Secure a development site with high occupancy rates.
- Secure a development site that has increasing rental rates.
- Secure a development site with established services/utilities.
- Select a development site based on market research, not emotion.
- Always perform a due diligence on the prospective development site.
- Always perform a pre-purchase viability study.

The don'ts

- Secure a development site on the down cycle.

- Purchase a development site if you have insufficient funding to carry any interest during the holding period.

- Secure a development site that does not have the appropriate zoning, unless there is a good chance of getting it rezoned.

- Secure excessive land unless it can be subdivided and sold to other parties or unless the land is cheap or required in a phased development.

Development site checklist

The site checklist template in table 4.1 can assist you with analysing the potential of a proposed development site. Although the form is fairly extensive, all items are unlikely to be applicable to a single site as the conditions for a residential site may differ from those of a commercial site.

Table 4.1: site checklist form

Property data				
Property address	No.	Street	Suburb	State
Legal description	Lot no.	Plan no.	Volume	Folio
Present owner/agent				
Address	No.	Street	Suburb	State
	Ph. (w)		Ph. (h)	Mobile
Local authority				
Zoning classification	Present		Future/potential	
Land size	Total m^2		Usable m^2	
	Frontage (m)	Left (m)	Right (m)	Rear (m)
Physical improvements	None	Other (describe)		
Easements	No	Yes (describe)		
Covenants	No	Yes (describe)		

Rental income	Income per month		Expenses per month	
Rates and taxes	Present		Future	
Land tax	Present		Future	
Reason for selling				
Type sale	Terms	Cash	Option	Joint venture
Sales price	Asking price		Per square metre	Per unit

Physical features

Site survey	Is a site survey available?			
Topography	Flat		Slope (describe)	
Vegetation	Dense			Sparse
Type of trees	Large		Small	Retain
Soils condition	Sandy		Clay	Rock
	Gravel		Limestone	Other
Soils test undertaken	Yes		No	
Are boundaries pegged	Yes		No	
Fences	Type		Condition	None
	Front	Right side	Left side	Rear
Views	Ocean	River	Lake	Other
	Front	Right side	Left side	Rear
Orientation	North facing	West facing	East facing	South facing
Neighbours (right side)	Vacant	Single storey	Double storey	Other
(left side)	Vacant	Single storey	Double storey	Other
(rear)	Vacant	Single storey	Double storey	Other
Street verge	Large trees	Telephone post	Electricity post	Other
	Do any of the above block the access driveway?			
Accessibility	Good	Bad	Heavy traffic?	
Noise levels	High	Low	Type	

(continued)

Table 4.1: site checklist form *(cont'd)*

Electricity	Yes	No	Overhead	Underground
Gas	Yes	No		
Water	Yes	No		
Sewerage	Yes	No	Deep sewer	Septic tank
Stormwater	Yes	No	Surface	Underground
Telephone	Yes	No	Overhead	Underground
Cable TV	Yes	No	Satellite	Underground
Broadband cable	Yes	No		
Refuse collection	Yes	No		
Neigbourhood characteristics				
Distance to CBD	Kilometres		Time	
Neighbourhood layout	Good	Poor	Comments	
Child care centres	Yes	No	Distance from site	
Primary school	Yes	No	Distance from site	
High school	Yes	No	Distance from site	
Technical school	Yes	No	Distance from site	
University	Yes	No	Distance from site	
Corner shop	Yes	No	Distance from site	
Neighbour shop centre	Yes	No	Distance from site	
Regional shop centre	Yes	No	Distance from site	
Medical services	Yes	No	Distance from site	
Hospital	Yes	No	Distance from site	
Churches	Yes	No	Distance from site	
Community centres	Yes	No	Distance from site	
Council offices	Yes	No	Distance from site	
Library	Yes	No	Distance from site	
Public parks	Yes	No	Distance from site	
Recreational facilities	Yes	No	Distance from site	

Rail public transport	Yes	No	Distance from site		
Bus public transport	Yes	No	Distance from site		
Freeway access	Yes	No	Distance from site		
Waterfront	Yes	No	Distance from site		
Crime rate	High	Low	Is police station close by?		
Governmental controls					
Local authority details	Council/shire			Ph.	Fax
	Address				
	Postal address				
	Planning department	Contact person		Ph.	
	Building department	Contact person		Ph.	
Other authorities	State planning				
	Main roads				
	Environment				
	Health				
	Fire				
	Water				
	Electricity				
	Gas				
	Sewerage				
	Telephone				
	Other				
Structure plan	Is there one available?			Can you purchase a copy?	
Zoning requirements	Zoning	Coverage	Plot ratio	Parking	
	Front setback	Right-side setback	Left-side setback	Rear setback	
	Height restrictions	Overshadowing	Privacy policy	Other	

(continued)

Table 4.1: site checklist form *(cont'd)*

Building requirements	Are national building codes used?		
	If not, describe		
Heritage	Does the property fall under a heritage ruling?		
	If yes, describe		
Environmental controls	Does the site fall under certain environmental controls?		
	If yes, describe		
Design criteria	Are there any special design requirements?		
	If yes, describe		
Council policy	Are there any specific council policy requirements pertaining to the site?		
	If yes, describe		
Attitude to development	Local authority	For?	Against?
	Community	For?	Against?
Comments from	Planning department		
	Building department		
Fees	Planning fees		
	Building fees		
	Other fees		
Council meetings	How often held?		

Councillors	Mayor	Ph.		Mobile	
	Councillor	Ph.		Mobile	
	Councillor	Ph.		Mobile	
Demographics					
Population	What is the population of the suburb or market catchment area?				
Income group	High (A group)		Middle (B group)		Lower (C group)
Average income ($)	What is the average income?				
Average age (years)	60 years plus	45 years plus		35 years plus	20 years plus
Average household size	2 members		3 members	4 members	5 members
Vehicles per household	1 vehicle		2 vehicles		4 vehicles
Owner occupied	What percentage of homes are owned?				
Renter occupied	What percentage of homes are rented?				
Economic trends					
Growth of area	Present growth			Future growth	
Property values	Values increasing			Values increasing	
Rates and taxes	Present rates and taxes			Future rates and taxes	
Unemployment rates	Present rate		Increasing	Decreasing	
Building approvals	Approvals increasing			Approvals decreasing	
Bankruptcy rates	Rates increasing			Rates decreasing	
Housing finance	Freely available?			Present interest rates	
Inflation indexes	Present index			Future index	
Real estate trends					
Rental rates	Average market rental			Average nett rental	
Vacancy rates	What are present vacancy rates?			What has been the past vacancy trends?	
Recent sales	Average recent sales			What was the average asking price?	
Absorption rate	How long are the properties on the market before they are sold?				
New building activity	Are there similar developments being built in the area?				

(continued)

Table 4.1: site checklist form *(cont'd)*

Highest and best use of property			
Renovation		Shopping centre	
Duplex, triplex		Showrooms	
Townhouses		Factory shops	
Retirement		Offices	
Apartments		Office park	
Land subdivision		Hotel/resort	
Holiday homes		Industrial	
Student accommodation		Medical centre	
Government housing		Mixed use	
Other		Other	
Purchasing cost			
Deposit	Lender 1	Lender 2	Lender 3
Bank application fees	Lender 1	Lender 2	Lender 3
Bank valuation fees	Lender 1	Lender 2	Lender 3
Bank ongoing fees	Lender 1	Lender 2	Lender 3
State stamp duty			
Conveyancing fees	Agency fees		
	Council enquiry fees		
	Water enquiry fees		
	Rates and taxes		
	Land tax		
	Disbursements		
Other matters relating to purchase decision			
Local building cost	Rate per square metre		

Professional fees	Project manager	
	Architect/ designer	
	Land surveyor	
	Quantity surveyor	
	Structural engineer	
	Civil engineer	
	Mechanical engineer	
	Electrical engineer	
	Geotechnical engineer	
	Town planner	
	Landscape architect	
	Interior designer	
	Accountant	
	Lawyer	
	Property valuer	
	Property manager	
Marketing fees	Marketing company	
	Commissions	
	Brochures	
	Advertising	
Additional items	Insurance	

CHAPTER 5
Negotiation and purchasing

Experienced property developers know that a lucrative development starts with the astute purchase of the site. Paying too much for a site means less profit for the developer. A successful outcome depends on the developer's knowledge of the property and its market value and sound negotiating skills. Aggressive developers do not necessarily always get the best outcome in a property transaction; smart and sophisticated negotiators seek a careful balance between the negotiating parties to achieve an outcome that is mutually beneficial.

As with all transactions, an important first step is to uncover the seller's motive. Are they selling because they need the cash owing to financial difficulty? Are they retiring or going through a divorce? In some cases sale properties are owned by a number of parties, so the developer needs to analyse all the parties involved in the transaction to find out who the ultimate decision maker is or whether a group decision is to be reached. Knowing as much as possible about the seller can help to determine the most successful negotiation strategy.

Before entering into negotiations with a seller, developers should do their homework on the property and establish strategies and options that are fluid for handling the various responses that may arise. Developers should anticipate any objection the seller might raise and have a well-thought-out response ready. Mental preparation for both positive and negative results is essential. How a developer responds to a negative outcome can influence the possibility of future talks. By handling a less-than-favourable outcome skilfully, calmly and tactfully, developers will enhance their general reputation, which may lead to future business with either party.

Structuring your offer

Before you can structure an offer you need to have a good understanding of the property for sale and of the motivating factors behind the sale. The best way to approach this is to ask a number of questions. This is all part of doing the due diligence on the property, some of which was covered in the previous chapter. The better the questions you ask, the more information you will obtain for structuring the correct deal. Ask the following questions during the initial negotiations.

About the seller

- Why is the property being sold?
- How long has the property been on the market?
- Who owns the property—a company or private individuals?
- How long have the present owners owned the property?
- Who is the person who makes the final selling decision?
- If the property is occupied, when and to where do the owners have to move?
- If the property is settled early, can you get a better price?
- Is the owner willing to participate in the development by offering land as part of the deal?

Price and terms

- What is the asking price?
- Is the asking price negotiable?
- Will the seller grant an option?
- When does the seller want settlement on the property?

Once you have a better understanding of the property and, more importantly, the seller's motives for placing the property on the market, you may need to consider the following.

If the seller is firm on price, negotiate your own terms

Some sellers are adamant about price and will not budge. Their focus is on a set price and they have not considered alternatives. This gives you the buyer an opportunity to buy on your terms. For example, you may offer the asking price but extend the settlement period so you can complete your designs and feasibility study without paying interest on the property.

If the seller is firm on terms, negotiate your own price

On the other hand, some sellers seek an early settlement because of personal circumstances. They may therefore look favourably on a cash offer below the asking price. In this case, at least factor the interest you would be paying during the feasibility studies, plans and various approvals as a discount on the asking price.

If the price is too high, dispel the seller's expectations

If you have done your research and found a property that you are keen to purchase but the price is too high and the seller and their agent won't budge, study the property carefully and look for all the negatives. You may decide that the deal is wasting your time and walk away, or you may want to show the seller or their agent that you are methodical and that you have found flaws in the property that require rectification. By pointing out the flaws you may bring the seller or their agent back to reality, persuading them to reduce the price in line with the market.

Position yourself for negotiations

When you have collected all the relevant information and, more importantly, understand the seller's motives you need to think about your own position and how best to set yourself up for negotiations.

Settle on what benefits you want

If you have been thorough in your research you will know the price that you should be paying for the property. Stick with your price and your terms. If the seller is not prepared to accept them, be prepared to walk away. The seller may realise that you are not bluffing and may back down. Property development is risky and if you cannot get a property that will deliver the correct financial outcome you will only be fooling yourself.

Keep it simple

It is advisable that you keep your offer and negotiations uncomplicated rather than risk confusing the seller or agent. There is also a possibility that the seller will walk away from the deal even if it would ultimately benefit them. Keep the deal simple and use terms that can be easily understood.

Try not to offer the figure first

Where a price of a hot property is not advertised or you are negotiating an 'off market' property, don't mention the number. Remember the old adage: 'The first person to mention a number loses'. Mentioning any figures may weaken your position. Let the seller expose what they are looking for and ask questions in order that the seller shows all their cards. From this position you will be able to strategise an offer that will benefit you.

Make the seller see the benefits

Most sellers focus only on price without considering the favourable terms you may be offering. Ensure that the seller or agent is made aware of the problems that you can save them from or the benefits you can offer.

Think laterally

Analyse different circumstances before you start negotiations or decide to make an offer, as not all property dealings are the same. Give the seller a number of options or alternative terms to select from. The seller needs to be convinced that cash is not the only form of property transaction. Show them that there may be solutions that will benefit both parties.

Prepare a pre-purchase feasibility report

After completing all the necessary research described in the previous chapter, you need to prepare a *pre-purchase feasibility report* before you make the final decision to purchase a potential development site unconditionally. The whole exercise should not be extensive, but should give you an overall idea of whether the site is worth the money the seller is asking for. The process should include the following exercises:

- Complete the property checklist (see table 4.1 on p. 86).
- Complete a schematic layout of the proposed development.
- Calculate the potential return if the development is sold.
- Calculate the potential rental return if the development is held.

Property checklist

The first principle is to avoid buying a property based on emotion and gut feeling. The best way to control the emotion factor is to draw up a comprehensive checklist and adhere to it conscientiously for every potential site you look at. Unless the property satisfies every aspect of the checklist either it should be dropped or you can use any negative findings as a powerful tool to negotiate the property down to the right price for you. The checklist will help to highlight any potential risks associated with your prospective development. Obviously there will be certain issues that you yourself may not be able to resolve, such as the subsoil conditions; however, you can then seek expert advice to clarify any outstanding issues raised.

Schematic layout

Although the zoning of a site may suggest a certain density this may not always be the case, as each site has its own characteristics (it may be oddly shaped, say). For example, the council regulations may state that, based on a certain site area, a total of 11 housing units can be built on the site. However, factors such as slope, irregular shape, orientation, impact on neighbours, streetscape, stormwater drainage, vehicle access, overshadowing and privacy may restrict the development potential to only nine units. It is therefore important to engage an architect to prepare a schematic or concept plan to see if this could be the case. If so, it would be best either to walk away or to negotiate a price reflecting the viability of nine units.

Potential profit

The potential profit is the prime reason for taking a risk in a development project. If there is no profit to be gained from the development then either the land is too expensive or the design is not cost effective. If the land is too expensive, try to negotiate a better price or better terms that will suit your feasibility. If the design is not cost effective, get your architect or designer to analyse the items that are too costly and look for more cost-effective alternatives (refer to chapter 11). If neither of these issues can be resolved walk away and look for another site. In calculating your potential return there are a number of formulas that you can utilise, and these are explained in chapter 10.

Potential rental return

Whether you intend to hold on to your completed development as a long-term investment or to sell it for pure profit, you should still undertake an exercise to assess the potential rental return. If your strategy is to sell, you should bear in mind that the market may turn and you could be caught in a position where you cannot sell your units and are forced to rent them out until the market turns again. The option of holding on to the property as an investment will obviously depend on the amount of equity you will allocate to the development. It is good business to ensure that you are not in a position where the loan is too highly geared, which would ultimately affect your cash flow.

In summary, these exercises do take time but they are well worth the effort. Unless you know the values in the area, a rash decision in purchasing a site could land you with a costly and stressful problem.

Items to consider before making an offer

The following list will provide insights into an offer that the developer must negotiate to gain control of a potential development site for sale.

Not all factors covered in this checklist will apply to every property transaction.

- *Name of the purchaser:* The name will depend on the entity under which you will be developing the property.

- *Name of the seller:* The property may be registered under a company name rather than the owner's personal name.

- *Legal description of the subject property:* This includes all legal details such as the lot number, street name, street number, suburb and title particulars, which include the volume number, folio number and plan number. In addition the type of the property should define whether it is freehold, strata title, green title and so on.

- *Purchase price:* After your negotiations you would have a price in mind.

- *Deposit:* This is the money required at the signing of the contract to demonstrate the buyer's sincerity.

- *Settlement date:* This is the date set for payment and transfer of the title.

- *Due diligence period:* This period, the time required to perform due diligence for evaluation and inspection of the property, should expire in a predetermined number of days after receiving all information requested from the landowner.

- *Settlement costs:* These are the expenses paid by the buyer or seller. Each party is responsible for their respective costs. Settlement costs include:

  - *stamp duty* — the tax due for transferring the deed from one owner to another, based on the sales price and a rate established by law

  - *mortgage registration fee* — the fee due to the state for the registration of the mortgage

  - *registration costs* — the fee charged by the deeds office for recording mortgage and deed documents

  - *survey cost* — the cost of the property survey that verifies the legal description

  - *attorney's fees* — usually paid by both the purchaser and seller.

- *Settlement extension:* This is an option to extend the settlement date should you not be able to settle on time. It may entail:
  - *additional money*—an additional amount of deposit money when the settlement time is extended, which can be either additional proceeds paid or included in the sales price
  - *notice to seller*—the time required by the contract for notification that you will exercise the extension option.
- *Shared settlement costs:* These are the expenses of the property, which will be shared between the seller and the buyer on the day of settlement, and include:
  - *revenue*—any revenue from the land, which is split as of the date of settlement
  - *real estate taxes*—the real estate tax due as of the date of settlement
  - *operating expenses*—any operating costs for the property should be prorated as of the date of settlement.
- *Sales commission:* If a real estate agent is involved in the sale of the property, he or she should be named.
- *Seller warranties:* These are the representations and warranties that you may require from the seller, including:
  - *authority to sell*—that the seller is the authorised party to execute the sales agreement
  - *conveyance*—that the sale of the property does not violate any government regulations
  - *utilities*—that the required utilities are available to the property
  - *soil conditions*—that the property was never used as a landfill site or as a repository for toxic waste
  - *liabilities*—that all liabilities that encumber the property are disclosed
  - *court proceedings*—that no current or proposed court proceedings are pending
  - *material defects*—that there are no defects that will adversely affect the property

- *road widening*—that there are no known current or proposed plans for road widening that would reduce the area being purchased
- *current leases or service contracts*—that there are no outstanding leases.

- *Conditional items:* These are items critical to the developer for the settlement of the transaction, and if not verified as believed at the signing of the contract or waived will cause the contract to be terminated. They include:
  - *land survey*—verification of the correct land area
  - *zoning*—required rezoning or variances for your intended use
  - *market studies*—confirmation of market supply and demand relative to your intended use
  - *financing*—evidence that financing for the land and the development can be obtained
  - *project viability*—time necessary for the developer to verify the project
  - *utilities*—availability of, or the costs to provide, needed utilities for the development
  - *site development costs*—if the site has unusual features, the liability is usually associated with site-work costs; estimates should be obtained and included in project viability
  - *soil and environmental tests*—studies to verify presence of rock or soil strength or the presence of other hazardous material
  - *raising the equity*—if the transaction requires additional equity, the developer may require time to raise the equity.

- *Terminating the contract:* In structuring the offer, you need to ensure that should certain events not occur prior to the settlement, the deal can be terminated. The following items should be considered for termination:
  - *lien free*—if the seller does not clear up all liens on the property prior to settlement, the transaction will be in default
  - *clear title*—the contract should state that at settlement the developer will receive land with a clear title.

Tendering for a development site

The tendering system is used mainly for larger development projects and where the state or local government has an area or zone that they are trying to promote to developers for economic reasons. At times private landowners also may offer their property for tender as they seek the best possible outcome for their land in terms of price and design or just a better price. In Australia, the government have a strict tender process for probity reasons; they focus on securing not the best price for the land but a better outcome for the local community, and on selecting a credible developer with the credentials to deliver.

The scope and process for each tender will vary depending on the type and scale of the proposed project. If you decide to participate in a tender, whether public (government) or private, you will need to understand the process and what is involved. The two more popular tender systems used are 'formal' and 'informal'.

Formal tenders

In formal tenders, also known as 'invited' or 'selected' tenders, a short list of parties are invited to participate and provided with documentation outlining the scope of the tender and an offer to contract. These parties are given a specified time to perform all due diligence requirements on the property. At the closing date the tenderer submits a signed offer to contract. Upon receiving the tenders, the seller has the right to accept the best tender or to negotiate with the other tenderers.

Informal tenders

In informal tenders a property is offered publicly in the marketplace and interested parties can request a copy of the tender documents. These parties will submit their offer by the closing date, including their capability, settlement date and a deposit cheque. From the list of submitted tenders a preferred party will be selected and given around two weeks to execute the contract of sale.

Proposal calls

Proposal calls or expressions of interest are normally offered by government bodies wishing to sell or lease government land but seeking the development that will best suit the community at large. At times the price and certain conditions are set. The proposals are normally displayed for public comment or objections before the governing body makes the final decision on the winning proposal.

How to secure a tender

If you participate in a tender, you must understand that you are competing with other tenderers. Therefore it is important to make sure that you have the right attitude and the ability to be a strong contender. Consider the following:

- Make your tender proposal unique by highlighting something special in your proposal that other tenderers may not be able to offer. This will give you a competitive edge.

- Prepare a professional presentation document. Remember that the adjudication panel will be reviewing several proposals and not you in person. Therefore a professionally prepared document will always stand out from other submissions.

- Abide by the rules and scope of the tender while at the same time keeping your proposal simple and easy to read.

Securing development rights

Under a development rights agreement, a developer negotiates a deal with a landowner to develop on the landowner's land. The developer provides expertise and erects the buildings. The landowner is paid for the land with accrued interest when the building or buildings are sold. These opportunities are not normally available to a novice developer as a landowner would usually be sceptical of a developer's inexperience and would look more favourably on an experienced developer with a good track record.

In formalising a development rights agreement both parties should consider the following aspects in order to prevent any misunderstanding during the period of the agreement.

The advantages of a development rights agreement

The advantages to the developer include the following:

- The developer does have to outlay large sums of capital or borrow funds to purchase the land, thereby reducing the total development cost.

- The developer's own cash is not at risk.

- There are savings on imposts such as settlement fees and stamp duty that will help to reduce the development costs and increase the profit.

- There is no pressure to build immediately so sufficient planning can take place, whereas with borrowed funds there is the pressure of the landholding cost.

- The developer who pre-sells the development is not actually paying for the land.

The advantages to the landowner include the following:

- The landowner does not have to wait for a potential buyer to secure funding for both the land and construction.

- The landowner receives a higher interest rate on equity owned than if they had sold and put the money in the bank.

- The landowner does not have to undertake development risks if they decide to develop themselves, and they are working with someone with more experience.

- If the developer defaults, the landowner still holds the title so retains the land.

The value of the land

An agreement should be reached as to the true market value of the land, and a sworn appraisal by a property valuer will help in this regard. If the project is a residential unit development, then the land cost per unit should be assessed and agreed. For example, if the land value is $1 million and 20 residential units can be accommodated, then the land value per unit should be $50 000. The developer should obviously negotiate a better price and at the same time undertake a comprehensive feasibility study to ensure a reasonable profit margin relative to the development risk involved.

The term of the agreement

The time set for the development to be completed will depend on the scale and area of the project and the prevailing market conditions. The developer should obviously aim for a longer period, as unknown factors may delay the project. There should be enough time for completing feasibility studies, planning approvals, development finance approvals, building approvals, construction, marketing and the conclusion of the sale of each unit.

The interest rate

Try to negotiate an interest rate with the landowner below normal bank rates with interest only. More importantly, try to set the start date of the interest after all approvals and outstanding conditions have been met or, better still, from the start of the first drawdown from the construction development loan. Allow for a six-monthly review in case rates undergo a general drop, but at the same time cap the rate at a reasonable level.

The development finance

The development finance will be for the construction of the units and for site infrastructure such as internal roads, sewerage, water, electricity, gas and telephone and any other incidental costs incurred to complete the development for sale and occupancy. These funds can be supplied either by the landowner or by another financial institution. If external funds are to be used there will be a mortgage over the property and the developer will be the guarantor of the loan. In this case, any debt owed to the landowner for the land will be a subordinated debt that will rank below the senior development loan. In some cases the landowner will borrow the development finance but will charge a higher interest rate to the developer.

The distribution of funds after the sale

After the development is completed and a number of successful sales have been concluded the distribution of funds will be calculated as in table 5.1.

Table 5.1: distribution of funds after sale

Item	Amount
Sale of unit no. 2	$300 000
Less development cost/unit	$180 000
Less land value per unit	$ 50 000
Less interest to landowner	$ 5000
Less commission	$ 9000
Profit to developer	$ 56 000

The process would be to pay out any money owing to the bank financing the development cost first and then to the landowner plus his interest. The balance would be the developer's profit on the unit.

Securing an option

An option to purchase a development site is simply a contract to buy a property at a specified price during an allotted period of time. Depending on the circumstances of the market and the property an option can provide advantages to both the seller and the developer. While options are not appropriate in every situation, property developers should be familiar with the basics of the transaction as it gives time for the developer to undertake the project's feasibility study without laying out too much cash for the land.

In legal terms, an option is considered a unilateral contract because it obligates only one party, the seller, who commits to sell the optioned property at a certain price. In exchange for this obligation, the seller usually receives the option payment immediately. But until the option is exercised, the seller retains use of the property and receives any resulting income.

Advantages to the developer

There are several advantages to the developer in securing an option:

- The developer can acquire the property without worrying that someone else will buy it.

- The developer does not have to manage the property during the option period, and this includes rates, taxes, insurance and other associated expenses.

- The developer need cover only the option money and is not responsible for a large mortgage and the associated interest repayments.

- The developer has sufficient time to complete a comprehensive feasibility study, arrange finance, invite partners or simply sell the property to another developer for a higher price.

- The developer who fails to exercise the option loses only the option money but cannot be sued for damages as would be the case in a normal offer to purchase contract.

- The developer gains the time to find the best financing arrangement.

For these advantages, the developer pays the cost of the option, which is usually a small portion of the total purchase price. If the buyer's option lapses, the seller usually keeps the option fee. Thus the seller is compensated for the fact that the property was taken off the market during the option period.

Granting an option

Generally, granting an option does not constitute an immediate taxable event to either the landowner or the developer. The landowner receives cash or other payment but does not report any taxable income; and the developer makes a payment that has no immediate tax consequences. An option is a non-taxable, open transaction that remains open until it is either exercised or expires. However, if the option payment will be assessed as ordinary income regardless of whether the option is exercised or is allowed to expire, then it must be reported as taxable income in the year it is received.

Option money

It is not always beneficial to place the minimum amount of option money on the table, as the landowner may not consider such an offer a serious one. Depending on the circumstances surrounding the option it may be better to offer more money but terms of greater benefit to the development. Once having agreed to the terms of the option the landowner cannot renege on the agreement. It is wise to structure the option around as many benefits to the development as possible rather than necessarily around the cash amounts, as this will provide an avenue to sell the option to a third party if required.

Exercising an option

Once the developer exercises the option to purchase the property, the option money paid is simply included in the amount paid for the property. The option agreement should recognise that the option money is part of the property's selling price. Accordingly, both the option money and the purchase price are included when calculating the amount realised on the sale.

Extension of time

Consideration should be given to what will happen at the end of the option term if more time is needed, for example if the funding for the land is not yet in place. There should be a provision in the option agreement for such an eventuality. It should be written into the agreement that the option can be extended for another year, or for whatever extended period is required, for an additional stated payment amount or an amount agreed by the seller.

Staged option

This option is used predominantly in land transactions where a developer does not want to buy a large tract of land all at once as the initial capital cost and interest could make the development unviable. Instead, the developer negotiates to buy the first stage or portion of the development with an option to purchase the other sections at a higher price at a later date. If the project turns sour then the developer is not obligated to exercise the options on the balance of the land. Obviously the option money will be forfeit but the developer will be able to look to better opportunities.

Lease with an option to purchase

Using this alternative option technique a developer can lower the option money and take out a lease with an option to purchase. The only investment the developer will have made in this situation is the time needed to find a tenant to cover the cost of the monthly lease arrangements. The benefit of this option is that it secures a property without a large capital outlay and the developer can decide the appropriate time to exercise the option and develop the property.

When buying a development site options are wonderful tools for the developer seeking to minimise risk. However, they are not easy to find. It is usually difficult to convince property owners to give you an option on their property, and it takes a great deal of time to research property that will increase value in the short term.

Summary

Development profit is made when purchasing the development site. Overpaying or settling on purchasing the property too early risk making the project unviable. Researching the market where the prospective property is located and its true market value will help you to establish the maximum price you should pay for the property. More importantly, you should undertake a prefeasibility study to ensure that the project is viable. Once this price is established, and adopting a strategy that takes advantage of a few options to buy the property, you will be in a better position to negotiate the terms of the offer.

CHAPTER 6
Making the numbers work

With the advancement of digital technology, developers can now access a variety of software offering digital spreadsheets, formulas and cash flows to assist them in determining the feasibility of their projects. One can purchase anything from a basic software package to a Rolls-Royce version or a typical Microsoft Excel spreadsheet application. I chose the last as I work with various types of projects and clients who like to view documents in different layouts. In addition, just as a hotel held for investment will differ from an apartment block to be sold to the public, the developer's inputs will require a very different financial result in each case.

Before entering the numbers, the developer and his professional team should first outline the various categories of cost and income items that will be encountered. More feasibility errors result from the developer or professional team overlooking necessary items than from their underestimating costs. From this data various formulas are used to analyse cash flows, capitalisation rates and so on to determine whether or not the development should proceed.

As developers measure their success based on profit and cost calculations, it is wise to add a number of safety factors to the assumptions and calculations of the proposed project. It is better to be surprised by an unexpected profit at the end of the deal than to be disappointed when the project comes in late and over budget. Evaluating the financial feasibility of a property development involves the following stages of analysis, each one more detailed than the last:

- preparing an income and expense spreadsheet

- preparing a prefeasibility analysis

- preparing a monthly cash flow
- sensitivity analysis
- refinement process.

Preparing a cost and income spreadsheet

Before applying the various formulas in the feasibility study, a spreadsheet (see table 6.7 on p. 127) with all possible income (cash inflow) and possible development costs (cash outflow) should be prepared by the developer and professional team. Each cost can be broken down into multiple subcategories as follows:

Possible Income (cash inflow)

- *Equity:* This is the amount of cash the developer and or investors will contribute to the development. The amount will either be determined by the developer upfront or be required by the lender based on the shortfall of the construction or long-term loan. The equity may be provided by partners, investors or joint-venture partners.

- *Finance loans:* These are the proceeds generated by the various loans obtained by the developer. They will cover the construction and any additional loans placed on the property. These loans may include a land acquisition loan, construction loan, mezzanine loan or long-term loan.

- *Rental income:* This income includes all the lease rental and additional charges made to the tenants. This income can include the *base rent, common area fees or parking.*

- *Interest income:* This is income on any funds left in the bank reflected as the *partnership account or operating account.*

- *Sale proceeds:* This is income generated by selling either portions of the development (strata title) or the total property. Sales can be defined as sales of residential units or sales of commercial strata units.

- *Miscellaneous income:* This includes any other proceeds not included in the above items.

Possible costs (cash outflow)

- *Land purchase:* This includes the cost of the land, the land conveyancing costs, stamp duty and the cost of carrying the land (interest). Items to be noted are *interest, settlement or conveyancing costs, real estate commission, and real estate taxes or insurance.*

- *Government and authority fees:* This includes all costs to local and state government and any other authorities who have jurisdiction over the approval of the project. Items to be taken into consideration are rates and taxes, land taxes, rezoning or planning application fees or developer's contribution.

- *Site costs:* These are the costs pertaining to developing the site, from clearing the land to final landscaping. Costs to be noted can include land survey, soil test, land improvements or landscaping.

- *Building construction costs:* These costs can be initially estimated per square metre by a quantity surveyor or building contractor. The final cost will be determined after a tender process. Costs to be accounted for can include the main structure, mechanical, electrical, plumbing, parking, interior finish, exterior finish, appliances, amenities and contingencies.

- *Furniture, fixtures and equipment:* If the planned project has furniture or equipment, there will be expenses for millwork and artwork, which must be included in the estimate.

- *Professional fees:* These fees include architectural, engineering and any other professional consultants' fees involved in the development of the property. This can include any of the following: project manager, architect, town planner, quantity surveyor, various engineers, landscape architect, interior designer, property valuer, market researcher.

- *Legal and accounting:* These professionals are kept as a separate cost as their work relates to the overall project rather than construction alone and can include sales and lease agreements, contracts, audits and taxes.

- *Marketing:* The marketing costs include the agency and production costs for brochures, media placement, promotions, market research, general and administrative office costs and displays. These costs are initially based on a percentage of the total budget or a flat dollar amount.

- *Sales expenses:* These are the costs associated with selling or leasing the property. Such costs are based on a brokerage fee, which is based on an agreed percentage of the sale or lease.

- *Management and administration:* Someone has to manage the development, and if it is not the developer it will be an appointed development manager, who will charge a fee. Additional administrative and office costs will be associated with the project.

- *Financing costs:* These are the costs associated with obtaining loans to acquire and develop the project. Most loans associated with the project, such as construction finance, have fees and charges additional to the interest charged. These costs can include *construction loan fees, construction debt interest, long-term loan fees, long-term debt interest, miscellaneous loan fees and charges, and loan mortgage broker fees.*

- *Taxes:* This expense includes any ATO taxes (including GST), ASIC fees and land taxes due during the development phase.

- *Contingency:* It is imperative that the developer have a contingency amount set aside that can be used for unexpected expenses. This amount is usually based on a percentage of the total development costs.

After undertaking the task above, the developer should create a data spreadsheet to include only items specific to the development project. From this data sheet, the items entered will be linked to other spreadsheets described in this chapter.

Preparing a prefeasibility analysis

After collecting all the relevant cash inflows and outflows, the developer or the appointed development manager will be able tabulate another spreadsheet inputting the relevant income and costs in order to establish whether or not the project is financially feasible. This is called a preliminary feasibility study (PFS) and calculates the income against the development cost. The objective of these calculations is to determine whether the project's net cash return in percentage terms against the total development cost (TDC) is within range of the risk associated with the type of development. In this exercise a number of formulas will be used to establish the correct figure, with the areas of interest being (a) the income of the project through sales or leasing, (b) the total development cost and (c) the returns on the development.

a. Income analysis

Under income analysis are two potential areas: (1) net potential sales of strata-titled units (apartments) and (2) net potential capitalised value from leasing commercial space or commercial strata-titled units.

Net potential sales

Total sales of units (this is the final sale price of total strata units to be sold)

Less GST (most developers are registered for GST and this amount is paid to the ATO)

Less sales commission (normally a percentage negotiated with the real estate agent)

Table 6.1 shows if a 20-unit development is sold at $250 000 per unit.

Table 6.1: income value from sales

	Apartments	Rate p/u	Net Income pa	Total
Sale of apartments	20	$250 000	$5 000 000	
Less GST		9.09%	$ 454 500	
Less commission		2.50%	$ 125 000	**$ 4 420 500**

Net potential capitalised value

Total rental per annum (the going rental rate × the leasable area)

Less outgoings/expenses per annum (any cost related to creating and maintaining the lease)

Multiplied by the Capitalisation Rate* (this is the expected return for the type of asset leased)

For explanation of the Capitalisation Rate refer to 'Other financial and measurement calculations' later in this chapter.

Table 6.2 shows the value if 8 strata units of 100 square metres are leased.

Table 6.2: income value from leases

	Area m²	Rate	Rent PA	Total
Strata units: 8 units at 100m²	800	$300	$240 000	
Less operating cost (10%)	800	$ 30	$ 24 000	
Net rental income per annum			$216 000	
Capitalisation rate		8%		$ 2 700 000

b. Total development cost analysis

There are not many complex calculations required under this section but rather realistic inputs investigated under the first stage. Some areas to consider while working in this section are as follows:

- Under land acquisition cost, check the stamp duty and conveyancing/settlement cost as it varies from state to state within Australia.

- Government and authority fees should be checked with the local council as they can vary between councils.

- An area some developers tend to neglect is the cost for the management of the development and administration even if the developer is doing the work on their own.

- After working out the total development cost, the GST of components such as building cost and professional fees should be deducted as this will be the net cost to the development.

c. Return analysis

Return on total development cost (TDC): This calculation is based on the percentage return of the profit/return after the deduction of the total development cost. For example, table 6.3 shows if the total income or capitalised value is $10 million and the total development cost is $8 million.

Table 6.3: percentage return on total development cost

Total sales or capitalised value	$10 000 000
Less total development cost	$ 8 000 000
Net return before tax	$ 2 000 000
Margin on development cost	25%

Return on equity: This calculation is based on the percentage return of the cash equity invested against the profit/return on a project. Using the example in table 6.3, table 6.4 shows the return on equity, if the developer has invested their own cash of $2.5 million into the project.

Table 6.4: percentage return on equity invested

Net return before tax	$2 000 000
Equity invested	$2 500 000
Return on equity invested	80%

Preparing a monthly cash flow

In line with prefeasibility analysis, a monthly cash flow will assist the developer to get a full picture of how the project will roll out, showing the flow of income and expenditure. It gives both the developer and the lender the most accurate picture of funding needs and serves as a useful tool for monitoring cash flows once the project starts.

Using the same headings as for the prefeasibility analysis, the developer or development manager should insert the estimated income and expenditure broken down into monthly intervals for the duration of the project until settlement of all cash flows. The monthly intervals can be broken into broader periods, including:

- purchase of property to development approval
- post-development approval to start of construction

- start of construction to practical completion

- practical completion to settlement of sales or tenant occupation.

Most monthly inputs are relatively simple except during the construction period when the drawdowns or payments to the building contractor are made. For a smaller, simple single- or double-storey development payments are made when the building reaches certain heights or levels, whereas for larger building contracts payments are made based on an 'S' curve. The name derives from the S-like shape of the graph, which is flatter at the beginning and end and steeper in the middle, as is typical of most projects. The start of construction is normally slow but progress accelerates to the peak before slowing down when completion is imminent. Working out the construction drawdowns is important as it is the major cost of most developments and in turn affects the interest cost being charged to the project.

Sensitivity analysis

In most feasibility studies the developer will use current building cost, development cost, sales and rentals. However, developers cannot control the future and nor can they predict where the market would be at the completion of the development. To try to address the risk of a different outcome from the one expected (as demonstrated in the foregoing models) the developer should carry out a sensitivity analysis on the development.

In simple terms, a sensitivity analysis is an economic projection that demonstrates a range of assumptions showing the developer the potential downside or upside of the development's project economics. Variables that can affect this study are:

- projected rental rates

- projected sale prices

- interest rates

- operating expenses

- development costs

- revenue and expenses.

By changing these variables, the developer can visualise how each will impact on the total profitability of the development. The sensitivity analysis is a 'what if' exercise that the developer can perform. Using the spreadsheets completed earlier, the developer can easily change these variables by adjusting the percentage items or create a separate spreadsheet demonstrating these variables. See table 6.5 for an example of a sensitivity analysis.

Table 6.5: sensitivity analysis of an apartment development

Activity		Sales	Total Dev Cost	Profit Margin	Return
Return on current PFS		$10 000 000	$8 000 000	$2 000 000	25%
Sales drop 10%	−10%	$ 9 000 000	$8 000 000	$1 000 000	13%
Sales increase 10%	10%	$11 000 000	$8 000 000	$3 000 000	38%
Cost increase by 10%	10%	$10 000 000	$8 800 000	$1 200 000	14%
Cost decrease by 10%	−10%	$10 000 000	$7 200 000	$2 800 000	39%
Interest rates increase by 2%	2%	$10 000 000	$8 100 000	$1 900 000	23%
Interest rates decrease by 2%	−2%	$10 000 000	$7 900 000	$2 100 000	27%

Refinement process

Refinement within the development process has to be constantly monitored and updated. This includes areas of planning and decision making within each discipline and the collecting of new knowledge about government regulations, design ideas, construction costs, market need, site planning and financing arrangements. The refinements become smaller and smaller as the development progresses until the project is financially viable relative to its market.

Massaging the preliminary numbers

Once all of the preliminary data has been entered, the developer should continue to update and massage the numbers. This process will continue even up to completion of the project. The developer and consultants should always try to obtain the most reliable numbers from the sources that have the answers.

To formulate the preliminary numbers as per the earlier models, a number of assumptions were made. Finalisation will simply be the process of eliminating assumptions and substantiating the estimates. In addition, through the sensitivity analysis, creative financing, and consideration of sales prices and rental rates, calculations will change. Constantly exploring ways to decrease costs and increase revenues over time will only increase net income or return.

Cutting costs without compromising quality

One method of cutting costs without losing quality is through value engineering, which is the process where the plans for a project are reviewed with a sharpened pencil and creative mindset. The objective is to take costs out of the project without compromising its functionality and durability or devaluing the aesthetics of its design.

In value engineering, the major challenge is not to find ways of cutting costs but to identify those strategies that deliver significant savings while improving the performance of the finished product. In other words, value engineering must be approached in a structured manner that begins with the 'big ticket' items, such as mechanical systems, exterior materials, structural design, excavation and site services. In the value engineering process, there are three prime areas in which savings can be found:

- *The developer's brief for the building can be altered*: For instance, canopies and other overhangs can be eliminated; less expensive finishes can be used; or the total number of square metres can be reduced.

- *The architectural and engineering plans can be reworked*: For example, shortening piping runs and ductwork can often reduce the cost of mechanical systems significantly. In another instance, a design may be reworked to replace custom-sized with standard-sized components, which is a sure way to reduce costs, or one type of structural element may be replaced with a less expensive alternative.

- *The components and systems used in the construction process can be revamped*: Working closely with subcontractors, it is usually possible to find less expensive construction techniques or materials that deliver equal or better results. In other instances, an essentially identical material can be substituted for the specified product at a healthy saving.

Frequently savings through value engineering depend on a firm grasp of the local construction environment. What materials will be most durable in this climate? When does using on-site labour offer a savings over pre-assembled or pre-cast components?

Other financial and measurement calculations

Below are additional calculations that can be used to analyse a development project. Some may not be required in residential developments if the buildings are to be sold on completion. However, with the increased densities in many inner suburbs, most developments are becoming mixed-use with apartments above and commercial below. While the apartments are sold the commercial units below can be kept as an ongoing income stream for the developer. These calculations could become useful when the developer is working with sophisticated investors or financial institutions.

a. Net yield

The net yield of a development is the percentage of the return on the development and is achieved by dividing the net operating income (NOI) or rental by the total development cost (TDC).

$$\frac{\text{Net operating income}}{\text{Total development cost}} \times 100 = \text{Yield (\%)}$$

For example, if the NOI of a proposed commercial centre is $1 250 000 and the total development cost is $18 000 000, then:

$$\frac{\$1\,250\,000}{\$18\,000\,000} \times 100 = 6.93\%$$

b. Capitalisation rate

The capitalisation rate or yield is the rate of return on the value of a completed property that a potential investor would expect when purchasing the property. Each type of property will have a different capitalisation rate, based on the associated risk and the level of management required. Remember, the greater the risk in the development the higher the capitalisation rate. Before using a capitalisation rate the developer should fully investigate the going rate for the type of property to be developed in its specific location. Listed here is a range of sample capitalisation rates used in the property industry at the time of writing.

- Residential: 4.5% to 7.5% or 0.045 to 0.075

- Offices: 8.5% to 11.0% or 0.085 to 0.11

- Retail: 9.0% to 11.5% or 0.09 to 0.115

c. Discounted cash flow

Discounted cash flow (DCF) analysis of the operating period is an important aspect of the financial feasibility of a development project as it is used by lenders, valuers and investors to determine projected returns of the proposed development. Even if the developer plans to sell the project as soon as it reaches stabilised occupancy, this analysis is the most widely used methodology to evaluate an income property investment or development.

Discounting a cash flow

This is the process whereby the 'time value' of money is taken into account in evaluating a particular yearly net after tax cash flow and residual to be received in the future. Discounting a cash flow is also commonly referred to as *present value analysis*. The basic premise behind present value analysis is that a particular cash flow or residual to be received in a future year can be replicated by an investment of some amount today at a specific interest rate. The amount required to be invested today (the 'present value') is less than the amount to be replicated at a future time because of the effect of compound interest.

By adding up the present values necessary to replicate a particular future cash flow and/or residual, valuers and investors are able to analyse more precisely a particular future cash flow and/or residual than if they merely used the traditional rules of thumb, which do not consider the time periods in which cash flows and/or residuals are to be received. For example, if the amount to be reserved in the future is to be $65 000.00, then the present value of such payment would be $50 700.00 ($65 000.00 × 0.78).

Sources of data for present value factors

Numerous tables have been published containing present value factors. Table 6.6 shows an example.

Table 6.6: sample present value factors

Year	5%	6%	7%	8%	9%	10%
1	0.95	0.94	0.93	0.92	0.91	0.90
2	0.91	0.89	0.87	0.86	0.84	0.82
3	0.86	0.84	0.81	0.79	0.77	0.75
4	0.82	0.79	0.76	0.74	0.71	0.68
5	0.78	0.75	0.71	0.68	0.65	0.62

Assume: Cash to be received in the future = $65 000.00

Discount rate = 9%

Year in which cash is to be secured = 4

Calculation: Present value factor = 0.71

Present value = (0.71) ($65 000.00) = $46 015.00

d. Internal rate of return (IRR)

Calculating the internal rate of return (IRR) of a project is a widely used method of assessing a potential project's viability. It is a similar calculation to net present value (NPV) and discounted cash flow (DCF) in that anticipated future income and expenditure are used to assess whether or not to proceed with a project. The IRR is the interest rate at which the net present value of all the cash flows (both positive and negative) from a project or investment equals zero.

Usually the project IRR must exceed the cost of capital by an agreed amount so that the risk of proceeding is seen to be within acceptable commercial parameters. It can be seen, therefore, that an accurate cash flow projection for a prospective project must be developed before an accurate IRR assessment can be made.

A general rule of thumb is that the IRR value cannot be derived analytically. Instead, IRR must be found by using mathematical trial-and-error to derive the appropriate rate. However, most spreadsheet programs such as Microsoft Excel will automatically perform this function.

e. Residual to land value

To analyse whether a potential development site for sale will deliver the expected profit when the project is sold, figure 6.1 shows a method that can be used to determine the site's residual value:

Figure 6.1: residual land formulae

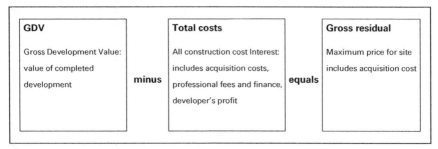

GDV		Total costs		Gross residual
Gross Development Value: value of completed development	**minus**	All construction cost Interest: includes acquisition costs, professional fees and finance, developer's profit	**equals**	Maximum price for site includes acquisition cost

Summary

Uncertainty is an integral part of the development process and this needs to be reflected in the feasibility studies undertaken. Without knowledge of development risk, developers are unable to determine the anticipated level of return that should be sought to compensate for the risk. The advantage of undertaking ongoing feasibility studies is that it allows the developer a better understanding of the possible outcomes for the development. Ultimately the decision will be made based on current expectations and current development constraints, but by assessing the upside and downside risks more thoroughly, the developer is equipped to make a 'better', more informed decision.

Income and expenditure checklist

Use the table 6.7 checklist form when evaluating the income and expenditure of a potential development. Once completed, these figures can be inserted into feasibility study software. Chapters 14, 15 and 16 include case studies in which these inputs have been used in prefeasibility study samples.

Table 6.7: income and expenditure checklist form

Proceeds/Income	$ Amount	Expenditure	$ Amount
Equity Partners, investors, joint venture partners		**Land purchase** Interest, settlement or conveyancing costs, real estate commission, real estate taxes or insurance	
Finance loans Land acquisition loan, construction loan, mezzanine loan, long-term loan		**Government and authority fees** Rates and taxes, land taxes, rezoning or planning application fees, developer's contribution	
Rental income Base rent, common area, parking		**Site costs** Land survey, soil test, land improvements or landscaping	
Interest income Partnership account, operating account		**Building construction costs** Main structure, mechanical, electrical, plumbing, parking, interior finish, exterior finish, appliances, amenities, contingencies	
Sale proceeds Sales of residential units, sales of commercial strata units		**Furniture, fixtures and equipment** Common area furniture and accessories, maintenance	
Miscellaneous		**Professional fees** Project manager, architect, town planner, quantity surveyor, various engineers, landscape architect, interior designer, property valuer, market researcher	
		Legal and accounting Sales and lease agreements, contracts, audits, taxes	

(continued)

Table 6.7: income and expenditure checklist form *(cont'd)*

Proceeds/Income	$ Amount	Expenditure	$ Amount
		Marketing Agency fee, production costs, brochures, signage, media placement, newspaper, magazine, radio, television, direct mail, public relations, promotions, entertainment	
		Sales expenses Real estate sales/leasing commissions	
		Management and administration Development manager, accounting, travel, entertainment, office supplies, office rent	
		Financing costs Construction loan fees, construction debt interest, long-term loan fees, long-term debt interest, miscellaneous loan fees and charges, loan mortgage broker fees	
		Taxes ATO (including GST) taxes, ASIC fees, land taxes	
		Contingency	
Total		Total	

CHAPTER 7
Development economics

An important goal for most developers is to find ways to save costs and maximise profits in their developments. Unfortunately this is the *only* goal for some developers, as is evident in some appalling developments in our cities. These developers approach the task with a philosophy of 'cost cutting' as opposed to 'cost-effective saving'. Successful developers approach cost saving intelligently. They advise their design team to analyse the economics of the structure without losing the concept and ambience that would make the development sell.

Intelligent cost saving can be achieved through an understanding of property development economics. Traditionally, a developer client approaches an architect to prepare sketch plans. If the architect is not experienced in building economics, invariably there is a cost blow-out that makes the development unviable. Through trial and error the architect and the design team will finally produce a scheme that can prove to be profitable, but the finished product may not look anything like the initial concept and is therefore not marketable.

By understanding the basic economics of a development, a developer can advise an architect—even one who is inexperienced in this type of development—on how to approach the design. However, care should be taken not to overemphasise the importance of economical design, as this may stifle the architect's creative abilities and you may end up with a bland and unmarketable product. The brief to the design team, therefore, is to create a functional building that will attract both tenants and buyers, with an exterior that is pleasant to the eye, but at the same time to consider the economics of the project. The architect and the rest of the design team should be reminded that without a return on investment, the capital invested in the design phase of a project is wasted. Good design may cost more, but if used intelligently the return will outweigh that cost.

In this chapter we will define development economics, analyse the economics of site selection, architectural design and alternative construction methods, and identify the most obvious issues the developer should consider when the tender price of the contractor is too high.

What is development economics?

Development economics can be defined as the process of guiding a development team towards producing an aesthetically pleasing, functional and cost-effective development, the value of which increases over time. The use of the development economics process is ongoing and should be followed from the initial inception to even after the project has been completed. The sum of the decisions made during this process must strengthen the project's success. Each decision, such as changing one item for another, must contribute to creating a product that will sell or lease successfully and perform efficiently for years to come.

The development economics process begins with the initial vision or idea of a project and the pre-purchase feasibility of the selected site and continues through the construction and long after the contractor has left the site. During the process the developer must be flexible and resourceful in finding solutions for every new challenge, no matter how big or small. With every piece of cost information accrued during the process, assumptions will be made. The key to good development economics is to minimise the number of assumptions. Eliminating these assumptions will strengthen the developer's confidence in producing the project within the budget.

Armed with a good understanding of development economics, the developer should involve all team members by clearly outlining the project's objectives and desired outcome. All too often team members pursue their own individual desires and goals for the project, and this tendency should be eliminated at the outset. The developer, as the key decision maker and each team member must understand that the key to a successful project is to meet the project's goals and to ensure that it is viable, producing the desired return. If this return is not achievable, the project cannot be financed and work will not continue.

The influence of site selection on cost

Finding a development site in the perfect location is a priority for a developer but it is only one element, as there can be physical cost factors beyond the developer's control that make the site unfeasible. These may include any the following.

Shape of site

A rectangular or square site is far more cost effective than an irregular one, as illustrated in figure 7.1.

Figure 7.1: cost impacts of site shape

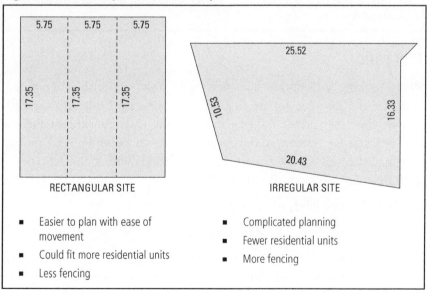

Slope of site

The steeper the slope, the more it costs to build on it. This is because foundations and supporting structures are more complex. Excavation and the need for retaining walls increase and drainage issues arise. As buildings step down a slope, the area of external walls increases (see figure 7.2).

Figure 7.2: cost impact of sloping site

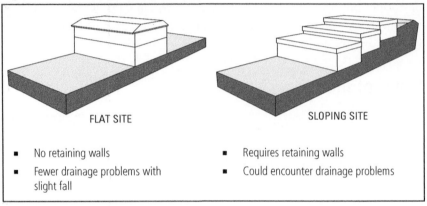

FLAT SITE

- No retaining walls
- Fewer drainage problems with slight fall

SLOPING SITE

- Requires retaining walls
- Could encounter drainage problems

Plot ratio

When looking at the price of a site for sale, a developer should not only compare the rate per square metre for the raw land but also carefully analyse the cost against the plot ratio for the total building(s) and the cost per unit for residential developments. As an example, if $1 million is being asked for a 1000 square metre site zoned with a plot ratio of 2.0 then the rates can be analysed as follows:

- Price for raw land: $1 000 000/1000 = $1000 per m^2
- Price for plot ratio: $1 000 000/2000 = $500 per m^2

Using the same example, if the site allows apartments to be built and if, say, the average apartment is 66 square metres, then 30 (2000/66) apartments can be constructed; therefore the land price per apartment is $33 333.33.

Subsoil conditions

Poor foundations may require additional engineering to support a structure. Sandy or clay soils can require deep concrete piles to achieve adequate support. Table 7.1 compares typical soil types and conditions.

Table 7.1: comparing typical development site soil types and conditions

Class	Foundation
A	Most sand and rock sites, with little or no ground movement from water changes
S	Slightly reactive clay sites, with only slight ground movement from moisture changes
M	Moderately reactive clay or silt sites that can experience moderate ground movement from moisture changes
H	Highly reactive clay sites that can experience high ground movement from moisture changes
E	Extremely reactive sites that can experience extreme ground movement from moisture changes
P	Sites that include soft soils, such as soft clay or silt or loose sands, landslips, mine subsistence, collapsing soils, soils subject to erosion, reactive sites subject to abnormal moisture conditions or sites that cannot be classified otherwise

Other site factors to consider

Additional items that may affect the cost during site selection include the following.

Access

Poor access makes materials handling more difficult and time consuming. Isolated sites such as those accessible only by water increase the costs of materials and labour dramatically.

Demolition and clearing the site

In some cases demolition and clearing the site can account for as much as 10 per cent of a new building's cost. Site contamination issues such as asbestos removal can add to the building cost significantly.

Excavation

Excavation is costly and time consuming, and often requires shoring up or underpinning adjacent foundations. Rock excavation can be very expensive and associated drainage issues add to the cost.

Availability of services

Some isolated sites do not have easy access to services such as water, electricity, sewerage, stormwater systems and gas. Provision of these services remotely can be very expensive. In less isolated areas the distance from mains can also be an issue.

The influence of design on building cost

Typically when we compare two buildings that have been designed to meet the same requirements in terms of floor area we may find one building costing, say, $1100/m² and the other $1000/m². Further analysis shows that they have the same external and internal finishes with similar roof and floor constructions. In fact, there seems no apparent reason why the rates should not be exactly the same, but it happens.

Various planning and architectural factors have cost implications that a developer and the design team should evaluate during the design stage of the development process. A number of design variables can create cost blow-outs, but if the developer and team understand the fundamentals it will assist in keeping costs under control.

Plan layout

The layout of a building has an important effect on cost. As a general rule, as illustrated in figure 7.3, the simpler the layout, the lower the cost.

Figure 7.3: cost advantages of simple building layout

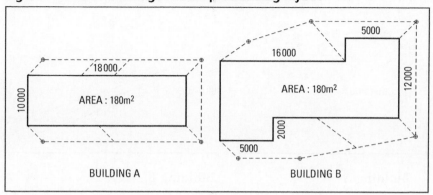

Note that both plans have exactly the same floor areas, yet Building B is more expensive because of its design layout. Reasons for the increase in costs include the following:

- Building B has a higher perimeter to floor area ratio (a term that will be explained later) and requires more external walling to enclose the same floor area as Building A.

- Setting out costs will be higher for Building B.

- Excavations will cost more for Building B.

- Drainage costs will increase for Building B because of the extra inspection holes and extra piping required.

- Additional costs will also result from other elements of Building B, such as the walling and roofing, because the work is complicated by the shape.

It can therefore be concluded that an irregular layout adds significantly to the overall cost of a building.

Plan form

Even though we may aim for a simple plan layout, there could also be a cost differentiation due to the plan form. The two drawings in figure 7.4 (overleaf) show a square and a long rectangular plan with the same floor area, yet there is a cost difference.

Figure 7.4: cost differences due to different plan forms

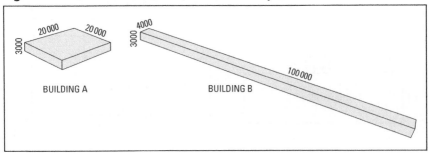

Building A	Building B
Area on plan = 400m²	Area on plan = 400m²
Length of walling = 80m	Length of walling = 208m
Assume 3m high walling @ $100.00/m²	Assume 3m high walling @ $100.00/m²
Assume internal cost @ $900.00/m²	Assume internal cost @ $900.00/m²
Then cost/m² = ((80 × 3 × 100) + (400 × 900)) ÷ 400 = $960.00/m²	Then cost/m² = (208 × 3 × 100) + (400 × 900)) ÷ 400 = $1056.00/m²

The length of Building B thus results in an additional expense of $38 400 over that of Building A.

It is important that both the design team and the developer are fully aware of the additional costs or savings that will arise from even small changes in the shape of the building. They can then adopt an elementary cost–benefit approach when considering the advantages of different shapes in achieving a suitable balance between cost, aesthetics and function.

Interior walls and wet areas

Another factor that adds to building cost is the quantity of internal walls and wet areas. Wet areas such as kitchens, bathrooms, laundries and toilets have a higher rate of cost per square metre. In the example in figure 7.5 it is obvious that the rate per square metre for a block of one-bedroom apartments will differ a great deal from the rate for a block of three-bedroom apartments.

Figure 7.5: rate per square metre comparison — one- versus three-bedroom units

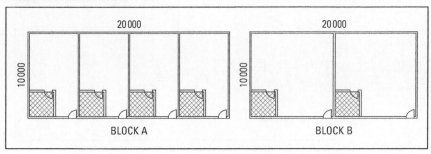

Assuming that an internal division wall will cost $2250.00 and a bathroom will cost $12 500.00 complete, table 7.2 outlines the influence of these elements.

Table 7.2: rate per square metre comparison — calculations

Block A				Block B			
Item	No.	Rate		Item	No.	Rate	
Division walls	3	$2 250 =	$ 6 750.00	Division walls	1	$2 250	$ 2 250.00
Bathrooms	4	$12 500 =	$50 000.00	Bathrooms	2	$12 500	$25 000.00
Total			$56 750.00	Total			$27 250.00
Cost/m²			$ 283.75	Cost/m²			$ 136.25

Although other, more complex relationships operate in such a comparison we can conclude that in general an increase in wet areas in a design will also increase the cost per square metre.

Perimeter to floor area ratio

We have seen from the previous example that a plan shape directly affects the outside perimeter walls. The perimeter to floor area ratio allows us to compare different plans to establish the more economical proposal — the lower the ratio, the more economical the proposal. Circular buildings have the best ratio but these savings are more than offset by the higher cost of circular work. Figure 7.6 offers another practical example.

Figure 7.6: cost impact of different perimeter to floor area ratios

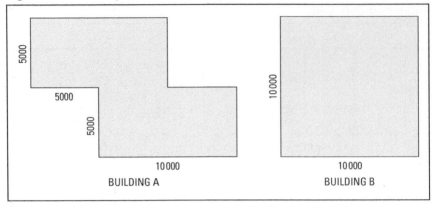

Table 7.3 assumes that both buildings have an identical floor to ceiling height of three metres.

Table 7.3: cost impact of different perimeter to floor area ratios — calculations

Building A	Building B
Area of perimeter walls ÷ Total floor area = 50m × 3m ÷ 100m² = 1.50	Area of perimeter walls ÷ Total floor area = 40m × 3m ÷ 100m² = 1.20

It should be remembered that the perimeter cost can be in the order of 20 to 30 per cent of the total cost, and an external wall is normally almost twice as expensive as an internal partition. Once again we should keep other design criteria in mind, but the perimeter to floor area ratio does allow the more experienced developer to identify the optimum ratio as part of the design criteria in the brief to the architect.

Dead spaces

Corridors, entrance halls, passages, staircases and lift lobbies are viewed as dead spaces that cannot be used profitably, yet they still need to be air-conditioned and provided with lighting, cleaning and maintenance.

Minimising these spaces during the design stage therefore provides a definite cost benefit. When analysing the cost of dead space, the functional and aesthetic values have to be considered as well; nevertheless substantial savings can be made by careful evaluation.

Amalgamating services

In high-rise buildings such as apartment blocks, locating bathrooms, kitchens and laundries (wet areas) adjacent to or above each other can lower the cost of providing services by reducing long runs of concealed plumbing and piping. Similarly, amalgamating several services in the same trench or conduit duct can reduce costs.

Other design variables

Other variables that could influence the cost of the design include:

- *Floor to ceiling height:* Increasing the height of walls will increase the rate per square metre.

- *Height of building:* A comparison of the unit rates for single-storey and multi-storey buildings will show substantial differences. With multi-storey buildings there is an increase in scaffolding and the rates of contractors working at higher levels.

- *Constructional differences:* Prefabricated concrete walls in lieu of brick walls or industrialised building methods in place of conventional ones will have a significant impact on the cost. This is also discussed later in the chapter.

- *Differences in finish and architectural detail:* Careful attention should be paid to the standard of finishes required, especially on the vertical components of a building.

- *Standard dimensions:* Many building products and fabricated components, such as aluminium windows and doors, come in standard dimensions. Designing with this in mind can reduce cutting and wastage. Standard sizes are always cheaper than custom sizes.

The influence of construction methods on cost

Construction is the area most focused on whenever cost savings are being considered even though, as pointed out earlier, other factors can affect the cost of developments significantly. There is a plethora of walling systems devised by many entrepreneurial minds in the building industry. However, walls are only one element of a building that includes flooring systems, roof systems, kitchen layouts and other features. When considering construction cost savings, the developer and design team should take a holistic view and not focus on one aspect only. Below are some methodologies that can be adopted, but before deciding on the building system you should consider the following points.

Low-cost building systems versus traditional methods

Depending on the location and type of your development, the cheapest and most acceptable building system uses traditional methods because the skills and materials are readily available. However, low-cost building systems that reduce the use of materials and/or save on construction time can provide significant savings. On the other hand, some newer products have yet to stand the test of time.

Low-cost materials

Materials that are low in cost more often than not look cheap; however, their appearance can be enhanced by the way they are subdivided, detailed and finished. A good way to reduce cost is to use low-cost materials where they are not visible, or where the performance of the material is not critical. A number of cheaper building materials are emanating from China, but the developer must ensure that these materials are compliant with local regulations and the Building Code of Australia.

City sites versus regional areas

For traditional construction methods, such as brick and concrete, the building rates in a city are lower than in regional areas because of the higher cost of labour and transport of building materials. Prefabricated systems or modular buildings in regional areas are cheaper than the local regional rates, but when prefabricated or modular competes with traditional construction in the city there is no significant saving unless there is repetition in the design and critical mass of the product. Regional areas do not have much in the way of choice, especially when it breaks down to price, but will the market in the city accept these alternative building methods?

Prefabrication

Fabricating building products in a factory is always faster and cheaper than building on site. This is because there is not always a good supply of shelter, materials, specialised machinery and labour on site. Prefabricated construction is a building method used to get buildings up faster and more economically, where only the foundations are constructed in the traditional way while sections of walls, floors and roof are pre-assembled in a factory, transported to the site, lifted into place by a crane and bolted together. The extent of prefabrication can range from individual components right up to fully prefabricated homes. Prefabrication cuts down on construction time and lowers the overall cost of a project.

Volumetric modular construction

Volumetric modular construction is a technique that has been proven over 30 years and is continuously evolving and fast becoming the world's preferred building method. Building elements are assembled in a factory to produce a completed three-dimensional room or space and then transported to the site where they can be connected to sewer outlets and power sources immediately. The benefits of pre-assembled, factory-manufactured building modules are akin to the efficiencies found in the automobile industry. Disadvantages of on-site building can include exposure to adverse weather and disruption to communities through traffic congestion and noise. Prefabricated modular buildings are increasingly providing solutions throughout

Australia, particularly for hotel rooms, apartments, offices, student accommodation and schools.

Bathroom and kitchen pods

Bathroom and kitchen pods apply similar principles to volumetric modular construction but are limited to kitchens and bathrooms. The advantage of this construction method is that while the main structural elements are being built on site, the pods are being assembled in a factory, ready to be installed when most of the onsite building is completed. Bathrooms and kitchens are the two most expensive elements in a building and command the highest rates per square metre owing to the amount of work completed in their limited floor areas. Delays in building programs most often relate to the completion of wet areas such as bathrooms and kitchens. Pod construction can save on interest due to delays.

Flat-pack systems

A flat-pack building system is similar to the Ikea furniture concept. All building elements are organised in a factory or warehouse. Building components are then transported to the site as a flat pack in a container and then assembled on site. The flat-pack building system is also known as a 'knock-down construction' or a 'kit home' in the residential building market. Unlike volumetric modular or pods, the flat-pack system involves two-dimensional systems that require a team of tradespeople to assemble on site. Flat-pack systems cost less in freight as they avoid transporting 'air'. The flat pack could cost less in terms of locality, distance and availability of trades, but a comparative analysis of the different products is needed.

Cost benefits of prefab, modular and flat-pack systems

The following is a list of broad benefits of using prefab, modular, pod or flat-pack buildings. This group of construction methods can also be defined as OSM (off-site manufacture), which is described further in the next chapter.

- *Speed of construction:* This means a quicker return on investment. Off-site construction allows for the building and site work to be completed simultaneously, reducing the overall completion schedule by as much as 50 per cent.

- *Indoor factory construction:* Assembly is independent of weather, which increases work efficiency and avoids damage to building material.

- *Favourable pricing:* With multiple similar components manufacturers can effectively bargain with suppliers for discounts on materials. Better construction times and reduced reliance on skilled labour on site contributes additional cost savings.

- *Improved quality:* Building modules are finished in a factory environment, which ensures improved quality control. Efficiencies in production and reliability are also achieved through fewer defects or call-backs.

- *Service remote locations:* In Australia higher costs are involved in building in a remote area or an area experiencing a construction boom such as mining towns. Off-site constructed buildings can be built in cities and transported to regional areas.

- *Minimum wastage:* With the same plans being repeated, records of exact quantities of materials can be established. On-site building generates a large quantity of waste that must be removed, whereas off-site buildings create less waste.

- *Environmentally friendly construction:* Off-site construction generates less materials waste, uses less energy and causes less site disturbance than comparable site-built structures.

- *Safety:* Constructing buildings in factories has proven to be safer as there are fewer components involved compared with traditional construction methods.

- *Self-supporting:* As most building components are ready-made, the need for formwork, shuttering and scaffolding is greatly reduced.

The influence of contractors on development cost

Building costs in Australia can vary considerably so you need to allow for site location in your feasibility study. In addition, tendered construction rates may vary within the same town or city as a result of conditions imposed on the contractor. Market conditions can also affect construction rates. During recessionary periods many builders are competitive, whereas during boom periods rates increase significantly because of the shortage of tradespeople.

The choice of building contractor can affect the building cost. It is known within the building industry that builders are only as good as the tradespeople they employ. A low-cost builder will usually employ low-cost tradespeople, and quality and workmanship will suffer. It is important that a careful, thorough due diligence is undertaken on the builder before awarding them the contract to build your project. Also important is the type of contract signed with the builder. A contract with minimal loose ends will ensure that costs are better controlled. In addition, the following elements could impact on the building cost.

Tenders

Although tender arrangements should be decided at the sketch design stage, tender conditions such as the competitiveness of the market and the quality of the tender documents also play important roles in fixing the final price of a project. The lowest tender submitted may not necessarily be the best tender. If there is a significant difference between the lowest and second lowest or other tenders, ask the lowest tenderer to check their figures again. A builder who has left out a major item or has miscalculated the cost will try to make up the cost elsewhere or risk bankruptcy. This could cause a multitude of problems as you would have to find another builder to complete your project. If you find out that the lowest tenderer intentionally left out an item and then tries to renegotiate the price, it would be better not to deal with them, as they have shown themselves to be unethical and someone you would not want to work with.

Completion date

An early completion date can save you money on interest. The construction period can be requested in the tender documents and the tender price should be assessed against this. In circumstances where it is imperative that a building be completed in a shorter period than would be reasonably expected, and where penalties are imposed for any delays, you may have to accept a higher construction price. It could well be that the higher tender is the most economical once construction time, earlier trading and savings on escalations are considered. Although most tenders make provision for a penalty for late completion, almost none provide the builder with an incentive bonus for early completion.

Variations

Variations, or changes to the design after the contract is signed, should be kept to an absolute minimum. Like any other business, builders aim to maximise their profits. They may have won your contract by being the lowest tender accepting the smallest profit margin, but they may try to make up the profit shortfall by charging preposterous rates for any variations. If you cannot minimise the variations, ensure that you and the builder agree on a satisfactory formula to calculate the cost for variations, such as actual cost plus a fixed percentage, before signing the contract.

Contracts

Make sure the contract price is fixed, with as many items finalised before the contract is signed as possible. The same applies to 'cost plus' contracts: ensure there is a mechanism for keeping a lid on the 'cost'. In chapter 12 various types of building contracts are analysed together with their benefits and pitfalls. The key with all building contracts is that the price must be stable with checks and balances for any potential variations.

Progress payments

Ensure that the progress payments meet the needs of the builder, the bank and your own resources. Most builders will want frequent payments because of their need for cash flow. On the other hand, you and your bank will want to ensure that the builder is not paid more than the value of the construction that has taken place on site. During the course of construction, if the builder asks for a deposit or any upfront payment, do not pay it unless it is in the contract and has been negotiated or explained prior to signing the contract.

The influence of finance on development cost

Banks aim to make as much profit as they can for their shareholders. Lending institutions differ tremendously in policies and practices. Some would not even consider a type of proposal that would be quite acceptable to another lender. A developer's success will depend on sufficient knowledge of the policies, practices and procedures of the different lending institutions and the various options available in the finance industry. Ignorance of these matters can cost money and affect the profitability of a project.

With many lending institutions competing for business the developer should look for the financial package that best suits the development. If the best two or three institutions approve a loan, the developer should review and analyse each loan offer. As each institution will be different, the respective terms and conditions of each offer should be compared to determine which one comes closest to suiting the project needs. Also take into account the following elements that could affect the cost of your development.

Interest rates

Interest rates can vary between banks and the smallest variation can affect the profitability of a project, especially if the construction period is long and protracted. A reduction in the rate may be considered if a developer is a good customer and has a reputable track record. But what if the developer is dealing with a new lender? In that case it is good practice to spend money upfront on providing a well-documented presentation of the project.

Bank fees and charges

The term *bank charge* covers all charges and fees made by a bank to its customers. Many banks charge nominal fees for various services, such as requesting a deposit slip or counter check or notarising a document. Bank fees generally constitute a major portion of bank revenue. These charges may take many forms, including:

- loan application fees
- valuation fees
- mortgage insurance
- legal fees.

Check the cost of each of these charges and where possible negotiate the cost down.

Finance brokerage fees

Using a finance broker to raise the development finance for your project may be helpful as they will be able to identify lenders with the appetite for the type project that is being developed. In addition, they will know which lender is offering better rates, fees and terms. However, before appointing the broker, verify their fees and charges, which can include the following:

- *Mandate fee:* Some brokers will not start work unless they have been officially appointed.

- *Monthly retainer fee:* Some may request this fee but unless they are providing ongoing or corporate advice it is not recommended.

- *Success/brokerage fee:* These fees can vary from 2.5 to 5 per cent for seed and equity capital and 0.5 to 1 per cent for debt, but ensure they are not getting paid by the lender as well.

The influence of authorities on development cost

As part of a developer's site due diligence, it should become a habit to check all fees and charges that will have to be covered during the early stages of the development process. Following is a list of some of the potential fees and costs imposed by local councils and other government authorities. Each jurisdiction has its own fees and charges so it is best to find out which authorities have jurisdiction over the development site and the fees that will be charged on the new development.

Development contributions

Development contributions are payments for a range of state and local government–provided infrastructure including roads, public transport, stormwater and stormwater run-off management systems, public open space and community facilities. Development contributions have been widely used in Australia and overseas to fund 'basic' infrastructure associated with the development of land. The scope of contributions varies significantly across jurisdictions in Australia. Contributions are generally required prior to construction, allowing more efficient timing of infrastructure provision.

Headworks

Headworks is a civil engineering term deriving from the traditional approach of diverting water at the start of an irrigation network and the location of these processes at the 'head of the works'. Headworks charges are integral to addressing increased development pressures and maintaining infrastructure standards within the community. Headworks contributions are a one-off fee for the provision of water and wastewater services for your development. These contributions, also referred to as standard infrastructure contributions (SICs), are exempt of GST and payable for works up to the connection point on a property that will increase the potential demand on existing water, wastewater or drainage schemes.

Submission fees

These could include development approval fees to the local council and fees to the state government if there is an amalgamation or subdivision of the development site. Building licence fees are generally covered in their contract price by the builder, who will pay this directly under their builder's registration number/licence.

Other approval fees

In addition to the fees and charges already mentioned, other fees could be charged by government authorities, and it is best to check with the local council's planning department and your development team. Additional fees could include:

- council inspection fees
- electrical power fees
- state planning commission fees
- estate fencing fees
- demolition fees (if existing building)
- council maintenance fees.

When plans exceed the budget

While the points covered in this chapter will provide a developer with the principles of development economics there will always be cases where even the best preparation fails to avert a crisis. After the project design and documentation is completed and the final tenders from the builders arrive, you find that the total construction cost has exceeded the budget set in your feasibility study. What do you do? Do you shelve the project or do you and your team revisit the plans and look for alternative ways to reduce the cost?

In my experience not all tenders received are within 100 per cent of the budget; some come in at 10 per cent above or below the set figure, while some are a lot higher than expected. Therefore, if the prices are beyond your budget, you and your development team need to analyse each aspect of the design for potential ideas. These ideas will be repriced and presented for evaluation. Then the total development team will provide input on the implications of each decision. Here are some possible cost-saving ideas.

Reduce the amount of siteworks

Changing the elevations to reduce cut and fill or raising the building to avoid rock excavation cuts costs. Relocating the roads to avoid excavation can also be helpful. Another viable idea is to reduce the quality of roadway design and drainage systems and reroute them to save piping. Also look at:

- revising the balance of cut and fill calculations
- reducing the amount of retaining walls and using natural banking
- using natural drainage techniques
- reducing the amount of paved surfaces
- keeping as many natural areas as possible
- locating building for the shortest distance for service connections
- using the natural contours of the land.

Construction of the exterior of the building

The building contractor can assist in trying to reduce the construction budget by suggesting alternative materials that have a similar appearance but cost less. In addition, look at the following:

- Consider alternative finishes for the exterior façade.
- Consider alternatives for the roofing material.
- Use a slope roof system instead of a flat roof and parapet walls.
- Redesign complicated details and simplify to suit standard construction techniques.
- Reduce the size and amount of glass.

- If gutters are not absolutely necessary, eliminate them or devise less expensive ways to control water run-off.

- Choose alternatives for exterior construction that require less installation time.

- Redesign the floor plan so there are fewer exterior perimeter walls.

Construction of the interior of the building

The design of the interior spaces should be reviewed by marketing agents to ensure that the layout options of floor plans are competitive in the market. The builder can review the plans for structural changes that can be made without altering the layout of the space, while the interior designer can review the interior floor plans to identify where less expensive finishes can be used. In addition, consider the following:

- Use more economical floor finishes, such as carpet instead of timber or tiles.

- Reduce the floor to ceiling height.

- Use less expensive plumbing fixtures.

- Use less expensive door hardware.

- Consider using less expensive alternatives to heating and cooling.

- Stack the plumbing fixtures within the building vertically to minimise distances for plumbing of water and sewerage.

- Use paint instead of wallpaper.

- Redesign the floor plan to minimise doors and the length of walls.

- Use alternative doors.

- Change the window treatment—use blinds instead of curtains.

- Reselect paint colours for less expensive paint.

- Reduce the number of electrical outlets.

- Select equipment not requiring separate electrical circuits.

- Eliminate skylights.

- Use standard cabinetry instead of custom design.

Landscaping design

The landscaping design will be critical to the final outcome of the development as it adds to the curb appeal, which helps sell the final product. Using less planting and smaller planting will often reduce these costs.

The landscape contractor can review the plans and specifications with installation costs and ultimate maintenance costs in mind. The landscaper can recommend revisions that take into account these criteria and the time of year for planting.

Amenities

Amenities will always add costs to the development and future operating costs, but without these amenities the market might not choose this development over its competitive. The architect can review the amenity plans with an eye to cost reduction and ease of installation, while the marketing agent should review the amenities provided to analyse if they offer a marketing edge over the competition.

Summary

Analysing and practising development economics in the early stages of design development will save a great deal of time and money. Reviewing the cost after the working drawings and specifications and tenders will prolong the development process and therefore cost more in interest owing to later delivery to the market.

The developer should use team members effectively in this process because their experience and creativity will generate solutions to every problem. The developer must be an effective leader in this process because of the sensitive personalities of the designers and the pressures on the team to perform.

The architect is there to give advice on design, the quantity surveyor's job is to keep an eye on the cost, but it is up to the developer to lay the ground rules. This can be achieved only through an intimate knowledge of what your needs really are, and what you are prepared to pay to have them satisfied. By defining parameters to the design and cost from the start, you will improve the probability of ending up with the development you envisaged.

CHAPTER 8
Utilising modern technology

The world is constantly changing and everything seems to be speeding up. It is hard for many of us to keep up with the pace of change in the twenty-first century. We are living longer but our daily lives have become overloaded. Emails, text messages and tweets have replaced real letters delivered by post. Instant gratification rules our lives and a flood of technological innovations threaten to overwhelm a society in which those who cannot keep up are left behind. Our smartphones control our lives: we are constantly checking for new messages or confirming our latest message has been received and will be responded to shortly. The very speed of progress means all that is current very quickly becomes obsolete.

No industry is immune to the frenetic pace of change. Any business that is not actively working to keep up with new technology risks being left behind by its competitors. There will always be someone who comes up with a leaner and meaner business model to interrupt an industry. It has already happened in industries such as advertising, marketing, music and print media; even the travel industry is almost entirely online today. The pace of change is only going to increase and a tough economy will actually help those who adapt to leaner, more efficient models. The property industry is not immune to these changes and has embraced new technology in research, marketing and sales through digital communication. As already noted, property developments are starting to use new construction methods that are faster and more cost efficient.

This chapter identifies the role of digital information and new construction methodologies in the property development industry. For the purposes of this discussion, the property development industry includes commercial and residential property, developers, builders, engineers, architects, suppliers, subcontractors and other related entities.

Modern technology in property development

The world of computers and information technology has become such an important aspect of our lives that it is unlikely that businesses will return to traditional methods. The primary benefits of technology are speed and efficiency. Property development as a business has changed too. Instead of locating and physically visiting a property, the developer can simply use a computer or smartphone to search for the property remotely and even log on to Google Earth to swoop down on the property from above.

Modern technology makes it possible to work from a virtual office and communicate with businesses and individuals around the world. Flexible work hours have become popular because so many duties and responsibilities can now be accomplished from the home or while travelling. For example, an architect can have their draftspeople working from home or contract a company overseas to provide digital perspectives of buildings they have designed. Building information modelling is streamlining the design process as more information is shared between the contractor, the architect and other consultants. Adopting the integrated design process model, the architect, contractor and developer all share information through new technology to expedite the development process. Cloud services such as Dropbox allow the development team to access files from any location, giving consultants and others the ability to be completely mobile.

Logistics enabled by better and more mobile technology has changed the construction industry. Information management systems allow more precise ordering and delivery scheduling. That makes staging and construction much more efficient. As we continue to refocus development activity on urban spaces, storage and logistics are premium so information management is particularly important in facilitating that transition. We are now seeing a different approach to building, with more factory construction and on-site assembly of buildings dramatically lowering costs and shortening construction time. Innovations such as nanotechnology in building materials and 3D printing will have a huge impact on building construction.

Social media are also having a profound impact on the way a property or project is marketed. Real estate agents and marketing groups are using blogs, Facebook, Twitter, YouTube, LinkedIn and ratings sites to market and sell. Now that most people have a smartphone and access to the internet, using social media makes advertising faster, easier and cheaper.

Using the internet for market research

The internet has presented property developers with a wealth of additional resources to use in conducting free or low-cost market research. Through search engines such as Google or Yahoo, with a few mouse clicks developers can use the following techniques to gather market information:

- *Conduct a keyword search:* By entering keywords for a building type or area of interest a developer can generate a wide range of useful information, including how many competing projects there are in the market for the type of development being undertaken. Keyword searches also help remind the developer of market niches they may not have considered.

- *Read blogs:* Blogs are updated much more regularly than traditional websites and can therefore be a good way to gauge current public opinion. Search blogs by using blog-specific search engines such as Technorati or Nielsen. Blogs tend to move at a faster pace and to be more informal. A developer can better follow a new product or need on a blog than on a standard website.

- *Conduct online surveys:* Another way to gauge public opinion is through online surveys. While not as scientific as in-person or phone surveys that use a random sampling of the population, online surveys are a low-cost way to do market research on whether an idea or product will appeal to consumers. Many companies will conduct online research for a fee or give your company the tools to carry out your own surveying.

Other websites provide topical, updated information or articles on the real estate industry, including the latest market trends and demographics that will give a developer an overview of the residential market. Here is a list of some of these websites.

REIA and subsidiary websites

www.reia.com.au, www.reiwa.com.au, www.reisa.com.au, www.reiact
.com.au, www.reint.com.au, www.reiq.com.au, www.reit.com.au, www
.reivic.com.au

The Real Estate Institute of Australia (REIA) is the national professional association for Australia's real estate sector. REIA is a politically nonaligned organisation that provides research and well-informed advice to the federal government, opposition and members of the real estate sector, media and the public on a range of issues affecting the property market. The association and its state counterparts regularly update information relating to market conditions in the residential market. The REIA websites produce a wide range of reports on current market conditions and events. The sites are a good source for rental yields, capital growth and other suburb data for analysis. Their data is useful for establishing demand in an area and trends in the market.

The Property Council of Australia

www.propertyoz.com.au

The Property Council of Australia is a prominent promoter of Australia's property industry. Members include investors, property owners, developers, professional consultants and trade providers. The organisation is governed by a board comprising key leaders from the industry.

The Australian Property Institute

www.api.org.au

The Australian Property Institute represents approximately 8600 property professionals throughout Australia and overseas. API members include residential and commercial valuers, property advisers, property analysts and fund managers, property lawyers, and property researchers and academics. The Institute's primary role is to set and maintain the highest standards of professional practice, education, ethics and conduct for its members and the broader property profession.

Australian Bureau of Statistics

www.abs.gov.au

The Australian Bureau of Statistics (ABS) produces a huge volume of statistics and data. The site has data relating to many particular industries, the economy, the environment and social demographics. The ABS is a useful source of information for real estate analysis as it provides the demographics of specific suburbs and historical census data, and also sometimes compiles survey data on targeted topics such as housing affordability.

Realestate.com.au, Domain.com.au

www.realestate.com.au, www.domain.com.au

Realestate.com.au and Domain.com.au are real estate search engines used by the general public to locate property listings on the market. Australia's two most popular real estate search engines provide information for real estate analysis. They give a detailed picture of current residential stock, as well as an idea of prices and how well properties are selling. Realestate.com.au attracts an average 18.6 million visitors each month. Like the REIA websites, the site also provides analysis by suburb to assist in understanding the demand factors for the area.

Property Data Solutions

www.propertydatasolutions.com.au

The Property Data Solutions group covers everything related to Australian property, from individual property research for property professionals to custom property mapping applications for large corporate and government departments. It offers one of the widest ranges of property information, listing every one of the 10.2 million properties in the country.

Residex

www.residex.com.au

Residex provides a range of property information to users in the housing and finance industries. It supplies automated valuation models to the banking industry, residential property price estimations and trend data to government and private enterprise, propensity modelling to large corporations, and property forecasting to institutions and personal investors.

RP Data

www.corelogic.com.au/products/rp-data-professional

RP Data is a subscription-based platform that provides access to rich property data collected by CoreLogic. RP Data reports are the most reliable source of information if one is planning on buying or selling properties. A typical RP Data report provides an estimated price range for the property, recent sale prices for similar properties in the area, details of nearby properties that are on the market, information on the suburb's performance and a suburb profile. The platform is commonly used by property professionals and financiers for information.

Using the internet for property information

In addition to general research, a developer may want to find out specific information on a property or site they intend to purchase or develop. Information on, for example, location and the surrounding neighbourhood, the size of the property, zoning and town planning zoning policies is especially useful. Following are some of the websites where such information can be found.

Google Earth

www.google.com/earth

Google Earth is a virtual globe, map and geographical information program. It maps the Earth by the superimposition of images obtained from satellite imagery, aerial photography and the geographic information system (GIS) 3D globe. Originally available under three different licences, it has since been reduced to just two versions: Google Earth (a free version with limited functionality) and Google Earth Pro ($399 per year), which is intended for commercial use. Developers can view a potential development site in 3D and even travel around the neighbourhood at street level. However, some of the 3D images may be a few years old so it is always best for the developer to visit the site physically.

Nearmap

www.nearmap.com

Similar to Google Earth, Nearmap Ltd is an Australian provider of high-resolution aerial imagery and is useful for developers looking for more updated, higher resolution images of a potential site. It uses a unique, exclusive process of image capturing, processing and publishing. The provider currently covers 2.26 per cent of Australia's landmass, primarily the capital cities and major regional towns. Imagery is normally updated around six times a year for 60 per cent of Australia's population in the metropolitan areas. Nearmap originally allowed free personal use of images for non-enterprise users. This free access ended in December 2012, when the company modified its business model to user-pays.

Council websites

Council websites are vital to the developer's research of a project. The planning section of the website provides the framework and town planning schemes for the area and in some cases online mapping tools to assist in finding specific information on the site. The tool is particularly useful for establishing lot details and zonings.

DMS IntraMaps

www.mapsolutions.com.au/intramaps/intramaps-public.aspx

Digital Mapping Solutions (DMS) specialises in the development and implementation of integrated mapping solutions for commercial and government organisations. DMS has created a product called IntraMaps that a number of local councils use to communicate spatial and business data to the general public. Developers can access interactive maps from a council's website for services and facilities, planning and zoning information, and to explore local topographical information. Currently mainly Western Australian local councils are using IntraMaps.

Software for feasibility studies

Essential for developers performing feasibility studies for property development is software that allows them to comprehensively calculate and display all the data required to make an informed decision. Several software programs on the market take all the confusion out of a development assessment. They are quick to implement and accurate, but it is up to the developer and team to provide the correct inputs to generate the correct results. Following is a list of the better known software products on the market.

Microsoft Excel

http://office.microsoft.com/en-AU/excel

Microsoft Excel is a spreadsheet application developed by Microsoft for MS Windows and Mac OS. It features calculation and graphing tools, pivot tables and a macro programming language called Visual Basic for Applications. Developers can create their own spreadsheets, from basic feasibility studies to cash flows. Several templates using Excel as the working platform are available on the internet.

Devfeas Pty Ltd

www.devfeas.com.au

This software was created for property developers by Mark Andrews of Australia. The company produces and markets the computer software programs Feastudy 7.0 Professional and Lite, which are used for the financial feasibility study of property proposals. Devfeas also provides property development feasibility consultancy services.

Estate Master

www.estatemaster.com

Established in Australia in 1991 by Martin Hill, Estate Master has been developing a suite of flexible and easy-to-use property development, valuation and investment software. Estate Master is used by companies and other users across the Asia-Pacific, Africa, Europe, India, Middle East, United Kingdom and United States. Estate Master provides a full range of implementation, support and training services to suit all project requirements on a global basis.

ARGUS Developer

www.argussoftware.com

ARGUS Software is an international software company that develops products exclusively for commercial real estate companies. Their software includes asset management, asset valuation, portfolio management, budgeting, forecasting, reporting, lease management, collaboration and knowledge management. ARGUS Software is an executive member of OSCRE, the Open Standards Consortium for Real Estate, as well as an active participant with the world's top real estate trade organisations.

Communicating with the development team

In property development, communication between team members is very important. Email makes life a lot easier for professionals as it is quick and easy while also providing written confirmation of communication. In most projects, drawings and documentation are circulated among the team members. These files can be fairly large and some email systems without a high upper limit on file size may reject them.

In the old days, if architects wanted to distribute files that were too large for email, they could buy some web-hosting space, burn a disc or copy the file to a USB drive and drop that in an envelope. Today there's a multitude of free services that offer tons of storage and bandwidth to and from which files can be uploaded and downloaded. These services are called file hosting, cloud storage, online file storage or cyberlockers. They involve an internet hosting service specifically designed to host user files. The files can be accessed over the internet from a different computer, tablet, smartphone or other networked device by the same user or by other users after a password or other authentication is provided. Below is a list of file-hosting services that can be used to distribute files via links or email. Each has a different mix of storage capacities, helper apps and quirks.

For general, personal-use file-storage services with mass distribution, try:

- **Box** www.box.com
- **Dropbox** www.dropbox.com
- **Google Drive** www.drive.google.com
- **Minus** www.minus.com
- **SkyDrive** www.skydrive.live.com
- **SugarSync** www.sugarsync.com

For corporate use, try:

- **MediaFire** www.mediafire.com
- **RapidShare** www.rapidshare.com
- **ShareFile** www.sharefile.com
- **YouSendIt** www.yousendit.com

Architects, project managers, engineers and other consultants should consider:

- **Media Lightbox** www.medialightbox.com
- **iShareDocs** www.isharedocs.com
- **Newforma Project Center** www.newforma.com

Using modern technology for marketing

Social media sites such as Facebook, Twitter and LinkedIn have forced many businesses to rethink the way they reach out to their markets. These sites offer a platform on which businesses can gain greater access to consumers. Social media are quick, easy and cheap to maintain, although negative or incorrect information supplied to your audience can spread just as quickly as your intended messages. Each social media site has its own niche. For instance, microblogger Twitter is useful for broadcasting short messages to its followers; LinkedIn focuses on business networking and connecting to like-minded professionals; Instagram and Pinterest are useful for displaying graphics; and on Facebook everyone can share news or personal information with their friends.

Developers marketing their project through the internet need to work out their media marketing strategy. There should be multiple ways for people to find the development project. Developers should also have a plan to keep track of who is visiting their Facebook page, blog or website and how to turn those leads into buyers.

Website

The internet is the ideal medium through which to get in touch with a broad audience at limited cost. A business website is a powerful communication tool and a unique way to communicate with the public. For the developer promoting a project, their website can be accessed from almost anywhere 24 hours a day. Through videos and lifelike perspectives, potential buyers can get a feel for what the development will look like when completed and can compare it with others on offer.

Blogging

Blogs are an informal medium for marketing and a great place for developers to show their offering. Rather than sending individual emails or letters, developers can let all potential buyers know about their project. A range of specific company information can be covered, such as new product releases, frequently asked questions and customer concerns, but the developer can also write about their industry in general, promoting their company as a known expert in the field. There are hundreds of free websites that will take you through setting up a free blog and linking to it on your website. Blogging software that includes analytics can record how many people are reading it.

Podcasts

Podcasts are another great trend in advertising. Using a cheap digital recorder or recording software on their computer, developers can record new developments and upload them to their website for visitors to listen to.

E-newsletters

Developers with a database of clients and interested parties should keep in touch with them by sending out an email newsletter every month or two weeks with content that is highly personalised. (These emails are more likely to be opened and acted on than junk mail, unless they are automatically directed into the recipient's spam box.) If buyers have any questions the developer can answer them personally, thereby creating a relationship with that buyer.

YouTube

Now that Google has purchased YouTube, the benefit of adding video content has increased for nearly all businesses, large or small. Including video content will increase the perceived quality of a developer's website and also move the site higher up in Google's search results. Another reason for creating videos for your company is the simple fact that videos are much more likely to 'go viral' than text-only social media posts.

New construction methods in development

Although traditional building technology is well developed, the construction industry continues to create improved competitiveness, cost efficiencies, sustainability, quality and safety of the built form. The demand for affordable housing in Australia has led developers, architects, builders and engineers to seek out new building materials and construction methods. With the need to save costs, these developers and their professional development teams have come up with several innovative housing construction methods in recent years.

As discussed in the previous chapter, one of the key focuses of innovative construction is OSM (off-site manufacture), in which parts of or whole buildings are manufactured in a factory remote from the actual construction site. Individually constructed parts or modules of a building are then transported from the factory to the site on specially designed trucks and trailers.

The types of products that can be manufactured in OSM process include:

- prefabricated building components (see figure 8.1)

- flat-pack buildings

- transportable buildings

- volumetric modular buildings

- bathroom and kitchen pods.

Figure 8.1: prefabricated building components

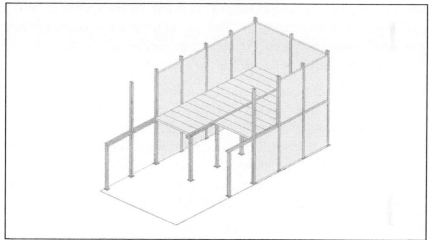

In addition to OSM, a number of new construction materials and systems are coming onto the market, such as lightweight concrete bricks and panels and lightweight steel frame structures that are easily assembled. One of the more recent innovations is 3D printed buildings. 3D printing, also called additive manufacturing, involves creating a solid object by layering thin slices of materials including plastic, metal and ceramic. The technology has been in industrial use for at least 20 years. 3D printing has caught the public eye over the past few years as the technology has become more refined, not to mention cheaper. Some of the proposed uses have drawn widespread attention in the media, from the ability to manufacture gun parts to the creation of new homes or buildings.

Prefabrication started more than a hundred years ago and gained popularity in the twentieth century. The most widely used form of prefabrication in building is the prefabricated concrete and steel sections in structures where a particular part or form is repeated many times. It can be difficult to construct the formwork required to mould concrete components on site, and delivering and pouring wet concrete to the site before it starts to set requires precise time management. Pouring concrete sections in a factory has several advantages, including being able to reuse moulds and mixing the concrete on the spot without the challenges of timing transportation and pumping wet concrete on a congested construction site. Prefabricating steel sections reduces on-site cutting and welding costs as well as the associated hazards.

Prefabrication techniques are used in office blocks, warehouses and factory buildings. Prefabricated steel and glass sections are widely used for the exterior of large buildings. The prefabrication process has now gone a step further: instead of small components manufactured in a factory and then put together on site, these components are now assembled in the factory into almost complete buildings, which are then erected on site. This technology is called the modular building system.

Transportable buildings or homes (see figure 8.2) have been around in Australia for some time. These structures are built in a factory and then transported to sites mainly in regional areas where skilled trades are not available. Typically they are constructed from wood, steel, gyprock, vinyl weatherboard and other materials that are not easily damaged during the moving process. Factory-built homes are usually not built from bricks or concrete. The homes are similar to standard suburban homes except they are built in sections of a particular width and length so they can be brought to the site by truck.

Figure 8.2: transportable buildings

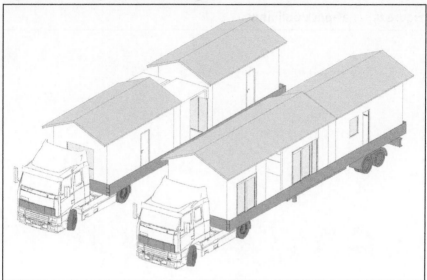

Transportable homes should not to be confused with mobile homes. Once they have been delivered to the site, stumped and connected to utilities, transportable homes are permanent. Portable versions of transportable homes are usually referred to as manufactured homes or relocatable homes and are situated in communities called manufactured home parks where the residents lease the land but own the house. Although relatively permanent, these houses could be moved far more easily than a large country homestead.

Depending on their intended purpose and which builder you speak to, transportable homes are known by several different names, such as modular homes, relocatable homes, prefabricated homes or factory-built homes.

Flat-pack buildings (see figure 8.3), or kit homes as they are known in Australia, comprise factory-produced building components that are broken down into smaller elements, packaged together, delivered to site and assembled by various skilled and unskilled tradespeople. In simple terms, they can be considered as the IKEA principle of building.

Figure 8.3: flat-pack buildings

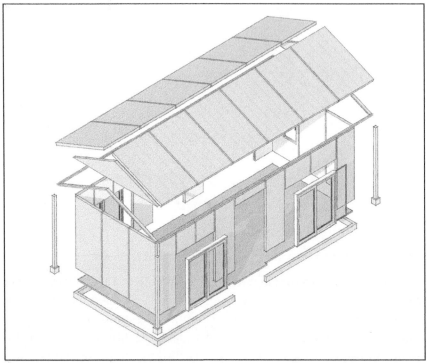

A flat-pack building should not be confused with a transportable building, as described earlier. Unlike transportable buildings, which are built in sections in a factory, a flat-pack building is made up of smaller, numbered components that are transported to the site. This eliminates the need for measuring and cutting, which saves both time and wastage of material. Flat-pack manufacturers claim their system saves the customer as much as 30 to 40 per cent on cost over traditional building methods.

With flat-pack buildings, all designs are standardised to maximise efficiency and reduce waste of both materials and labour. Steel frames and hardware are purchased in bulk. A flat-pack factory employs skilled tradespeople and uses modern machines to cut the lightweight steel frames and other components that can be packed and assembled later. The steel frames are pre-cut, pre-holed for easy bolting and labelled. Gyprock, steel rafters, roof sheeting or tiles and other components are supplied to finish the walls and roof.

Although the lightweight steel frame and main components are standardised, the designs are not. This allows buyers to design their own building or choose from various models, from a single-storey building to one of three storeys or more. The exterior can feature various finishes such as timber or steel cladding or face-brick. Walls, windows and doors can be moved, added or eliminated.

Volumetric modular buildings (see figure 8.4, overleaf), similar in concept to transportable homes, are mass-produced modular units designed for apartments, hotels or mining camps where the same module is produced in numbers — the more modules produced, the more cost effective the production process.

The modular units, which are six-sided boxes constructed in the factory then delivered to site, may form complete rooms or parts of rooms.

The big advantage of volumetric buildings is that while the modules are being manufactured in the factory, on-site works such as foundations and podiums can be completed. Using a crane, the modules are lowered onto the building's foundation and joined together to make a single building. The modules can be placed side by side or end to end or stacked, allowing a wide variety of configurations and styles in building layout.

These processes automatically compress the building program, meaning the project can be delivered in less than half the time of a traditionally constructed facility.

Figure 8.4: volumetric modular buildings

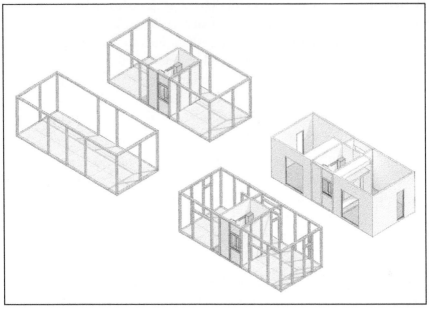

Most volumetric modular buildings are manufactured overseas in countries such as China and shipped over on a container ship. In the early days these modules were designed to fit in a standard shipping container, being 2.4 metres wide and 6 or 12 metres long. However, over time the manufacturers have introduced other sizes, subject only to the strictures of ship and road transport. Sizes can now vary from 2.4 to 4.5 metres wide to 18 metres long. Besides overseas manufacturers there are now a few factories in Australia that supply volumetric modular buildings to various parts of Australia. With the growing acceptance of this form of construction there will certainly be more local manufacturing. Although the cost of overseas modules may be lower, the developer has to ensure that the overseas product complies with the Building Code of Australia.

The concept behind the prefabricated bathroom pod has evolved over the years and has also led to the prefabricated kitchen pod (see figure 8.5). The pod is similar to the volumetric module.

Figure 8.5: bathroom and kitchen pods

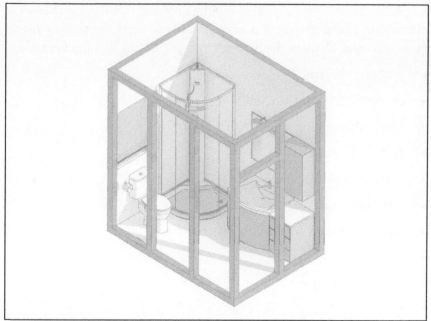

The most expensive elements in any residential building are the kitchen and bathroom areas. In addition, these areas cause the greatest delays to a development as different tradespeople wait for others to complete their part of the job before the next portion of the works can start.

A pod can be used in applications such as kitchens, bathrooms, en-suites, laundries and robes to reduce the need for on-site trade work. Most common are bathroom pods used in the construction of hotels and apartment buildings, although they are used increasingly in residential housing. The main drivers for choosing a modular pod method are that they are cost effective (if there is sufficient repetition), feature higher quality finishes applied in factory conditions, are quick to install and require less trade work on site that can cause delays.

Benefits in OSM in property developments

OSM construction is fast becoming the world's preferred building technique that has been proven over 30 years and is continuously evolving. As outlined in the previous chapter, the advantages and benefits of pre-assembled factory manufactured building modules are comparable to the efficiencies found in the automobile industry. Recapping the key points in the previous chapter, the benefits using OSM in a development are:

- speed of construction
- indoor factory construction
- favourable pricing
- improved quality
- service remote locations
- minimum wastage
- environmentally friendly construction
- safety
- self-supporting.

Risks with OSM in property development

Whilst there are many advantages to using OSM construction, developers should also be aware of the risks involved with using anything new in their projects:

- *New to market:* OSM buildings have so far not been particularly marketable when compared with standard on-site buildings.

- *Market perception:* The consumer is either not familiar with the concept or does not favour it. Social prejudice is linked to the inferior quality of some mass-produced designs used in the past.

- *Compliance:* Most prefabricated and modular buildings are imported from Asia and do not comply with the BCA (Building Code of Australia).

- *Financing:* Difficulties obtaining finance are associated with stricter guidelines being used by lenders to assess prefabricated and modular building loans.

Most of the risk outlined here relates to the market's reaction. If there is a cost saving, however, developers would be wise to lower their prices to reflect this as it will give them an edge over their competitors.

3D printed buildings

Printed buildings refers to technology that uses 3D printing as a way to construct buildings (see figure 8.6, overleaf). Advantages of this technology include quicker construction, lower labour costs and less waste produced. 3D printing has recently emerged as the tech topic with the greatest expectations. Technically, 3D printing, or additive manufacturing, is the process of creating almost any three-dimensional object with various materials, such as plastic, metal or carbon fibre. For the past three decades, 3D printers have been used primarily by engineers for rapid prototyping.

Recently a Chinese company, WinSun, built a number of houses using large 3D printers using a mixture of quick drying cement and recycled raw materials. Ten demonstration houses were built in 24 hours, each costing US$5000. This technology could be used to build cost-effective, environmentally sustainable affordable housing. Large buildings, including high-rises, are expected to be built using this technology. Dutch and Chinese demonstration projects are slowly constructing 3D-printed buildings to educate the public to the possibilities of the new plant-based building technology and to spur greater innovation in 3D printing of residential buildings.

Figure 8.6: 3D printed buildings

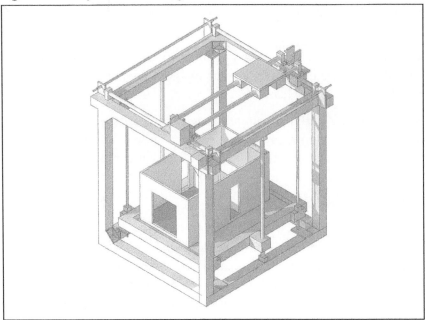

While this innovative technology could ultimately change the way we build, the time when we will be able to print buildings in line with today's architecture and market tastes is still a long way off. Over time, however, with new materials and new printing methods the process could find acceptance in the marketplace.

Summary

For most people trying to keep up with new technology that is being created, introduced and promoted virtually daily can be a daunting task. However, developers need to keep abreast of what is new in the high-tech and building industries as it may affect the market that a project is targeting. This does not mean that developers should automatically accept these new ideas; rather, they should take a cautious approach by undertaking a due diligence study of the new technology before adopting it in their development process or project. Being seen as innovative can help a developer to achieve a dominant position in the market, but if the technology is not accepted by the market it could lead to financial difficulties.

CHAPTER 9
Raising development finance

Finance is the key to most property developments. Almost all developers need it, as the capital requirement of most developments is usually significantly greater than the developer's own equity. Developers need a range of funding at each stage in the development process, including seed capital for development approval, land finance to secure the land, construction finance for implementation, and long-term finance to hold and operate the development.

Regardless of its location, design and pre-sales, the development will not proceed without finance, and the financing package must be in line with the development's roll-out. Not only must the loan rate and terms fit the project, but the terms and conditions must also give the developer the flexibility needed to successfully develop, manage, build, market and ultimately sell the property.

When seeking finance, property developers should take into account all aspects of lending, including the status of various capital sources, outside factors and trends that influence lending, and the types of properties that lenders prefer. While capital is not available for every developer and every project, enough money is flowing with the right rates and terms to meet the needs of most developers.

To secure development finance, the developer must understand how to identify potential lenders for the particular type of project, how to present the finance proposal and how to negotiate the loan. In searching for the ideal loan, you should negotiate with more than one lender at the same time as you will not know if your loan is approved until it passes through the loan committee.

The lenders

Since the recession in the early 1990s we have seen a variety of lenders starting to populate the property finance market in Australia offering loans for residential and commercial properties. These lenders include commercial banks, savings institutions, credit unions, life insurance companies, superannuation funds, finance companies and mortgage companies. They also include private wealthy individual investors seeking good returns and a growing number of foreign investors.

Since the 2008 global financial crisis (GFC) most of these lenders have taken a conservative and disciplined approach to financing. However, by 2012 more money was becoming available and once again these lenders are starting to compete for the best deals while innovative lenders are offering special products, including equity and mezzanine financing. Finance companies, which often have a higher appetite for risks, are taking up the slack as more conservative lenders pass on deals they might have seized two to three years ago.

While pricing is important in financing, relationships are important as well. Good financial partnerships with lenders can help developers identify and maximise available opportunities. The current status of primary lending sources varies. Following are some of the main lenders.

Commercial banks

These are mainly national banks that are regulated primarily by the Reserve Bank. In Australia the 'Big Four' are ANZ Bank, Commonwealth Bank, National Australia Bank and Westpac Bank. These commercial banks specialise in predominantly short-term commercial credit, placing more emphasis on liquidity than on savings, and tend to be more conservative in their appraisal. One of the main forms of short-term finance is the overdraft facility; however, some banks have become more involved in property financing through various subsidiaries.

For property development, most banks will lend between 65 and 80 per cent of the valuation, which is generally considered to be conservative and below market value. Interest rates may vary according to the amount borrowed, the type of loan and the risk profile of the borrower. These banks will prefer a principal and interest monthly repayment. This may not be suitable for development finance, especially where a short-term interest-only loan may be required. Developers should look carefully at the number of different loans offered together with the accompanying terms and conditions and negotiate what best suits their project.

Savings banks (general bank)

These banks provide finance mainly through their depositors. The operation and involvement of general banks in property finance is similar to that of institutions previously known as building societies. The past number of years have seen the conversion of leading building societies into banks. The proportion of total home lending provided by building societies has declined and as a result a number of these societies have merged operations as well as diversifying into insurance, advisory services and commercial financing. A general bank is mainly involved in residential property mortgages and suburban development.

Investment banks

The Banking Act controls the rules of operation of investment banks, which are also known in Australia as merchant banks. An investment bank is a financial intermediary that performs a variety of services and specialises in large and complex financial transactions such as underwriting, acting as an intermediary between a securities issuer and the investing public, capital raising, facilitating mergers and other corporate reorganisations, and acting as a broker and/or financial adviser for institutional clients. Many investment banks also have retail operations that serve small, individual customers. In property development, investment banks can provide bridging and permanent capital financing but they focus mainly on larger projects.

Life insurance companies

These institutions are mainly interested in long-term investment projects with growth and capital appreciation potential. With large, stable cash flows from contracted depositors (their policyholders) they are not interested in small development projects. As a general rule, insurance companies prefer to buy into completed developments undertaken by other developers at a fixed price with guaranteed returns. Some of the larger companies have subsidiaries that will finance developments and sell them on to the holding company on completion.

Superannuation funds

Superannuation funds are in a similar position to the life insurance companies with regard to their large, stable cash flow situations. These funds are generally interested in long-term property investments that are profitable and stable and show a potential for increased capital growth. Some superannuation funds are subject to the trust deed and may be restricted to a maximum investment of 5 per cent of the value of the fund in any single project.

Property trusts/unit trust companies

These are different from mutual fund operators, which only deal with portfolios of shares and don't invest directly in the property industry. Some unit trust companies only invest in the shares of property and construction companies on the stock exchange, such as property mutual fund equities. These unit trusts cover a portfolio of shares across a broad spectrum of the property development industry.

Syndications

Syndications offer private investors participation in quality properties by way of property syndication memberships that combine the best features of property ownership with reduced risk. As investment into property syndication will afford the purchaser ownership of only a particular property and not a spread over a range of different properties, the risk is higher than investing in a property trust, for example.

Finance companies

These companies mainly lend funds to new developments rather than providing long-term ownership, but this can be negotiated. When dealing with finance companies, be careful of the interest rates offered as they may charge 1.5 to 3.5 per cent above the variable rate. It is wise to shop around unless you cannot find finance elsewhere.

Joint-venture arrangements

An alternative means of financing a development project is through a joint-venture agreement. Often lenders are not willing to lend money at low yields, but they may be willing to 'joint venture' with the developer. The form of such joint ventures can vary according to the project. Some lenders may enter into a partnership, fund the purchase of the land and finance the development cost in return for a portion of the profits. Other lenders may buy the land and sign a contract with the developer for their services and then parcel out the potential profits to the developer. Either way, developers are given the opportunity to utilise their skills with other people's money.

Offshore finance

Offshore money is often sought in times of high interest rates, similar to those experienced in the early 1990s. Interest rates abroad were comparatively low, but investors often require additional security in the form of 'forward cover', which is an additional cost on the rate of interest to cover the lending institution or investor against any currency fluctuations that may occur. Offshore finance is acceptable for short-term funding, such as development or construction loans, subject to interest rates being lower than local banks. For long-term property investing this finance would not be suitable because of the instability caused by currency fluctuations.

Solicitors and accountants

High-profile solicitors and accounting firms have a large base of wealthy clients who are always on the lookout for good investments. If your scheme is viable, a solicitor can arrange a loan in the form of a mortgage — part equity part mortgage, or equity only. With the latter the investor will become a shareholder in the development. The part equity part mortgage will be arranged on a short-term basis, while the mortgage held by the investor will be viewed over a longer term.

Types of development loans

The following are loans that may be required during the various phases of the development.

Seed capital loan

Depending on a developer's own personal finances, seed capital may be required in the conceptual stage of a new development. This initial finance, which is relatively small, is required to cover the cost of consultants and disbursements for the initial design and submission for development approval. It is considered a high-risk loan and is often obtained in exchange for an equity stake in the project. Seed capital often comes from the developer's personal assets or from friends and family or private investors seeking a higher return on their capital. The higher risk stage of the project means interest rates are a lot higher than from other lenders.

Land acquisition loan

A land acquisition loan is used to secure the purchase of raw land or a potential development site. The borrower's track record and ability to secure the debt with collateral will weigh heavily on the lender's decision to provide for this financing. For a built-form development on raw land, most lenders do not like funding the land only, which they view as 'land banking', and will consider the loan only as part of a full development loan. If the development site has a building with an income, the developer would apply first for a longer term loan and then for a development or construction loan after securing development approval. For a land subdivision development, the land developer is advised to secure the raw land without any debt, as the long approval process can be costly and any future profit will be eaten away by the interest over this period.

Construction loan

A construction loan generally operates as an interest-only, drawdown facility to finance the building as required. Often the interest on a construction loan is capitalised during the building period, with the entire loan inclusive of interest charged being repaid upon the sale of the development and/or the refinance of any residual debt.

Construction loans are considered risky by most lenders. This is because at this stage of the development the construction costs can escalate; the building program can be delayed; or the builder may run into financial difficulty requiring another builder, whose cost may be higher, to take over. Depending on the type of development, these loans are usually for a short period of time (9 to 36 months). The rate is normally higher than prime, and there is usually an origination fee.

When considering a construction loan, most lenders will require that the developer has a source of permanent financing secured, or an exit by way of sale to a third party, before agreeing to provide this financing. In some instances, the construction lender may not require that the developer (depending on financial strength and development experience) have a permanent investment loan to repay their construction loan.

Bridging loan

Bridging loans are often used to close on a property quickly or to take advantage of a short-term opportunity in order to secure long-term financing. Bridging loans on a property are typically paid back when the property is sold or refinanced with a traditional lender, the borrower's creditworthiness improves, the property is improved or completed, or there is a specific improvement or change that allows a permanent or subsequent round of mortgage financing to occur. A bridging loan is often obtained by developers to carry a project while permit approval is sought. Because there is no guarantee the project will happen, the loan might be at a high interest rate and from a specialised lending source that will accept the risk. Once the project is approved a construction loan would be obtained to take out the bridging loan and fund completion of the project.

Mezzanine loan

A mezzanine loan is basically debt capital that gives the lender the right to convert to an ownership or equity interest in the company if the loan is not paid back in time and in full. It is generally subordinated debt provided by private lenders or venture capital companies. This type of loan is advantageous because it is treated like equity and may make it easier to obtain standard bank financing. Mezzanine loans are often used by developers to secure additional financing for development projects where there is a shortfall of equity required by the senior lender.

Mezzanine loans are often a more expensive financing source for a developer than secured debt or senior debt. The higher cost of capital associated with mezzanine financing results from its being an unsecured, subordinated (or junior) debt in a project's capital structure, which means that in the event of default the mezzanine financing is repaid only after all senior obligations have been satisfied. In compensation for the increased risk, mezzanine debt holders require a higher return for their investment than secured or more senior lenders. This type of financing is aggressively priced, with the lender seeking a return in the 20 to 30 per cent range.

Non-recourse loan

Non-recourse debt or a non-recourse loan is a debt (loan) that is secured by a pledge of collateral, typically real property, but for which the borrower is not personally liable. If the borrower defaults, the lender can seize the property pledged as security, but the lender's recovery is limited to that property. The lender cannot seek out the borrower for any further compensation, even if the collateral does not cover the full value of the defaulted amount. This is one instance where the borrower does not have personal liability for the loan. Therefore, non-recourse debt is typically limited to 50 or 60 per cent loan-to-value ratios, so the property itself provides *overcollateralisation* of the loan.

Commercial bills

This facility is to cover short- or long-term requirements. A commercial bill assists the developer to raise finance through the drawing and discounting of negotiable bank bills. Under this facility the lender agrees to both accept and discount the customer's bills. The developer can choose from an array of facilities utilising the latest financial market techniques to suit their individual requirements, including:

- finance for amounts over $500 000

- facility terms of one to five years

- drawdown terms ranging from a minimum of 30 days to a maximum of 185 days

- choice of a floating or fixed interest rate

- a facility commencing on any business day with drawdown dates being monthly, quarterly, half-yearly or tailored to suit their cash flow requirements.

With the floating rate bill, the drawdown rate and the term to maturity of the bill are agreed at the time of the drawdown. The interest rate applicable is determined by the term of the bill. The lender accepts the bills and discounts them on the required date at the lender's bank bill drawdown rate of the day. On the other hand, with a fixed bill rate the drawdown rate is fixed for the term of the facility. The aggregate face amount of the bills to be discounted and the drawdown dates are established prior to the first drawdown date.

Risk participation loan

In situations where there is a large sum of money to be invested in a development and the lender desires to reduce risk or is unable to fund a construction loan of the size required by the lender, the lender may assemble a syndication of other lenders to fund the construction loan. Usually in this situation the lead lender will take a larger share of the upfront fees for putting the deal together as well as a monthly servicing fee to service the loan. The lenders may also provide finance for up to 100 per cent of the project costs. Typically, two-thirds of the funding is treated as notional debt, the remaining third as notional equity.

Builder's design, construct and finance loan

Builders with a significant balance sheet are in a position to offer a design, construct and finance loan to approved developers. This will also depend on the amount of work the builder has on their order book and how much they want the project. Before the builder enters into this type of loan they will require an unconditional bank guarantee that all the costs paid by them will be repaid at completion. The benefit to the developer is in not having to fund the full equity required by a commercial bank, especially if the equity required is 30 per cent or more. All the developer has to fund is the land and development approval cost plus running and overhead costs. The disadvantage with this type of loan is that the builder will add a margin over their own bank's interest to cover the risk of providing the finance to the developer. In some cases this could be higher than the current available rates. Entering into such a loan contract, the developer should have an independent quantity surveyor verify the builder's cost and ensure that it is in line with current construction costs.

Loan characteristics

In taking out a development or construction loan with any of the lenders mentioned, the developer should consider the following characteristics of a typical loan. Bank conditions will vary and will be based on the developer's reputation and track record and also the project itself.

Loan-to-value ratio

For loan-to-value ratio (LVR), the rule of thumb for both development/construction (short term) and investment (long term) loans for most property types is a maximum of 75 per cent. A reappraisal or valuation may be required for the investment loan after the completion of the development, with the condition that the loan will be revised if the 75 per cent LVR is not met. In addition, for the investment loan some form of principal and interest payment is required, if not during the initial term of the loan then certainly during any subsequent extension options. The amount may be based on a 25-year amortisation or may be dictated by the property's actual net income.

Pre-sales

For larger residential projects, typically three or more units, most lenders require a certain level of pre-sales to minimise their risk. The percentage of the project they require to be pre-sold before they are prepared to hand over development finance varies but is typically around 80 per cent of the debt to be provided by the lender. Obviously this is a way for lenders to minimise their risk. An alternative way to overcome a pre-sales condition requirement is to secure a pre-sale underwriting product, also referred to as renounceable pre-sales, such as put options and standby pre-sales. This enables the construction finance facility to commence immediately instead of waiting for pre-sales requirements from the construction loan lender to be met.

Pre-leasing

This is mainly for commercial development projects, such as offices, retail outlets and industrial properties, for which the preferred pre-leasing should be at least 75 per cent. For other types of properties, such as residential or serviced apartments, the pre-leasing requirement is on a case-by-case basis and will depend on the strength of the borrower, the project and the structure of the loan itself.

Analysing loan issues

Before selecting a lender, the developer should consider the following issues relative to lender response:

- type of property you need on which financing is needed
- location of the property
- extent of loans that lender normally provides
- lender's quoted interest rate.

If the answers to these issues are encouraging, then the following should be considered:

- percentage of total development cost on which the lender will provide financing
- equity required
- funding of development and professional fees
- terms of the construction loan

- interest rate for the construction loan

- interest payment schedule

- construction loan personal liability

- estimate of loan settlement costs

- reimbursement of pre-development costs

- time required for underwriting and funding the loan

- submissions necessary for the underwriting of this loan

- construction drawdown schedule

- letters of credit of contractor

- phasing of property funding

- property valuers approved by the lender

- loan extensions costs and terms.

Packaging a loan proposal

The packaging of a development project has increased in importance for obtaining development finance. A submission consisting of various documents gathered in a loose-leaf binder no longer generates a favourable response from a lender. The information should be presented in logical order and in a professional manner. Every step in the process requires significant time and effort. Many developers may not have the available time or the experience to collect the abundant information and organise it in the necessary form, but doing so is critical to successful presentation.

When preparing your loan proposal ensure that you have all documentation in place for the completed submission. This will decrease the loan processing time and give you the best chance of acceptance. It is also important to consider the sophistication of the lender to whom you are submitting your proposal. For the more sophisticated lenders, you will use all of the following items. (For other, smaller lenders with whom you have existing relationships, your presentation may be shortened.)

Finance document criteria

The finance document is the culmination of months of work undertaken by the developer and team. The aim is to present a proposal that is both comprehensive and professional to ensure that lending institutions or investors are confident of the professionalism of the group they are dealing with. The following guidelines may vary somewhat between different types of developments:

1 general information
   - outline and goals of the development
   - background (history of the site)
   - site information (location, title particulars, land area and so on).

2 town planning report—include a copy of rezoning or development approval

3 market research—a copy of the research findings, demographics etc.

4 illustrations—maps, diagrams and photographs of site and neighbourhood

5 architectural documents—plans and specifications by the architect

6 economic viability study—prepared by the quantity surveyor or development manager

7 schedule of leases / offers to lease (for commercial projects)—prepared by commercial leasing agents

8 schedule of sale prices / sales contracts (for residential projects)—prepared by marketing and sales agents

9 valuation of the land or sale contracts—prepared by property valuer

10 the developer and support team
   - profile of the developer
   - developer's past projects
   - capability statements of the supporting professional team.

11 financial information (can be separate document)—include balance sheets and/or statements of assets and liabilities of the directors

12 other supporting information—land sale contract, construction contract, management contract and so on.

In support of the documents provided to the lender, the credibility and track record of the developer is of great importance. If you as the developer do not have the track record, it is advisable that you employ a team of professionals with the necessary experience of the type of project to be developed. A key team member would be an experienced development and project manager. Alternatively, you could partner with a developer who does have the credibility and track record.

How a lender evaluates a development loan

Before any lender can determine the cost and fees that can be charged for the loan, it must consider the credit history of the borrower and all of the relevant information provided on the proposed development. In addition, the lender's offerings will be valued against the present market conditions and the risks associated with the development. The risk is usually based on:

- type of project
- projected sales if applicable
- type of tenancy (length of lease and the creditworthiness of the tenant), if applicable
- expected future income streams to repay the loan
- financial strength of the developer
- track record of the developer and team.

The lender will propose various terms and conditions relative to the risk, including the following.

Interest rate

As the use of money has a cost, lenders will review the costs of raising funds and determine the profit margin they must receive on the use of these funds. The profit margin is based on the risk taken by the lender, the length of time these funds will be outstanding and the repayment schedule. If the developer is a good customer and has a substantial balance in the lender's institution, this profit margin may be reduced.

Fees and charges

These fees and charges are in addition to the interest rate charged by the lender and provide another way for the lender to increase its profit margin and lessen its risk. They generally range from 1 to 4 per cent, as determined by the magnitude of the risk.

Construction loan period

The construction loan period is usually determined by the amount of time necessary to construct the building(s). In most instances lenders will include additional time for the property to achieve a steady occupancy or sales, which will allow the developer to obtain a larger permanent loan or settlement of sales.

Conditions applied in the loan agreement

The lender may add extra conditions into the loan documents. These may require the developer to support the loan with additional collateral through securing the property with a mortgage or even by adding the borrower's personal guarantee of the loan repayment. Each lender's requirement will vary according to any problems they have experienced in the past. The developer should negotiate carefully in this area to ensure the most favourable terms are accepted.

Guarantees

In most financing transactions, further security may be required by lenders to minimise their risk should the developer default on the loan. This security or guarantee can take various forms. Some guarantees involve the following.

Jointly and severally

When more than one borrower is involved in borrowing funds for a development, the lender will usually require that the borrowers sign the personal guarantees both personally and jointly and severally with the other borrowers. Each borrower should be made aware that if these loans are ever called early or if they are in default of the loan terms, then each borrower is responsible not only for their own share of the loan but also for the shares of the other borrowers should they not be able to honour the financial commitment to the lender.

Recourse versus non-recourse guarantees

As noted, most lenders today will require a personal guarantee from the developer or directors of a development company, whichever is applicable. In addition, full or partial financial guarantees will be required for the permanent investment loan. The developer should reduce these financial guarantees as much as possible. Many developers have lost their fortunes as a result of personal guarantees on properties they developed that failed. Some methods of minimising these risks are as follows:

- Find substitute or additional guarantors. These additional guarantors will reduce the developer's risk exposure by reducing their guarantee portion. Using this method, the developer will probably have to share ownership of the project.

- Negotiate a reducible amount of the personal guarantee relative to the achievement of a predetermined net operating income for a specified time period.

- Negotiate a guarantee for only the upper portion of the loan balance. For example, a $1 million loan might have only the top 10 per cent or $100 000 personally guaranteed by the borrower.

- Negotiate or accept a higher interest rate or charges from the lender for a reduced or no personal guarantee to be provided. If the project is profitable enough on paper then it is well worth considering this option.

Additional collateral

Often the lender will require not only that the developer sign the loan with a personal guarantee, but also that additional collateral of other property or assets (such as stock and bonds) be provided as security. Upon default, the developer may lose these other assets. It is advisable to keep them under a separate entity and not to have a relationship with the development entity, which can be a separate ownership vehicle.

Negotiating loan document details

When reviewing the written loan offers from the various banks you have approached, analyse the terms and conditions from each lender, as they could be different. Take special care to analyse your obligations as most lenders structure terms to their benefit. Some of these clauses will not be subject to negotiation, while others can be reworded to your benefit or in some cases can be totally removed. It is more common to negotiate these clauses in a development project loan than it is in residential home loans. As in any negotiation, if you find a problem clause, ask that it be removed. In selecting the most suitable candidate from your list of potential lenders, consider the following issues.

Know your lender's position

Develop a sense of whether your lender is lending on the project or on the experience and integrity of the developer. The key to obtaining a loan is to develop a lasting relationship with the lender. Lenders are conservative individuals who must have the utmost confidence in the borrower's ability to pay back the loan.

Interest rates

Institutional lenders typically price long-term fixed-rate mortgage loans based on yields available on comparable term Australian Treasury notes or bills plus a spread to compensate for the additional risk associated with making a mortgage, as compared with buying a Treasury note. Currently spreads of 250 to 270 basis points (2.5 to 2.7 per cent), depending on property type, are the norm. Institutional lenders establish a floor rate that they will not go below, regardless of the Treasury yield. Negotiating the bank's spread will depend on your project's risk profile and your financial standing.

Prepayment fees

If you take out a longer term investment loan after you complete your development, you should be aware of what will occur when your loan matures and if it is paid before it matures. Most long-term, fixed-rate loans require a prepayment fee if paid off early. This fee typically decreases as the loan approaches maturity. You should negotiate a prepayment fee that is not payable should you give at least 90 days' notice before you settle the full loan.

Bank fees and charges

Bank fees and charges generally constitute a major portion of revenue for most banks, particularly regional and local branches. Most banks charge nominal fees for various services and these vary from lender to lender. These fees and charges can include monthly charges for the provision of an account, charges for drawdowns on your loan, line fees, capital raising fees and so on. Carefully review these fees when you get an offer, compare them between banks and negotiate lower charges if possible.

Be creative in structuring your loan

As there are many options, be creative when structuring your loan by refining the terms and conditions to suit your needs. Each developer has specific needs in relation to their project and a knowledgeable accountant or finance broker can assist you in reaching your objectives. For example, if 70 per cent LVR is the standard, that does not mean that 85 per cent is not possible. Lenders are keen to offer loans. If one proposal doesn't work, search for other possibilities with the lender until you find the one that meets the needs of both parties.

Using finance brokers

If as a developer you do not have the time, knowledge or network needed to locate the best available development financing, you may choose to use the services of an outside professional such as a finance broker. A finance broker has:

- specialist knowledge of who the best lenders are for a specific project
- access to the best interest rates and charges
- knowledge of how to present a project and to negotiate the best terms and conditions.

Finance brokers act as mediators between the developer and the lender. Brokers deal not only with the major commercial banks but also with other known financial institutions and private lenders. In addition to negotiating loans with third-party lenders, some brokers will also perform the role of a lender and self-fund loans. With a larger number of lenders and programs to choose from, brokers can often find the ideal balance between cost, loan terms, liberal underwriting standards and speed.

Most brokers are very knowledgeable about all phases of the loan process and, as they are paid only when they conclude a loan, they have great incentive to package the loan applications correctly and to intercede when the inevitable snags occur. Brokers typically maintain good working relationships with property valuers, title companies, underwriters and other professionals often needed in the finance process. In addition, most brokers know when to contest a low valuation, when to dispute the refusal of a loan application and, failing those challenges, which lender to approach next.

Most brokers charge a success commission for their services. The commission, based on a percentage of the loan proceeds, can range from 0.5 to 2 per cent depending on the size of the loan. Good brokers can put the initial loan proposal together and use their list of relationships in the financial community to find the best possible loan. In addition, the broker can help structure the business terms and can offer sophistication within the process that you as a developer may not possess. Remember, if you decide to use a mortgage broker, choose one who is qualified, accredited and experienced with the type of financing for which you are searching.

Summary

This chapter has stressed the important role of finance in property development. Without funding there is no project. If you decide to take up property development as a career, you should study and learn to understand finance and the parties involved. As an architect I was never concerned about development finance. There was no finance course as part of my curriculum at university. When I decided that I wanted to build and develop my own projects, I realised I had to negotiate with banks. Knowing that I needed to secure the best terms and conditions from my bank, I decided to study finance and read as many books and articles on finance as I could. Today, with this knowledge, I'm confident and comfortable when negotiating finance either for my clients or for my own projects.

CHAPTER 10
Raising equity finance

In most instances a developer seeking debt funding from a lender will be able to secure only a certain percentage of the overall project cost as a loan. The balance will have to be provided by the developer as equity. The lender will require the cash equity in the development deal on the front end, by purchasing the land or part of the land, by depositing a cash equivalent with the lender or by using another property as equity. Depending on the developer's cash position, they may contribute the equity themselves, borrow funds or have other individuals contribute the equity needed to close.

For developers involved in larger projects where funding generally runs into the millions, a proportionally larger equity will be required. Not every private developer will have the necessary equity to initiate a project. A developer who cannot secure the equity needed must raise the necessary capital from other sources. This chapter provides guidelines for the developer to follow in this endeavour. In finding these resources the developer will need to go into partnership with others, usually as the 'managing partner' (to avoid the risk of losing control of the development) with the new partners becoming limited partners.

Developers who invest their own cash in a development, either for the land or to cover the gap between the costs and the loan, are likely to pay closer attention to the project, which increases their chances of success. In most instances, lenders use loan-to-value ratios (LVR) to determine the amount of equity required, which places the developer at a certain level of risk and avoids the lender carrying the total risk for the development.

What is equity?

Equity is normally that cash at-risk from either the developer or their partners that bridges the gap between the lender's loan and the total costs of the development. It is also the value remaining in the property after payment of all debt or other charges on the property. An owner's equity in a property is normally the monetary interest the owner retains over and above the mortgage debt. If the property is encumbered with a long-term mortgage, the developer's equity in the property increases with each monthly principal mortgage payment, not including the increased value through appreciation.

Sources of equity

Once the amount of equity is determined, the developer should list potential equity investors, such as:

■ friends

■ business associates

■ brokers/dealers who specialise in property

■ financial planners who specialise in property

■ brokers who have contacts with private money

■ accountants who have clients who desire to invest in property

■ attorneys who have clients who desire to invest in property

■ bankers who have clients who may be potential investors

■ insurance agents who have clients who may be potential investors

■ property investment firms or funds

■ syndications

■ joint-venture partnerships.

Developers seeking potential equity investors should gather information on the interested parties, including their investment experience, income, financial resources and net worth. This information should give developers an in-depth understanding of the potential investor and a sense of whether they might be an asset or a liability to the project.

There is an adage that one should never involve family or friends in business. If you are inviting family or friends to become investors, be sure to explain the risks involved in the project and in property development in general, and your role and remuneration in the project. If their knowledge of property development is limited, this could cause misunderstanding should the project fail. Do not oversell the benefits of your development or they will blame you for the collapse of the scheme or for its failure to reach its financial targets.

Other sources of equity

There is no shortage of investors in property development investment, especially if the returns look good. Besides the list of investors listed earlier in this chapter there are three other sources of potential equity partners: new or prospective migrants, financial institutions and building contractors.

New migrants

Wealthy migrants arriving in Australia are always looking for business and investment opportunities. In some cases prospective business migrants need to establish a business in order to qualify for permanent residency. Migrants who invest in a development opportunity can benefit on two fronts: they acquire a return on their money and they also gain an understanding of how developments work in Australia. However, persuading migrants to invest in your project is not always as easy as it sounds. Being unfamiliar with the country and the economic conditions, they are likely to be overcautious and tend to double-check every detail. This could lead you to waste a lot of time and effort only to find out that at the last minute they have found another opportunity. In addition, migrants, especially those coming from Asia, expect a high return on their investment. In Australia a return of 20 per cent is considered good, whereas some migrant investors want 30 per cent or more.

Financial institutions

Depending on the location, the profile of the development, the credibility of the developer and the financial feasibility, some financial institutions will provide the equity on a larger project. The institution will provide

100 per cent funding, apportioned as 25 per cent equity and 75 per cent interest-only debt finance. If the development is sold, the institution will share 25 per cent of the net profit. If the development is planned as a long-term investment, the institution will want the developer to purchase their 25 per cent equity at a price calculated by a licensed property valuer within a five-year period. During this period the developer can either invite other investors or refinance the property.

Building contractors

Builders are always looking for new building contracts, and if the size and type of project fits well into their building program they may at times inject equity in return for securing the building contract. Their source of equity could be their own cash resources, their balance sheet or investors they know. When entering into such a contract you need to ensure that you have your own independent quantity surveyor verify that the contract price provided by the builder is within an acceptable range.

What is sweat equity?

Equity is defined as earned real money you put towards a property or an asset, whereas *free equity*, also called *sweat equity*, is money that is created or built up over a period of time. It is this free equity that all property developers aim for; the more free equity you create in the early part of a project, the less risk you will encounter and the less cash you will need for the deposit on the property.

If you have a career in the building industry, you certainly have an advantage when it comes to property development. As an architect, builder, building estimator, engineer, bricklayer, plumber or carpenter you will be able to provide the cost of your job on your own development project for free, thereby creating the sweat equity.

Following are some ideas for creating this sweat equity. Please note, however, that not all lenders would consider these as equity as they would prefer to see cash injected by the developer.

Generating fees

As a professional developer you will be spending a great deal of your own time and energy in researching and evaluating potential developments. You will also be responsible for supervising and managing the project from inception to completion. For your effort you should be rewarded in the form of a fee payment, which should be factored into the development as an outgoing. These fees can be used to cover your overhead cost or they could be left in the development as part of your equity. Some examples are outlined here.

Project procurement fee

This fee is paid to developers for their initiative in finding a viable project, which includes using their personal time to research the market, networking with various people within the property industry, creating the vision and structuring a deal with the landowner. The fee for this service is usually based on a percentage of the development cost and is a fixed figure. Fees can vary from 1 to 2 per cent of the development cost depending on the size, type and complexity of the project.

Development management fee

For large or complex projects, development managers are normally employed because of their skill and knowledge of such projects. Their role is to represent the developer or investment group and to direct the development to ensure its viability so it can be financed and the projected returns achieved. In addition, they would analyse the development's potential, set up a strategic policy framework and ensure that the appointed project manager is doing their job. Development management fees range from 1.5 to 3 per cent of the total development cost excluding land.

Project management fee

A project manager can also be employed to ensure the smooth operation of the project. Their role is to manage the professional team and the building contract on behalf of the developer or development manager.

Their fees are normally based on a percentage of the building contract sum, which is around 1.5 per cent for larger and complex projects and around 3 per cent for smaller and less complex projects.

Marketing or leasing fee

The developer who undertakes the marketing and leasing of the development should be paid accordingly. Fees are based on industry standards—that is, the going market rate. Unless a developer has the time, resources and marketing expertise, it is wiser to employ the services of a third party with the right credentials so the developer can concentrate on 'developing'.

Property management fee

Some developers who hold on to their developments and have a sufficient portfolio take on the role of property manager rather than employing a third party. Their fee is usually based on a percentage of the collected revenues.

Partnership or director's fee

The developer could be the appointed managing partner, or a managing director of the development company will usually charge a fee or be paid a salary for managing the project, administration, accounting, tax issues and general correspondence. The fee can be based on a monthly time basis or a fixed monthly amount.

Syndication fee

These fees are for services rendered in creating the investment syndication, negotiating with potential investors, arranging a new partnership or company, negotiating debt finance and setting up of the management and accounting systems. The developer or managing partners could take a small fee and larger shareholding. The fee can be either a flat fee or based on a percentage of the equity raised in the range of 2.5 to 5 per cent of the monies invested by the syndicate members.

Rezoning

Developers who research an area or suburb of interest will be aware of future town planning proposals and rezoning of certain streets. Such new proposals could involve, for example, an increase in residential densities in a particular zone of a growing suburb or a corridor strip along a major arterial road being converted from residential to commercial. However, some property sellers will not be aware of these proposals and will sell their properties under their current zoning at a lower price than had they been rezoned. It is here that an alert developer can take advantage of the situation and place an offer on a property 'subject to rezoning', allowing a reasonable time for council approval. Should the rezoning be approved then the value of the property would increase significantly and the developer would have created his free equity.

Subdivision

Subdividing semi-rural lots into new suburban lots, or suburban lots in older suburbs into smaller green title lots, can create huge financial benefits for a residential property developer. As noted, studying the local town planning scheme and looking for the growth areas will certainly give you an advantage when new properties come onto the market. Here again, when an opportunity arises, place an offer on a property conditional on subdivision approval by your state planning commission, but allow a reasonable amount of time for approval. The approval time can be checked with a town planner or land surveyor.

Equity through the landowner

This is a simple concept used when a developer is considering developing a site and the seller is prepared to become part of the project by (a) becoming a joint-venture partner, (b) granting the developer development rights over the land or (c) providing vendor finance to the developer with settlement at a later date. The land then becomes part of the equity required for the overall development. The balance of the funds required to complete the project is financed through a bank that secures a first mortgage on the property.

Benefits to the parties

Not every landowner or seller will look at this type of proposal, as they may require the equity to purchase another property, but those who are able to be part of the project will benefit by obtaining:

- a potentially higher sales price
- a better interest rate on their money from the bank
- a quicker sale.

From an equity point of view, the developer also benefits for the following reasons:

- The equity is immediate and the project can start earlier.
- As the land is part of the project, less money is required upfront to secure development approval.
- If there is an equity shortfall, other investors will feel more comfortable as the landowner will also be willing to take the risk.

Items to consider in relation to this opportunity

If the landowner is not willing to be a joint-venture partner who takes the same risk as the developer, but would rather agree to grant development rights or offer vendor finance, you should consider the following issues before committing to the agreement in writing.

Interest rates

If the landowner is charging interest, try to negotiate a better rate that is below the standard rate offered by financial institutions. If possible secure an interest-only loan with the final payment at the completion of the project or at the end of the agreed term.

Term

Ensure that a longer term is provided in the agreement for the project to be completed or for you to pay out the money to the landowner. Have a clause making allowance for an extension without any penalties or change of the interest rate.

Construction finance

Ensure that the landowner is made aware and agrees that you will be seeking a construction loan from a senior lender and any debt owed to them for the land will be a *subordinated debt*, which means the land debt will rank after the senior loan should things go awry.

Dealing with an equity partner

Many people have substantial amounts of money in savings accounts earning low interest. A developer who can convince them that the development will bring higher returns will soon have a queue of potential partners, as most people are motivated by greed and are always looking at avenues that offer a better return.

Fledgling or undercapitalised developers need to foster investor partner relationships for the times when they find they are financially stretched. It is best to have at least four or five potential partners who can be approached when the need arises. Developers who prove to be successful with their developments will find they are never short of prospective partners; best of all, they may never have to use their own capital for future developments.

While it is easy to convince people to become partners, these relationships can generate problems if some basic rules are not adhered to. Stick to the following principles and you will experience fewer problems down the track:

- *Form partnerships only if necessary:* It is important that partnerships are formed only when totally necessary. New partners should contribute where the developer's resources are insufficient, such as through a lack of funds. A partnership functions a lot better when partners complement each other and work as a single unit.

- *Be selective with partners:* Developers considering relatives, friends or business associates as partners should be very selective and make sure their personalities do not clash. Preferred partners will understand the property industry. There is nothing worse than if the development does not reach the expected returns and a partner who does not understand the issues involved accuses the developer of being reckless.

- *Define the role of each partner:* If the developer's role is to manage the development based on their knowledge and the partner's role is to provide or raise the funds based on their financial standing, then these roles should be defined before the partnership is formalised and signed off.

- *Define early how the profits are to be split:* If the project is profitable, the developer should negotiate a fair arrangement for both parties related to their roles. There are several models that can be used. For example, the finance partner can be offered a percentage return per annum on the capital injected with the balance of the profit split, say, 50:50.

- *Reduce the fear of the partner:* If a partner is putting up the money, it is important to allay any fear they may have of losing their money. This can be resolved by placing the property in joint names or setting up a company with agreed shareholding. Also have an agreement on how the development should be managed and what fees should be paid to the manager.

- *Maintain control of the partnership:* If, as the developer, you found the project and have the knowledge on how to deliver the development, it is important that you retain control. If your partner proves not to be compatible and is limiting the progress of the development it would be best to dissolve the partnership as soon as possible.

- *Retain a partnership for one property at a time:* Each development project should be assessed on its own merits. At the end of the project the profits should be split and the partnership should be dissolved. Following this rule allows flexibility when another property development opportunity arises. It should be clarified from the outset that the partnership is temporary and applies only to a specific development.

- *Work out resolutions for if the partnership has to dissolve:* Not all partnerships work out successfully and there can be misunderstandings or personal conflict along the way, or one partner may pass away. It is imperative to decide at the outset what procedures should be followed in such circumstances.

If you are developing property based on your own knowledge and expertise but without your own cash, then it is important to build up a level of credibility and trust. Treat partners fairly and don't abuse the relationship, as if you do word will spread fast and it will be difficult to find future partners.

Preparing an investor information package

In order to persuade investors to part with their money on a development you have to convince them that it will be worth the risk. To make this decision the investor needs all the facts and relevant information on the project presented in an investor package. The package should include details of the terms of the land transaction, the financial projections, the capital debt required and any other information needed to raise the equity for the development to proceed. The following list is a generic outline of items that can be included in the package but it need not be limited to this, as the more quality information provided the better when helping the investor reach a decision.

1   introduction to the development

    –   a brief summary of the property

    –   a brief summary of the land transaction.

2   locality overview

    –   map of site location

    –   state information—population, income, employment, government etc.

    –   city information—demographics, income, employment, government etc.

    –   neighbourhood information—demographics, income groups, traffic information, housing, local government and so on.

3   site details

    –   site survey

    –   title details and address

    –   zoning type and approvals

- building regulations
- site description—size, topographical information
- local climatic conditions
- environmental issues.

4 development team
- developer
- development manager
- project manager
- town planner
- architect
- quantity surveyor
- engineers—structural, civil, mechanical, traffic
- environmentalist
- marketing consultants
- solicitor/accountant
- any other consultants giving advice.

5 design information
- design concept
- site development plan
- sketch plans and elevations
- perspective
- any other architectural visual information.

6 construction
- type of construction
- type of external material
- type of internal finishes
- landscaping and parking.

7 leasing information

- tenant profile

- gross leasable floor areas

- rental rate per square metre

- lease terms

- rent escalation

- common area charges

- tenant allowances and concessions.

8 investment vehicle

- details of current owner

- type of new investment vehicle.

9 program

- design program

- construction program

- leasing program.

10 investment feasibility

- estimate development cost

- estimate income

- capitalisation rate

- internal rate of return.

11 financial forecast

- forecast of investment performance

- sources and sources of proceeds

- forecast of cash flow

- forecast of taxable income (loss)

- forecast of resale.

12 offer

- – type of shareholding
- – investment unit size
- – closing date
- – risk warning.

Developers offering equity or shareholding in a development by way of investment should abide by the regulations of the Australian Securities and Investments Commission (ASIC). There is a limit to the number of investors who can participate in an investment group before it becomes a public offering. ASIC has specific rules in this regard.

The investor package, presented in an attractive brochure, should be professionally written and supported with graphics and photographs. Use a graphic designer or an architect to assist with the layout and make sure the document is professionally printed and bound.

Guide to raising equity

Finding suitable investors is one of the biggest challenges for the developer in a project's early stages. Major hurdles include identifying the right potential investors, convincing them to invest and achieving this before the market opportunity is lost. Listed here are some valuable tips on the procedure and dealing with investors that will help you achieve a successful outcome.

Be prepared

To target and pursue suitable investors, the developer must understand their investment strategy and preferences. Developers tend to be over-optimistic about their project but it may not be the same with the investor. To communicate successfully with investors, a developer needs to understand the way they think. Investors think in terms of business and finance, and evaluate you and your project based on these concerns. Learning investor language and demonstrating sound business skills will place you in a stronger position. This requires the following of you.

- ■ *Communicate effectively*: When seeking equity for a development, it's easier to gain the confidence of a potential investor if the developer understands the investor's requirements and their background and, more importantly, listens more and speaks less. The biggest obstacle to good communication is the one-sided nature of over-selling. To find out exactly what will motivate the investor to part with their money, it is far better to listen than to talk.

- *Read body language:* Communication is not just about the words said. In fact, we all communicate more through gestures and facial expression than speech. Paying attention to the body language of the potential investor will give a good guide to where negotiations are heading and their level of interest in the project.

- *Avoid misunderstandings:* It is vital to prevent any misunderstandings during negotiations. This can best be achieved by paying close attention to the prospect's responses.

- *Sell trust:* When dealing with prospective investors for the first time, convincing them you are a trustworthy and credible person is half the battle. Be frank and answer all questions in a professional manner even if some of them are intimidating.

Be selective

A developer should select an investor based not only on the money they can bring but also on the value they can add to the development through:

- their experience in similar projects
- the management role they have taken in investment projects
- their links with other potential investors
- their contacts with service providers that will be useful for the project
- their profile in the community
- their personality and compatibility.

Introduction to an investor through referral sources will improve the odds of securing financing. All developers should have a trusted and credible referral base.

Introducing the project

At the very first meeting a developer may have less than three minutes to introduce the project to a prospective investor. Investors are busy people with little time to spare. This introduction will therefore either make or break the deal. A developer who is professional and well prepared for this meeting with a brief, thorough, oral presentation will make an impact. Key information that should be covered on a single page will outline:

- the development project
- the development's potential and returns
- the market research undertaken
- the marketing strategies planned
- the key managers, consultants and their backgrounds
- the amount of financing you require and the way in which you will use it.

If interested as a result, the investor will probably ask to see the feasibility study or the investor package described earlier in the chapter.

Negotiate and close the deal

Developers should be flexible in their approach as most investors prefer to structure deals themselves. The investor may propose a funding package that contains various forms of finance. Because the question of the funding package is both complex and very important, it is worth consulting an attorney beforehand. Investors will value a proposed development project and combine this with the required rate of return to decide on the type and level of investment they are prepared to make in exchange for a percentage of equity proportional to the risk it will incur.

Using a professional finance consultant

For the novice developer who has not raised money for a project before and does not have the confidence that comes from experience, an alternative is to find an experienced finance consultant or broker to raise the equity. These consultants will have direct connections in the property industry, but ensure they have successfully raised money in the past. While the investor will want to hear directly from the developer, a properly selected consultant will help with the introduction. With some of my own projects, I use a professional licensed finance broker as I do not have all the investor networks and nor do I have the time to nurture these associations. It also gives me more time to concentrate on what I do best.

Increasing your equity in a staged process

Property development is one of the few businesses where enterprising entrepreneurs can be rewarded exponentially for their efforts in adding value. They take the greatest risk in the creation of a new development and should therefore receive the greatest rewards. It is an art to utilise the least amount of capital and through vision, expertise and commitment make significant returns for equity participants.

The following outlines the staged process by which you can increase your equity value during the development of a project you initiated. The strategy demonstrates how with each step you control the process, selling a percentage of your shareholding only after you have added value to the project. This strategy is applicable mainly to larger scale residential or commercial developments where substantial capital is required.

Stage 1: Land purchase

As noted in an earlier chapter: 'Developers make their money when they buy the land'. Buying and settling on a development site is not wise and carries risk, especially if you have not secured a DA (development approval) for your intended project. The alternatives are to secure development rights over the property, to establish a JV (joint venture) with the landowner or to negotiate to buy the land subject to securing a DA. Each of these options has its own idiosyncrasies and should be evaluated accordingly; however, the aim is to secure and control the land with minimal capital from your own pocket.

Stage 2: Pre-development approval

Once you have control of the land, the next step is to raise seed capital for the documentation required for the DA. The amount of seed capital required is generally around 1 per cent of the development cost. There are several sources where seed capital can be raised, but what can be offered in return? Below are a few structures:

- A convertible loan entitles the lender to convert the loan to equity after the approval of the DA. As a DA application is still risky to the lender they will expect a much higher return on their money, ranging from 20 per cent per annum to 3 per cent per month. Security can be provided by way of a caveat over the development property or some other asset that you can provide. Some lenders may ask for a personal guarantee on top of other security provided.

- Class 'A' Preferred Shares can be converted into ordinary shares after the approval of the DA. The value of Class A shares varies and depends on the type of project, the risk and projected profit. If the seed investor is providing 1 per cent of the development cost then typically they will be looking at a 5 to 10 per cent share of the development company.

Stage 3: Post-development approval

Securing a DA takes one of the main risks out of the development process and adds value to the project. Equity investors will therefore be more comfortable to invest. What percentage of the development company you are prepared to part with for the additional equity required will depend on new valuations. If you have done your numbers and show a good return on the project you should demonstrate to the investor the return on their cash invested rather than the actual return on the total development cost. Table 10.1 shows a theoretical example:

Table 10.1: acceptable return on equity to investor

Total development cost (1 year construction)	$10 000 000
Say, profit margin on development 20%	$ 2 000 000
Equity required 30%	$ 3 000 000
Return on equity	67%
Say, additional equity required for project	$ 2 000 000
Expected return by investor of minimum 30% pa	$ 600 000
Therefore investor's shareholding is (based on $2 million profit)	30%

Using this table, in general circumstances one should be offering a 60 per cent shareholding based on the $2 million investment of the $3 million equity required for the project to move ahead. As the developer has spent time and effort in finding the opportunity it is reasonable to offer a shareholding based on return on equity rather than equity against equity.

When assessing these values, employ a good accountant or lawyer with property development knowledge and expertise as they will be able to structure the shareholding of the development company and at the same time explain to the equity investor the justification of their shareholding.

Summary

Many people can afford to take an equity stake in a development. While it is easy to convince people to become investment partners, these relationships can give rise to problems if some basic rules are not adhered to. Stick to the following principles and you will have less tribulation down the track:

- Choose investors very carefully.

- Turn to investors only if you need to.

- Define your role and their role in the development.

- Define early on how the profits are to be split.

- Reduce the fear of your investor.

- Maintain control of your equity position.

- Retain investment agreements with one property at a time.

- Establish protocols for if the investment agreement has to dissolve.

- Always explain the risks.

On a personal level, start building a level of credibility and trust, and always act professionally. Treat all investors fairly and don't abuse the relationship or you may find it difficult to find partners willing to invest in your future developments.

CHAPTER 11

The development approval process

A broad overview of the development process was outlined in chapter 3. The process is actually more complex than this, with a number of actions required before the next step can happen. The development process can be broken down into three stages: (a) the development approval (DA) process, (b) the construction process and (c) operations. At the end of each stage the developer has to make some important decisions. This chapter deals specifically with the development approval phase, whereas the next chapter covers construction. These chapters explain the various actions required to complete the process and provide guidelines to achieve this. They have been divided into two chapters because in each case the information provided is reasonably comprehensive and is best examined separately.

The development approval process is critical to the financial viability of a project. During this period the developer has to ensure that the pre-purchase viability assumptions are kept to an absolute minimum while creating the most effective design and projecting the most accurate cost estimates and schedules. The work undertaken during this period will minimise risk to the developer and set in motion the forces needed for a quality project. In this chapter we will analyse the creation of a development brief, the selection of the team, feasibility studies, budget control, programming and managing the process.

The DA process

The development approval process happens after the development site has been selected and before the start of construction. During this stage further design, cost estimates, project economics, financing, market studies and schedules are performed to determine the viability of the project. It is also the period when 'seed capital' is required to control the site and to prepare feasibility studies. As this money is at risk, the developer must focus on all of the factors that can affect the success of the development. This means the developer and team must gather all the facts, analyse various development options and decide whether to proceed or shelve the development. Table 11.1 outlines the process and the actions required by various team members.

Table 11.1: the development approval process

Stages	Action	Team members
Step 1	Legal due diligence	Lawyer
Step 2	Site information	Town planner, architect, engineers
Step 3	Market research	Marketing consultants
Step 4	Create the brief	Developer, development manager
Step 5	Development team selection	Developer, development / project manager
Step 6	Development approval budgeting	Developer, development manager
Step 7	Programming work tasks	Developer, development manager
Step 8	Master plan, architectural design	Town planner, architect, engineers
Step 9	Feasibility analysis	Developer, development manager, quantity surveyor
Step 10	Preliminary development finance	Various consultants
Step 11	Development approval application	Town planner, architect

Step 1: Legal due diligence

Before starting the development approval process it is important that a legal due diligence be undertaken. All legal matters are usually managed by a lawyer who is an expert in property development. Areas that should be covered by the lawyer include the following:

- *Land sales agreement*: Initially, the lawyer will prepare and help negotiate the land purchase agreement.

- *Title search:* The lawyer should undertake a title search to verify the existing owner and identify any restrictions on the title such as easements. As most developers will not be able to finance property with limitations on the title, the sooner they are aware of potential title problems, the more time there will be to correct them.

- *Zoning classification:* The property's zoning should be verified through the local planning department. This can be done by the appointed architect or town planner. It is important that the zoning and related information is confirmed and verified in writing.

- *Existing leases:* If the property involves any current leases, the lawyer should review their terms and conditions. If the developer must terminate the existing leases, the lawyer can give guidance into legal procedures.

Step 2: Site information

Before the design team can start on more detailed schematic architectural plans it is important that certain engineering information is gathered. The commissioned consultants collect and study data and then provide recommendations as to existing conditions to suit the development. It is important that they uncover problem areas to help minimise the developer's risks. The engineering information covers the following areas.

Planning regulations

During the development approval stage, the architect or town planner will meet with the developer to discuss the development concept. The developer will then give the architect basic property and development information such as location, property size (area), current zoning, a copy of the topographic survey and the design brief. After the review, the architect will contact the local planning and building department to verify the current zoning and determine the necessary building codes to which the development must conform. The architect should obtain the following information (overleaf):

Local planning department

- current land zoning use
- zoning restrictions
- possible future zoning
- building restrictions
- plot ratio
- coverage
- units per hectare
- height limitations
- setback requirements
- parking requirements
- open space required
- procedure for rezoning or variations
- approval of variations

Local building department

- plan approval process
- necessary licences and process
- cost of licences

Local utility departments

- contacts for information
- current or proposed moratoriums
- permit process
- utility connection fees
- easements required
- construction timing
- monthly charges
- services guarantee or allotments

Local fire department

- fire safety requirements
- interpretation of regulations
- applicable regulations

Local department of transportation

- new layout requirements
- bond requirements
- road specifications

Site survey

A land surveyor should be appointed to complete an updated topographical and feature survey of the site. The surveyor will undertake on-site field work and then provide a drawing that will illustrate the topography and other features of the site plus the adjacent neighbours' structures. This drawing will assist the architect in evaluating the design against the features of the site. A typical site survey should include the following information:

- title particulars
- property location
- date of survey
- true and magnetic north
- scale of drawing
- existing easements
- rights of ways
- adjacent property buildings
- location of any existing structures
- location of existing fences
- existing trees and vegetation
- existing pavements
- existing streets and parking

- street lighting poles
- location of stormwater
- location of sewer systems
- location of water supply
- location of gas supply
- location of electrical power supply
- location of telecommunication service
- direction of views
- water features: lakes, ponds or streams
- utility pole locations
- rock outcropping locations
- predetermined contour intervals
- existing building locations

Geotechnical report

The geotechnical engineers will be responsible for this work. Unknown soil conditions can have a significant cost impact on a new development. The conditions can include rock formations, underground water, clay conditions and toxic soil, which could be costly to remove or remediate. Should any of these conditions be found then the price for the site should be renegotiated. The following are used to determine the soil conditions:

- *Soil samples:* Samples are taken at different underground depths and tested to analyse the soil contents.

- *Seismic tests:* If rock is found, seismic tests are conducted using sound waves to verify the depth of rock formations.

- *Compaction tests:* These tests are used when the dirt has been moved to another area of the property. They determine the compact strength of the new soil.

- *Water tests:* These tests are used to measure the absorption of water into the soil.

Traffic analysis

Most new development generates an increase in people and motor vehicles. Traffic engineers study the movement of traffic in response to the growth of communities. They have the expertise to design roadways in response to the projected traffic problems. When a DA application is made most authorities will require a traffic impact analysis to accompany the other documents.

Utility services

The hydraulics engineer should confirm if there are existing utility services such as water supply, sewerage and gas, whether the new development will have an impact on these existing utilities and, if so, at what cost to the project. Similarly, the electrical engineer will evaluate electrical power and telecommunications.

Stormwater retention and disposal.

Civil engineers will work with regulatory authorities who control the preservation of wetlands and waterways. Local authorities will require a plan for releasing water from the development site.

Environmental Site Assessments (ESA)

Depending on the scale and location of a new development there are a number of environmental issues to be addressed. In a built-up area where an older building is demolished environmental testing may be used to verify the presence of chemical pollutants in the air or soil. With a new ('greenfield') project on virgin soil, a number of environmental issues have to be addressed involving both government and public bodies. An environmental consultant can be appointed for these environmental studies, which might include analysis of the environmental impact of a development site or recommendations to create an environmentally sustainable project.

Step 3: Market research

In chapter 2 it was stressed how important market research is to the success of a development. To direct and brief the design team, the developer will need to undertake market research of the tenants or buyers of the proposed development. The research applies to data collected by the marketing consultants on market trends, demographics, competition and current market conditions. Marketing consultants may be market research companies, real estate agencies or property valuers. Accurate and objective market research is the foundation of all good development decisions. Areas of research that should be considered include:

- demographic and target market analysis
- market profile and trends
- geographic market information
- project analysis, including product and pricing recommendations
- competitive project activity analysis
- pricing and sales analysis
- rental and investment property advice, such as return analysis
- economic indicators
- social research, including focus groups.

Step 4: Creating the development brief

A clearly defined development brief is essential as it provides a guideline for the project's outcome. The developer and/or the appointed development manager should decide precisely what is best for the site and target market and then specify these conclusions in writing. These decisions, assembled in a formal document, will help the team members to understand the objectives of the project and provide accurate design proposals for costs and programs.

A development brief contains a series of key points outlining the objectives of the project and the way in which to achieve these goals. A well-informed team who clearly understand the motives of the project will be better able to deliver a quality project within budget and on time. The following is a list of items to be included in the brief.

- *Introduction:* The introduction describes the project and the key objectives. It should outline the vision of the development and how it responds to the market.

- *Site description:* This includes the site plan, aerial photographs, location maps, existing boundary and topographical drawings, site analysis studies and any other site specifics.

- *Town planning regulations:* This section should include the applicable town planning regulations complete with zoning, amendments, conditions, covenants and any applicable drawings.

- *Scope of the project:* In this section a full description and the extent of the work should be documented. This includes tasks to be accomplished during the preconstruction process with clearly stated objectives.

- *Developer's philosophy:* This should include the developer's strategies, objectives, beliefs and value system, and any specific developer requirements related to the project.

- *Building description:* An inexperienced developer should use experienced consultants to assist with this section. The following is a list of data that will be required:

  - height restrictions
  - building form
  - preferred floor to ceiling heights
  - external theme and aesthetics
  - internal character and design
  - gross building area
  - telecommunications
  - fire protection
  - ceiling systems
  - handicapped provisions
  - mechanical systems
  - communications provisions
  - energy optimisation

- tenant area sizes, unit sizes, unit mixes or room mixes
- floor sizes or number of units or rooms per floor
- parking requirements
- open spaces
- service areas
- security systems
- exterior and interior lighting
- special features
- art, graphics and signage systems
- materials and colours desired
- furniture, fixtures and equipment provisions
- future expansion or phasing
- landscape concept relative to overall intent of the project

- *Existing data:* If available, any existing data from the previous owner of the project site that will provide insight for the team, such as existing drawings, should be included in this section.

- *Technical data:* If available, any geotechnical and environmental assessment studies should be included together with topographical surveys. If not, these should be tasks to be undertaken.

- *Marketing:* An outline of the marketing strategy for the project will give the team an insight into the methods to use in the sale or leasing of the project. The preliminary marketing research and conclusions should be included, as should competitors' products so the team can provide amenities and features that are more appealing to the market.

- *Programming:* In order to prepare accurate proposals and schedules for the project, the developer must prepare a preliminary program that outlines all activities relating to cash flow needs. This program will be updated as the project progresses.

- *Team and team relationships matrix:* This section of the brief should list all team members selected, along with their addresses, phone numbers, email addresses, mobile numbers and chief representative. If some members have not been selected to date, their generic titles can be used at this stage. Because it is essential that each member knows their responsibilities, a team matrix can be included to describe those relationships.

Step 5: Development team selection

Professional help is essential to any developer, so great care should be taken in the selection and employment of the development team. The developer must bear in mind that development is a risky business and that only the best players should be in the team. Select experts who:

- *Have specific experience:* Developers should work only with professionals who have knowledge and experience specific to the type of project that is being developed. They should not let them learn by the mistakes they make on the developer's own project.

- *Have appropriate qualifications:* Ensure that each expert has the qualifications for their given specialty. This is not an overriding prerequisite but it does provide a guide to the person's expertise.

- *Charge reasonable fees:* Check that the professional's fees are reasonable and in line with the going rate for the services they offer. Obtaining a few quotes from similarly qualified parties will help.

- *Care about the project's goals:* Potential team members who ask about the project's goals show that they care. Those who seem unengaged are the type of consultant only interested in getting to the end of the project and collecting their fees.

- *Provide positive interaction:* A good development team is one in which all parties work in unison. Each member should believe that the project outcome comes before their ego. Those who put their ego first should not be employed at all as they will cause problems as the project progresses.

The size of the team will depend on the scale and type of project to be developed. Obviously a larger project, such as a high-rise apartment block or a mixed-use development, will require a larger team. Chapter 3 includes a list of potential team members along with a description of their roles in the development process.

In my experience there are two key individuals who will help the project move in a positive direction—the development or project manager and the architect. These are the developer's principal agents and representatives. Getting these selections right makes the rest of the team selection easier, as these two individuals have experience in working with other consultants. With their working experience and contacts with other industry members, they can recommend appropriate consultants who have knowledge and experience relevant to the type of project.

For the development approval application, not all professional consultants may be required. The developer's town planner or architect should check with the local council for a list of documents required for the application, as the requirements can vary between councils.

Step 6: Development approval budgeting

After the team members have been selected, the budget for development approval costs should be prepared based on the brief. Each consultant should prepare a proposal covering the following areas:

- The scope of each consultant's responsibilities should be broken down into the various services to be performed, listed under:

    – preconstruction services

    – contract documentation services

    – contract administration services.

- The time schedule necessary to perform their duties should also be determined. As most projects will be on a tight schedule, each consultant must be committed to performing their duties in a specified time.

- Part of the consultant's agreement is the fee and payment schedule. The fee schedule can be negotiated as a fixed fee, an hourly rate or a percentage of the costs. It is advisable to have the consultant quote a fee with a guaranteed maximum cost for the service but accounting only the actual costs until the ceiling has been reached. This allows the developer to terminate the service at any time and pay only for work accomplished to date.

- The consultants should carefully define their services in their contract. Expensive architectural models and renderings, and multiple copies of reports and construction documents, must be accounted for. If the consultant is from out of town, expect extensive travel and communication costs.

Development approval budget

With a list of the work required during the development approval process and proposals from the individual team members, the developer can now formulate a budget (see table 11.2). This will help in programming a cash flow analysis and management requirements for the development application. This very simple budget format can be expanded or reduced. If one of the items listed is not used, simply leave blank. If others are needed from your team listing, add them.

Table 11.2: development approval preconstruction budget

Item	Consultant	Description	Amount
1	Development manager	Client's representative and adviser	$
2	Project manager	Project leader and team manager	$
3	Town planner	Master plan, rezoning and planning	$
4	Architect	Architectural design and planning	$
5	Quantity surveyor	Costing, estimates and feasibility studies	$
6	Structural engineer	Structural design	$
7	Civil engineer	Roads, parking, stormwater	$
8	Mechanical engineer	Air-conditioning, heating, escalators, lifts	$
9	Electrical engineer	Electricity, lighting	$
10	Geotechnical engineer	Soil studies and analysis	$
11	Traffic engineer	Traffic analysis and impact studies	$
12	Surveyor	Topographical and site survey	$
13	Environmentalist	Environmental scoping and impact studies	$
14	Lawyer	Legal representation	$
15	Accountant	Tax issues, accounting	$
16	Market researcher	Market survey and research	$
17	Finance consultant	Development finance	$
18	Development approval	Application fees	$
19	BCA consultant	Building compliance	$
20	Other	Disbursements	$
21	Other	Contingency	$
TOTAL			$

As a guide, the budget for this phase is around 1 per cent of the total development costs. In order to firm up the budget the developer or appointed town planner or architect confirms with the council what documentation other than that covering architectural work is required for the development application. Once established the relevant consultant's report can be budgeted for.

Managing the budget

Once the pre-development approval budget has been completed, the developer must identify sources for these funds. They may already have used some of their own resources, such as the deposit for purchasing the site, so the balance of the budget must be funded before the consultants begin their work. These funds, the 'seed capital', will be at risk so the developer must manage them carefully. This money comes from the developer's funds, joint-venture partners, lines of credit or investors.

To manage the seed money effectively, a system must be structured for the developer to use to expedite approvals, initiate work efforts, control expenditures, approve invoices and accurately report expenses. There are various accounting software packages on the market that the developer can utilise to suit the project and/or the organisation.

Step 7: Programming work tasks

The best way to manage the pre-development approval process is to program all the activities to be accomplished by the team. By using a software package such as Microsoft Office Project, the developer or project manager can prepare a schedule that will show various stages of the project and tasks undertaken by each member of the development team, thus identifying critical path sequencing. In this way the developer can understand the complex set of work tasks to be completed and gain valuable insight into the relationships between concept design, financing, planning, marketing, construction and a host of other activities. Using the schedule will allow the developer to manage the team so that vital input is received when critical decisions are necessary.

These schedules will be used for different reasons at different times during the process. Some formats will be similar but be used for different objectives, depending on the composition of the team at that time. The initial schedules will be broad or summary types listing major work tasks with few details. As the team grows and the activities increase, the schedules will become more detailed. During the pre-development approval process, the project manager should be able to develop detailed schedules to help the process to flow smoothly. Although the process will be analysed, other activities will come into play after the start of construction so the developer can see what is needed ahead of time. Figure 11.1 shows a typical scheduling program, also known as a Gantt chart.

Figure 11.1 Gantt chart

APARTMENT DEVELOPMENT 27th July 2014	Mth 1 Aug-14	Mth 2 Sep-14	Mth 3 Oct-14	Mth 4 Nov-14	Mth 5 Dec-14	Mth 6 Jan-15	Mth 7 Feb-15	Mth 8 Mar-15	Mth 9 Apr-15	Mth 10 May-15	Mth 11 Jun-15	Mth 12 Jul-15	Mth 13 Aug-15	Mth 14 Sep-15	Mth 15 Oct-15	Mth 16 Nov-15	Mth 17 Dec-15	Mth 18 Jan-16	Mth 19 Feb-16	Mth 20 Mar-16	Mth 21 Apr-16	Mth 22 May-16
Land Sale Contract																						
DADocumentation																						
DA Application																						
Marketing preparation																						
Marketing																						
Land Settlement																						
Construction Documentation																						
Tender																						
Construction Finance																						
Select Builder																						
Construction																						
Strata Titles																						
Settlement of Apt sales																						

Figure reproduced courtesy of AYR International Pty Ltd.

231

Step 8: Master planning and architectural design

After the development approval budget is assessed, the development team selected and the overall work tasks scheduled, a startup meeting of the team is recommended before the work begins. In this meeting the program should be established together with relationships and lines of communication.

The town planner and architect, together with required engineers, are responsible for analysis of the design program in the context of the community and building codes to create a product that the developer can market.

- *Master planning:* Where larger sites are involved such as residential land development, an architect or a town planner will analyse and prepare a master plan for the whole site.

- *Schematic drawings:* After the legal and site information is researched, the architect can lay out the preliminary plans and sketches. The preliminary plans and specifications will then be incorporated into the developer's financial package, which will include the following:

  – site plan

  – exterior elevations

  – interior floor plans

  – wall sections

  – rendering

  – outline specifications.

- *Cost control:* These preliminary plans will then be handed over to the appointed quantity surveyor to provide the developer with an estimated cost for the development. If satisfied with these costs, the developer will instruct the architect and engineers to prepare design development drawings for more detailed costing.

- *Design development:* These drawings are produced by the architect and engineers as the second stage and expand on the concept drawings. They have enough detail to allow for cost estimates of the development and marketing.

Step 9: Feasibility study

After the design and preliminary costings have been completed, a feasibility study is undertaken by the developer or the development manager. This is probably the most important task in the development approval process. Essentially, a detailed feasibility study will tell the developer whether the proposed development will be financially viable. It will tell the developer whether the projected returns add up and the profit margin that can be expected at the completion of the project. Without a clear understanding of whether the development is viable there is really no point in proceeding to the next stage.

As noted in chapter 8, there are several available software packages that can simplify the calculations. However, the developer's conclusions and analysis are only as good as the input information and numbers entered into the program. Chapter 6 includes an income and expenditure checklist form containing a list of possible inputs. It is only a guide and, depending on the type and scale of building and whether the building is to be sold or leased, further inputs may be required.

If the feasibility study concludes that the project is not financially viable, the architect and the rest of the design team should reassess or refine their design. They will need to identify and eliminate inessential costs while not compromising function and quality. This will involve the consideration of materials available, construction methods, transportation issues, site limitations or restrictions, planning and organisation costs, profits and so on. Chapter 7 discusses methods and solutions that can assist in this exercise.

Step 10: Preliminary development finance

With the feasibility study completed, the developer should start approaching a few financial institutions to gauge their interest in financing the development. Obtaining preliminary development finance in principle, together with terms and conditions, will give the developer confidence in progressing to the next stage of the development process. A preliminary finance offer will also give the developer an idea of the level of debt that can be secured and whether additional equity may be required. The developer will either obtain the financing needed or contract with a mortgage broker to find it. Should additional equity be required there is time to raise this while the development proposal is reviewed for development approval. Chapters 9 and 10 provide additional information on finance and equity.

Step 11: Development approval application

Either the appointed town planner or the architect will coordinate the submission and application for development approval, having discovered from the planning services department of the council which documents will be required for them to make the planning assessment. They may require reports from other consultants, such as a traffic impact analysis, noise impact study or environmental assessment. Before the formal submission the town planner or architect should arrange a meeting with the planning services officials to present the development proposal and ask for their input and recommendations. I have found this to be very useful in helping to facilitate the approval process.

Summary

The development approval process can be a lengthy and costly exercise if the developer does not have a professional and effective design team. In some cases, controversial projects that generate community disapproval can take up to a year or more to clear. However, should the application be approved, the developer will have added financial value to the project and can either sell the project to another developer or proceed to the construction phase. Alternatively, the developer may have found that because of the long delays the project has missed the market opportunity and may therefore decide to shelve the project until the market conditions improve.

CHAPTER 12

The construction process

Once the development approval has been granted and a decision has been made to proceed with the construction, the developer's consulting team will prepare and issue tender documents to contractors, who will then submit a price or tender for building the project. Before delving into the tender and construction stages, there are a few areas that the developer should understand and should take into consideration in order to make the correct decisions. These include the role and responsibilities of building contractors, types of contractors, contractor selection criteria and the type of building contract.

The role and responsibilities of a contractor

The contractor's duty is to construct the project according to the architect and consulting team's plans and specifications within the time and price specified in the contract. This should be done without sacrificing either the quality of the work or the safety of the workers. In general terms, the contractor purchases the materials, hires the tradespeople and brings in subcontractors to get the work done. The subcontractors are responsible to the contractor, not to you, the developer. Their role in the building process is explained further under the headings below.

Estimating and bidding the project

One of the main jobs that a contractor undertakes is prepare the building cost that is to be presented to the developer. If the cost is not accurate, valuable trust between the contractor and the developer can be lost. A contractor should prepare a realistic cost plan and review it for accuracy with several subcontractors and other people in their office. This step is especially important when the contract is at cost plus a specific contractor fee.

Interpreting plans and specifications

Any misinterpretation of the plans and or specifications could be costly to the contractor and/or the subcontractors. In addition to interpreting plans and specifications, a contractor has to analyse how best to construct the building, where to place the site office, access for materials and trucks, fencing and so on.

Interacting with the architect

Where an architect or architectural designer is involved, the contractor will work with that person to ensure the project is implemented as planned. The architect and the contractor will review the plans together before any work begins. If problems arise, the architect will often look to the contractor to suggest workable solutions.

Coordinating with subcontractors

The supervision — hiring and negotiating contracts with subcontractors then slotting them into schedules in line with the building contract — is not an easy task. Contractors with good leadership skills have loyal subcontractors who help the construction process run more smoothly because they understand what is required of them.

Arranging licences and inspections

Various licences are required before the contractor or any subcontractor can demolish, build or improve any building. The contractor, being familiar with the process, will know which licences are required. The contractor will also coordinate the required inspections, arrange meetings with the building inspectors at the job site and work with them on any requested changes.

Implementing the construction program

The activities of a building contractor revolve around making sure that the program for completion is implemented on a daily basis. This involves ensuring that all employees and subcontractors are working within their prescribed area by creating a schedule for workers and subcontractors, and that all materials are delivered on site on time.

Scheduling payment

The contractor has to establish a payment schedule based on work progress, and review and analyse the budget to ensure that the construction is proceeding within the budget outlined at the beginning of the project.

Resolving issues and providing answers

The contractor has to be on site regularly, inspecting the work as it is completed, providing answers and resolving issues. If not, a subcontractor may have to wait or guess at what is required, which will often result in delays or mistakes that can disrupt the flow of work.

Ordering building materials

The contractor is responsible for negotiating and ordering building materials designated to a specific subcontractor. Timely delivery and proper on-site storage of materials are important, as is payment.

Troubleshooting jobsite problems

A contractor should always be aware of the changing nature of a building project, reviewing progress, and be ready to troubleshoot any on-site problems, implementing changes as needed. The contractor is accountable for on-site emergencies that may arise throughout the course of construction.

Types of contractors

Before selecting a building contractor, the developer should first consider the size and scope of the development. Like other industries, construction has its own classification system. Building contractors are basically classified as Tier 1, Tier 2 and Tier 3. The tier system rates building contractors according to their capacity to undertake certain projects. This takes account of their staffing numbers, resources, experience and, importantly, their financial capacity. In simple terms, Tier 1 contractors are the big established organisations, whereas Tier 3 contractors are the more modest companies who could move up to the next tier over a period of time. The following sections explain the three tiers in more detail.

Tier 1 contractors

Tier 1 building contractors are the largest, wealthiest and most experienced operators in the industry. These contractors take on major commercial projects such as motorways, railways, hospitals, universities, office towers and shopping centres. They have the expertise, resources and finances to take on such large-scale projects. Tier 1 contracts are usually in the hundreds of millions or even billions price range.

Tier 2 contractors

Mid-tier building contractors are still key players in the construction industry. As a general rule, Tier 2 companies are more likely to take on commercial than smaller residential projects. Some specialise in a specific type of construction, such as shopping centres, industrial buildings or residential apartment complexes.

Tier 3 contractors

Tier 3 contractors, the most numerous category, take on the smaller projects. Typical contracts are for residential buildings, including rebuilding and refurbishing, and small-scale commercial work such as small office blocks. These contractors are essential to the industry, and as they build up their portfolio they have the opportunity to start moving up the tier ladder.

Contractor selection criteria

Finding, qualifying and selecting a building contractor is one of the first steps towards a quality development project. A developer could ask an architect or project manager for assistance. If they have been in the industry for some time, they would have worked with many contractors in the locality of the project and would therefore know which contractors are suitable. The following list outlines the due diligence that a developer should undertake to qualify a contractor.

- Ask the contractor for a capability statement, which should include:
    - contractor's licence and registration number
    - legal name, business address, telephone numbers and email
    - number of years in contracting business, education and training
    - company profile, including responsible staff members
    - financial stability of business and relationship to their bank
    - details of past and current projects
    - references of previous customers with projects similar to yours.

- Visit the contractor's current site to see if the contractor:
    - executes their trade in a skilful and professional manner
    - provides adequate site supervision
    - maintains a steady and reliable work crew
    - has a strong relationship with subcontractors and other trades
    - uses materials efficiently and effectively
    - keeps the construction site clean and safe.

- Interview the contractor's current client and ask the following questions:
    - Is the contractor reliable and efficient?
    - Is the contractor maintaining the project's building program?
    - Is the contractor's team adequate for the size and scope of the work?

- How does the contractor respond to problems both on and off site?

- Have the various stages of the work passed inspections successfully?

- Is the contractor readily available by telephone, voicemail and email?

Once a contractor is selected, the developer and consulting team must exercise the management skills to schedule, coordinate and control the contractor's work so that work proceeds on time, within the established budget and to the quality specified. The developer should be prepared to pay fair market value for work performed so the contractor can maintain cash flow, pay for overheads, suppliers and subcontractors, and still make a profit.

Understanding building contracts

Selecting the right building contract can be critical to the successful completion of a project. A building contract should suit the specific requirements of the project by taking account of its complexity and value. Too often the selection is based on an architect's previous experience with a particular contract. Selecting a contract simply because one is familiar with the terms and conditions may do little to assist in overcoming the difficulties that can arise if the contract is inappropriate for the project.

What should be in the building contract?

Before signing a building contract, ensure that the contractor is currently licensed and registered with the appropriate authority, such as a Building Registration Board. Ensure that your building contract includes the following:

- The contract must be in writing and be written in clear English.

- It should set out in full all the terms and conditions of the contract.

- Your name and the contractor's licence number should be included, along with addresses of both parties to the contract.

- The scope of work must be described clearly and comprehensively in the contract, including plans or specifications and any other relevant documents.

- The contract price and whether or not it includes GST should be clearly stated.

- The commencement and completion date of the project is clearly stated, with allowances for delays. If the start date is not known, the contract must state how the start date will be determined.

- The number of days allowed for unforeseeable delays and inclement weather should be stated.

- The dollar amounts and timing of progress payments are clearly stated and in line with the completion of works and according to the bank's approval.

- All provisional sum items or prime cost items are clearly stated and adequate costs allowed for (see note below).

- A clause should state that all work will comply with the Building Code of Australia as well as any other standards required by law.

- All definitions of words and key phrases used in the contract are included.

- All implied warranties and necessary insurances have been set out.

- The contract should also include a set of plans and specifications containing enough information to get a building permit for the work.

- If a deposit is required then the amount should be within the legal limit.

- The contractor acknowledges that the site is suitable for the proposed work and has obtained foundation data and a soil report. It is their responsibility to satisfy themselves that the foundation data is accurate.

It should be noted that the contract begins on the day when the last signature is added and the other party is made aware of this signing. This is the *contract date* and should not be confused with the starting date for the project.

Prime cost items are those for which the contractor is unable to give a definite price at the time the contract is signed, despite making reasonable enquiries, and include items such as tiling and landscaping. A *provisional sum item* is one that has not been decided at the time the contract is entered into, such as whitegoods and light fittings. In both cases, an allowance will be made for the cost of the prime cost or provisional sum item under the contract. If the amount allowed is more than the cost of the item, then the owner will receive a credit. If the amount allowed is less than the cost, then the contractor can charge a margin on the cost exceeding the allowance and this margin must be stated in the contract.

Types of building contracts

In the construction industry there are basically two avenues when contracting a building contractor to undertake your project. These are either a readily available conventional or standard contract or a custom contract drawn up by a construction lawyer to suit the special needs of a specific type of project.

A conventional contract is one in which the developer employs a team of consultants to design the works and to supervise a contractor in the performance of these works. The contractor is selected on the basis of their capability for the type of work and the competitiveness of their price relative to other contractors. The architect or project manager acts as the developer's expert and manager with delegated responsibilities, and as initial mediator between the developer and contractor. However, a conventional approach is not appropriate when:

- there is insufficient time for the conventional processes owing to time constraints or early completion

- the project is complex and the scale of the project warrants an early start before completion of the technical drawings

- there is restricted access

- the work is of high risk

- there is inadequate definition of the work.

Following is a list of the several of contracts that can be negotiated with a contractor.

Lump-sum contract

In a *lump-sum contract*, also known as *fixed price contract*, a contractor agrees to build a project with a specific scope for a fixed price. This is the most common type of contract used for residential buildings. A lump-sum contract is suitable if the scope and schedule of the project are sufficiently defined to allow the contractor to fully estimate project costs.

It is important to be aware that there are several ways in which the lump contract price can be changed. These include 'variations'—that is, changes or additions to the scope of works such as prime cost or provisional sum adjustments. It is also possible that one fixed-price contract will not cover all of the work that is to be done. For example, you may wish to have a separate contract for any landscaping work conducted.

Cost-plus contract

An alternative to the lump-sum contract is the *cost-plus contract*. It is essential to consider such a contract carefully before entering into it as there is no upper limit for the final price and therefore it can become very expensive!

Cost plus is a contractual agreement by which the developer agrees to pay the cost of the work, including all trade contractor work, labour, materials and equipment, plus an amount for contractor overhead and profit. These types of contracts are used where the scope of work, such as labour and materials, is uncertain or where the developer likes to include or purchase their own materials and select their own subcontractors. The contracts may be specified as:

- *Cost + Fixed Percentage:* Payment is based on a percentage of the cost.

- *Cost + Fixed Fee:* Payment is based on a fixed sum independent of the final project cost. The developer agrees to reimburse the contractor's actual costs, regardless of the amount, and in addition pay a negotiated fee independent of the amount of the actual costs.

- *Cost + Fixed Fee with Guaranteed Maximum Price:* Payment is based on a fixed sum of money. The total project cost will not exceed an agreed upper limit.

- *Cost + Fixed Fee with Bonus:* Payment is based on a fixed sum of money. A bonus is given if the project finishes below budget or ahead of schedule.

- *Cost + Fixed Fee with Guaranteed Maximum Price and Bonus:* Payment is based on a fixed sum of money. The total project cost will not exceed an agreed upper limit and a bonus is given if the project is finished below budget or ahead of schedule.

- *Cost + Fixed Fee with Agreement for Sharing Any Cost Savings:* Payment is based on a fixed sum of money. Any cost savings are shared between the developer and the contractor.

Design and construct contract

In a *design and construct (D & C) contract* the developer awards the entire project to a single contractor. Once the contract is signed, the contractor is responsible for all design and construction work to complete the project. With this type of contract the contractor must hire all architects and engineers required to complete the design work. The developer is still given the right to approve or reject design options, but is no longer responsible for coordinating or managing the design team. Once the developer has approved the design, the contractor supervises the construction process.

This type of contracting method is preferred by many developers because it facilitates fast-track schedules. The final project can be completed faster and the return of investment capitalised sooner. The design process can be scheduled in phases. The advantages of a D & C contract include:

- single point of responsibility for the developer

- reduced design timeframe

- simplified construction drawings

- reduced construction program

- variations kept to a minimum

- project easily customised to actual site conditions

- greater cost certainty, making the project more acceptable to lenders

- reduced conflict between contractor and developer's own team

- overlapping programs for design and construction
- fewer time extensions.

D & C contracts also have some disadvantages, including the following:

- The project outcome might not be as expected.
- A project that is not scheduled correctly might experience substantial delays.
- These contracts have no impact on labour costs.
- The final cost can be higher than the original estimate.
- An integrated design cannot be used.
- The architect's design could appear to suit the contractor.
- If the contractor does not have an experienced team, problems can occur that can be costly.

There are also alternative methods from the standard D & C contract:

- *Turnkey:* The contractor designs, finances and completes the project. At completion the developer pays the full cost of the building and the contractor hands over the key to the developer.
- *Bridging:* The developer employs their own architect and consultants to prepare the preliminary design to secure development approval. The approved design is then passed on to the contractor to complete the rest of the design, either with the same design team or their own, and complete the construction process.

Unit price contract

In a *unit price contract* the developer and the contractor agree on the price that will be charged per unit for the major elements of the project. The developer's quantity surveyor typically provides estimated quantities for the project, asking contractors to bid on the job by providing unit prices for these items and calculating a final price. Contractor overhead, profit and other project expenses are included within the unit prices. The developer then compares the final price and selects the low bidder.

The advantage of this contracting method is that in many projects it is difficult to accurately quantify the work necessary. In excavation work it is often hard to figure the actual amount of rock versus earth that must be excavated. To eliminate risk to both the developer and the contractor, the quantity surveyor will estimate the quantities and then ask the contractors to provide a unit price for each type of excavation. Payments will be based on multiplying the actual quantities excavated by the unit price.

This contracting method provides the developer with a competitive price that is fair and reasonable for the work. It also eliminates the risk of negotiating a fixed price but then having to renegotiate because of unexpected site conditions. With this contracting method, work can begin before the design is complete, thus speeding up the project.

Guaranteed maximum price contract

A *guaranteed maximum price (GMP) contract* is a cost-type contract (also known as an *open-book contract*) by which the contractor is compensated for actual costs incurred plus a fixed fee subject to a ceiling price. The contractor is responsible for cost overruns, unless the GMP has been increased via formal variation, which can occur only as a result of additional scope from the developer, not of price overruns, errors or omissions. Savings resulting from cost underruns are returned to the owner. This is different from a fixed-price or lump-sum contract where cost savings are typically retained by the contractor and essentially become additional profits.

Tender phase

To get the best price for a project, the tender process is a better method than a negotiated contract. Tendering is the process of interested parties making an offer, bid or proposal, or expressing interest in response to an invitation or request for tender. Developers will seek building contractors to respond to their specific development or building and will select an offer or tender that meets their requirements and provides the best value for money.

Tenders can be issued through:

- *Expressions of interest (EOI)*: Used to shortlist potential contractors before seeking detailed offers

- *Request for information (RFI)*: Used in the planning stage to assist in defining the project, but not used to select suppliers

- *Request for proposal (RFP)*: Used where the project requirements have been defined but an innovative or flexible solution is needed

- *Request for tender (RFT)*: An invitation to tender by public advertisement, open to all contractors.

There are three main types of tenders:

- *Open tender*: An open tender is an invitation to tender via a public advertisement. There are no restrictions placed on who can submit a tender; however, contractors are required to submit all required information and are evaluated against the stated selection criteria.

- *Selected tender*: A selected tender is open only to a select number of contractors. The contractors may be shortlisted from an open tender or from contractors recommended by the architect or project manager.

- *Invited tender*: The developer contacts a select number of contractors directly and requests them to perform the contract. It is generally used for specialist work, emergency situations or low-value, low-risk and off-the-shelf options.

There are six main steps in the tender process:

1 *The tender process is determined*: The developer and development team requesting the tender will determine the type of tender to be used, as well as what will be involved in the tender process.

2 *The tender documents are prepared*: The tender documents include the drawings and specifications, and the contractual terms and conditions, plus how the tenderer should respond.

3 *Tenders are invited*: The developer should agree with the architect on the contractors who will be invited to submit tenders.

4 *Close of tender*: On the tender documents there is a closing time when all tenders should be submitted, and any late tenders should not be accepted. Depending on the type of tender, the tender prices are normally read out.

5 *Notification and debriefing:* When a contract has been awarded, the successful tenderer will be advised in writing of the outcome. Unsuccessful tenderers are also advised of the outcome.

6 *Contracts established and managed:* Once satisfied on all matters, the developer authorises the placing of the building contract. Once ready the contract documents should be signed before work starts on site.

Construction phase

Before construction can start the contract between the developer and contractor should be signed. In addition, the developer and team should ensure that the documents and working drawings are adequate and the following information is obtained from the contractor:

- *Construction draw schedules:* The construction draw schedules provided by the contractor will give the developer a guide to the flow of funds required during various stages of construction.

- *Site meetings schedule:* This schedule will help the developer and team organise their meetings and ensure they are available for such meetings.

- *Program:* A bar chart or Gantt chart showing the flow of trades and completion of various stages will give the developer and his team strategic dates, especially for the coordination of occupier fit-out and occupation dates.

Phases of construction

The construction process can be broken down into the following main steps. Depending on the design and specification of the building, the process can vary in some parts. For the sake of clarity the process described here is for a conventional concrete, brick and frame construction:

1 *Site mobilisation:* This involves clearing of the site, pegging it out by the surveyor, and setting up temporary utility services, site offices, lay-down areas, site parking, temporary fencing and benchmarks.

2 *Site works:* The site workers will start preparing the site for the major works, which includes levelling as per the plan for levels,

installing underground utilities and site drainage systems, and building retaining walls if required.

3 *Foundations and slab:* Excavation, forming and placement of the concrete foundations, footings, columns, beams, elevator pits and walls (if applicable), installation of anchor bolts and other required activities—except the forming and placement of the first floor slab (if applicable), which is completed later. The plumber will need to lay plumbing that will be located beneath the ground concrete slab of the development, which needs to be done before the slab can be formed up.

4 *Brickwork:* The bricklaying team will start with both the interior and exterior brickwork of the building, including the elevator and utility cores (if applicable), ready for the plasterer. Door and window frames are placed in position and the brickwork erected fixing these frames in position.

5 *Form and pour concrete floors:* If applicable and if there are additional floors, before the concrete floors are poured, the reinforcing bars are installed, and in-floor utilities and conduits placed. The brickwork will continue once the concrete on each level is cured.

6 *Wall frames and roof trusses:* If the internal walls are lightweight frames, these would be generally prepared before being delivered to site. The same applies with roof trusses.

7 *Roofing:* Some contractors prefer to complete the roof before starting the brickwork or internal wall framework, and other contractors work the other way around.

8 *Rough in:* This involves the electrical and plumbing wiring and pipes to be installed before the internal linings to the frames. If there is air-conditioning the ductwork is installed.

9 *Internal linings:* After the rough in is complete, the insulation will be installed in the walls and ceilings then the plasterers will start on lining the walls and ceilings.

10 *Waterproofing and tiling:* The wet areas will be waterproofed in preparation for the tilers to start work, generally after or even during the finishing carpentry.

11 *Finishing carpentry:* This stage involves the finishing carpenters installing the skirting boards, architraves, door jams and doors with door furniture.

12 *Lockup:* During the lockup stage all external doors and windows are installed and access is limited only to the contractor trades that are finishing the building. This is also the stage when the plumber installs items such as tapware, baths, mirrors, vanities and other accessories. Cabinetwork is installed in kitchens and bathrooms, with tiling and internal painting following.

13 *Final clean-up and occupancy including inspections:* The contractor's final clean-up is undertaken for the final and certification for occupancy by the council building inspector.

14 *Practical completion:* The developer or his architect will walk through the development with the site supervisor and point out any items that still need attention. By this time it should be limited to touch-ups and minor items requiring installation.

15 *Handover:* At this stage the developer is happy with the construction, which is completed to specifications and expected quality. A certificate of completion is handed over, the contractor's final invoice paid and the keys handed over to the developer.

16 *Maintenance:* Depending on the type of contract, but typically after a three-month period, another inspection is undertaken by the developer or their representative to list any items that require further fixing. If retention has been held back, then this will be released after these maintenance items have been attended to.

Summary

The construction process can be either an enjoyable experience or a nightmare, depending on the contractor selected for the project. Positive contractors always look for a solution should a problem occur on site, whereas a litigious contractor will have submitted a low tender price to secure the job and then try to make up ground through variations or delays. It is best to avoid the latter type of contractor, and this can be achieved by following the builder selection process explained in this chapter.

CHAPTER 13

Marketing and selling

In a development project, marketing is not purely appointing a marketing team to market and sell the completed buildings. It starts from the inception of the development with a developer who has the ability to understand the market, and the personality and attributes to sell their vision to others such as the council, investors and bankers. In essence, developers are entrepreneurs who are risk takers who at the same time monitor and control the development activities. They are visionaries who take advantage of development opportunities and then sell their vision to all those involved in the development process with the ultimate goal of profiting financially from their efforts.

The developer's marketing role does not stop when they have made their project bankable (that is, they have secured a DA and development finance). They have to find and appoint the most effective marketing and selling group to sell their product. They need to be totally market oriented. All their decisions should consider the context of the market and their potential buyers and tenants. From the inception of the concept, the selection of the site and the design of the building to the final finishing touches, they should be focusing on the needs of the end user.

Whether marketing a small residential project or a golf course estate, a range of marketing activities beyond advertising and face-to-face selling is needed. Developers must have a comprehensive knowledge of the real estate market, consumer behaviour and the development process.

Understanding the residential market

In chapter 2, supply and demand and the property cycle were discussed. Following are a few more fundamentals specific to the residential property market. Understanding these, a developer will have a better understanding of the residential property development industry.

The housing market pyramid

The residential market can be broken into three broad categories, namely affordable, mid-price and luxury (see figure 13.1).

Figure 13.1: sales activity pyramid

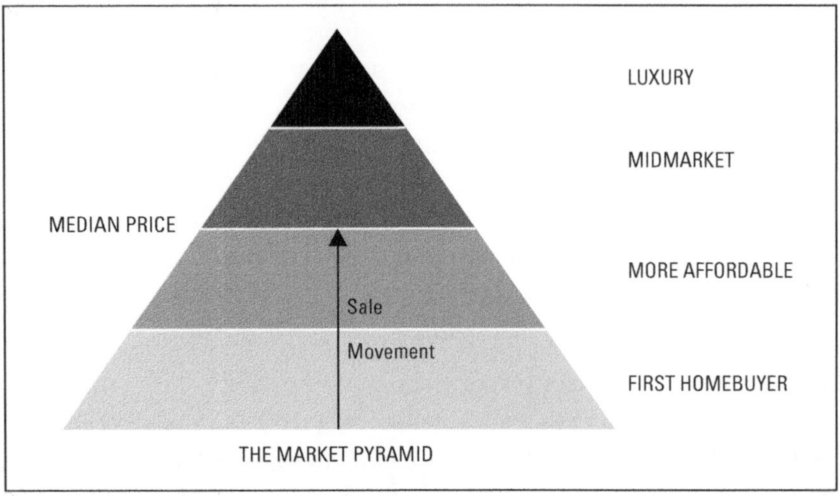

LUXURY

MIDMARKET

MEDIAN PRICE

MORE AFFORDABLE

Sale

Movement

FIRST HOMEBUYER

THE MARKET PYRAMID

Affordable

At the base of the pyramid is 'affordable' housing, a healthy market that accounts for about 40 per cent of all home sales. The buyers in this category are mainly first-time buyers, blue-collar workers, young professionals and retirees who are scaling down.

Mid-price

The middle of the pyramid represents mid-priced homes and primarily second or third home buyers. The buyers in this category are middle class, including highly educated, salaried professionals and managers, semi-professionals, skilled craftsmen and lower-level management. They commonly have a comfortable standard of living, significant economic security and considerable work autonomy, and rely on their expertise to sustain themselves.

Luxury

The top of the pyramid represents the smallest number of buyers and the most expensive part of the housing market. The buyers in this category include the wealthiest 5 per cent of the population. The sector is distinguished by immense wealth.

As first-time home buyer activity increases at the base it sets off a chain reaction of sales up the price points. It is this process that drives and sustains a healthy housing market. However, affordable housing is a significant problem in major cities in Australia. The decline in house purchase affordability is a structural problem created by house prices growing faster than incomes over the past half century. The supply of affordable housing is impacted by planning, regulatory and financial barriers.

The 80:20 principle

The Pareto Principle, named after economist Vilfredo Pareto, identifies an unequal relationship between inputs and outputs. The principle states that, for many phenomena, 20 per cent of invested input is responsible for 80 per cent of the results obtained. Put another way, 80 per cent of consequences stem from 20 per cent of causes. The Pareto Principle can be applied in a wide range of areas such as manufacturing, management and human resources. Pareto used it to explain how 80 per cent of property in Italy was owned by 20 per cent of the country's population.

In the marketing of property development the principle can be applied to sales: about 20 per cent of your buyers produce 80 per cent of your sales (see figure 13.2, overleaf). In essence, two out ten prospective buyers will be converted into genuine sales. It can also be applied in a slightly different way. When researching the demographics of potential buyers near a proposed project, 80 per cent of potential buyers will come from within 20 kilometres of the project.

Figure 13.2: property market forecast

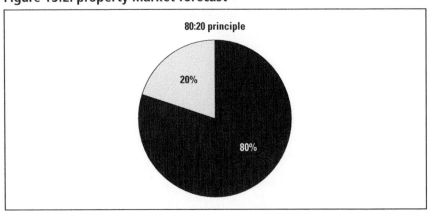

Before starting and marketing a development, a property developer should have a good understanding of the property supply chain, which is the source of future property demand. This is easier said than done, however, as forecasting future property demand is arguably the single most difficult task for any property developer. Most forecasts made by experts are inconsistent as they are generally done on a time lag basis. Therefore, rather than looking for a specific forecast, in order to make development decisions developers should look at the fundamentals of the market and the probabilities. The following are a few of the fundamentals to consider.

- *Population increase:* The population of Australia is predicted to increase dramatically to somewhere close to 42 million by 2050.

- *Immigration:* Most immigrants will be heading for the capital cities, in particular Sydney, Melbourne, Perth and Brisbane.

- *Supply and demand:* Statistics on this vary significantly, but it is generally acknowledged that Australia has an acute shortage of housing, especially in the affordable category, and is not building enough new properties to house the expected increase in population.

- *Demographic change:* In general, people are marrying later and living in smaller, two-income households for longer. Younger people overwhelmingly want to live near the CBDs of cities, creating a demand for apartment developments.

- *Population density:* The increasing population will mean denser traffic, and rising fuel prices will increase the importance of transport links to the CBD.

Based on these fundamentals there will be a consistent demand for housing, which will continue to increase in value. This bodes well for residential property developers in the long term. However, given the cyclical nature of property, how does a developer analyse the demand for their product in the short term? A developer needs to study the property market and ask the following questions:

- What are the latest house price trends?

- Why are prices rising or stagnating?

- What is driving demand?

- What is driving supply?

- Are investors distorting the market?

- Are SMSFs distorting the market?

- Are foreign investors distorting the market?

- Will dwelling prices keep rising?

Marketing yourself as a developer

A market-driven developer will always be more successful than a developer driven by self-interest. A successful market-driven development is achieved by undertaking thorough research before committing financially to proceed. In this instance, the developer can appoint third-party researchers or undertake the task themselves by using various media formats to get a good understanding of the market without having any interaction with people. However, for other activities in the development process, the developer has to create a personal market profile. After all, property development is an entrepreneurial activity and developers have to win the confidence of bankers, investors, councillors and the development team in order to achieve their goals. The following is a list of qualities that developers should aim to attain in order to sell themselves and their project.

Become an expert

Some people may think that it takes a special, inborn talent to become a successful property developer. In reality, if you are interested in this career you can learn much from reading books and talking to people in the industry, and you can gain experience by being involved in a project, either on your own or through a partnership. When I decided to become a property developer after obtaining my degree in architecture, I found that the main expertise I lacked was in the area of finance. I decided that I needed to become an expert in this area. With this in mind I read any finance book I could get my hands on and talked to people in the finance industry. Today I have a thorough understanding of the finance industry and am confident in negotiating with people and institutions within the finance industry.

Stay focused

One of the biggest challenges of being a developer is being able to stay focused long enough to see the results of a development. After a successful project, a developer will start looking for more opportunities and will be offered many more by real estate agents. With more development opportunities on offer, staying focused can be tough. I have seen developers tackling too many projects (especially in boom times) and not focusing on what has been successful for them in the past, which ultimately leads to failure or at least lower profits. The best ways to remain focused are (a) write down your goals and policies, (b) prioritise your goals and work out a daily plan for achieving them, and (c) don't tackle another project unless you have the time and resources to handle it.

Work with disciplined, ethical and effective people

Working with people who are disciplined, ethical and effective will help you to develop these traits. When you look at peak-performing experts, you'll often see that either they have coaches or mentors or they surround themselves with growth-oriented friends who help them excel. In my 43-year involvement with the building and development industry, I have seen and worked with a wide variety of people and have found that only those who have strong discipline and ethics are respected. There are no short cuts in property development, and those who achieve wealth by unethical means do not survive in the long term as they will be caught out on the next project.

Learn from your mistakes

To learn and grow in property development, a fledgling developer has to tackle a project that will suit their resources. Without doubt they will make mistakes along the way, but if they are careful these will not be major mistakes. Learn from the first project and the next one will be a lot easier. I started off with a small residential development, grew to tackling larger housing projects and later moved into the commercial sector, developing shopping centres and office blocks. I definitely made mistakes along the way but learned a great deal from them, and now it is second nature to know where potential mistakes can be made in a development.

Be confident

In general, people want to work with developers who are confident and successful. Investors and bankers will be willing to part with their funds if they feel comfortable that the developer has the confidence and ability to deliver a project. Confidence in the property development industry is not a trait that happens overnight. A developer has to be prepared to devote a great deal of personal time to learning and gaining experience in the industry and to take risks. Every piece of knowledge gained will increase your confidence.

Become a problem solver

In the early stages of my career as an architect, I was told by a senior architect that a problem is not a problem unless it is impossible to resolve. Today I still believe in this philosophy and always look at difficult issues in a positive light in order to find a solution. The property development process is fraught with problems and the developer who is not prepared to search for solutions may as well find a job in a factory doing only one task at a time. The way to resolve a problem is first to fully understand it, second to step back and examine it from a broader perspective, and third to look at a number of possible solutions by thinking laterally. If the problem cannot be resolved immediately, sleep on it and a solution will occur the following day when there is less clutter in your brain. Some of my best solutions come to me in my sleep, in the shower, while taking a walk or while engaged in some other activity.

Keep motivated and enthusiastic

Motivated and enthusiastic people are positive people, positive people are confident and confidence sells. A developer with these traits has a far better chance of convincing and selling their project to councillors, investors and bankers. So how does a developer stay motivated? *Be happy.* People with problems are generally unhappy, so whenever you have problems work to resolve them early. *Be energetic.* Keep healthy and fit, as this will keep your energy levels up. *Be efficient.* Without efficiency you will have zero motivation to do anything. And when things really get bad, remind yourself of your goals.

Always be personable

A smile goes a long way, and acknowledging another person by name goes further. In the property development industry, you will be meeting people from all levels, from tradespeople to senior bankers, and to be remembered you have to use the common language of being personable. Never look down on or ill-treat someone you believe has a lesser skill set or profession than you, as these people will speak about you negatively in the industry. Dress smartly and neatly as this is an indicator of your character. Exuding a positive, professional image by the clothes you wear builds credibility.

Be flexible

Flexibility is very important in the development industry, because sometimes changes have to be made from plans to strategies. Being able to adjust accordingly and always having the ability to do so will make your project less vulnerable. In order to correct mistakes and inefficiencies swiftly, you must have flexibility. Flexibility means having the power, authority and system to change as needed with ease. Listening and talking to various people within the property industry, especially on the market for your project, will improve the viability of the development.

Be honest

In the long run, it is always best to speak the truth. A developer's integrity is their most valuable asset. Having once acted dishonestly, it is very hard to rebuild their credibility in the marketplace. The value of honesty in business has obvious and subtle implications. Honest business practices inspire the development team and business associates. Honest business practices build foundations of trust with colleagues, competitors, staff, buyers and every other party within the property development industry. Bankers and investors express confidence by funding the developer and the developer's product is viewed in a positive light.

Ask and listen

Successful developers listen. They listen to the current market for their development and they listen and take good advice from others within the industry. They ask questions and listen carefully to the responses, often taking notes and summarising their understanding of the responses they receive. They know that by asking the right questions they will get a good understanding of where their development fits in the marketplace. In turn they will know the most effective way to design and present their product. This practice applies not only when providing a product to a market but also when speaking to and negotiating with bankers and investors.

Build trust

People do business with people they trust. Developers seeking repeat business and high-quality referrals must focus on building a business network of people who will trust them. To gain this trust, the developer should always act in the best interests of business associates and the community at large. To build trust, the developer should demonstrate competence and tell the truth. If they don't know the answer to a question, they should not make one up or they will soon be found out. If they commit to something they must complete that task in a timely manner. Promises should not be made if they cannot be fulfilled. Remember, it takes three positive experiences to create trust and only one bad one to jeopardise that trust.

A developer's approach to marketing

The main goal of marketing a residential development is to generate sales. For the marketing to be a success a holistic approach should be taken, and this means developing a marketing 'package'. This package should include the design, planning, legal, financial and physical aspects of a development project.

A developer should take a systematic approach to creating a comprehensive marketing package. In practice, the many marketing tasks and activities that collectively form a project marketing package include seven specific stages:

1   Conduct comprehensive market research.

2   Establish the project's marketing goals.

3   Develop a market-oriented strategy.

4   Create a marketing budget.

5   Appoint the marketing team.

6   Execute the marketing and sales activities.

7   Check and evaluate progress.

Stage 1: Conduct comprehensive market research

In chapter 2 I stressed the importance of market research. Obtaining statistics and conducting market research give the developer a better understanding of the market, and the buyers and their needs, as well as giving you a better insight into your competitors. As a developer, before you establish a marketing strategy that suits the project to be developed, you need a clear idea of the project and the position it holds in the market. The following questions can also help in establishing the project's position:

- Who are the target buyers?

- What are these buyers interested in?

- What are the buyers' likes and dislikes?

- How do competitor developers meet the needs of the target customers?

- Does the proposed project offer anything better?

The key is to establish a marketing edge. The developer should create a product that is better than or different from the competition, whether in architectural design and planning or in price.

By gathering this information, developers will be able to establish where their proposed project is positioned in the market (for example, whether it is high-end, competitive or low-cost) and if the project has a unique selling position or distinctive edge.

Chapter 8 provided information on how to conduct your own initial market research through the internet. However, the developer should not rely totally on these sources and should speak to real estate agents and other marketing groups to gain a clear understanding of the market being targeted.

Stage 2: Establish the project's marketing goals

Once the market research has been undertaken and the developer has a clear understanding where the development is positioned in the marketplace, they should start thinking about what sales are to be achieved as well as when, and more importantly how, these targets will be achieved.

Unless developing to hold, most residential developers plan to sell, and in most cases sales targets are set by their bank. Depending on the project and the developer's experience, banks will generally require pre-sales before releasing any of their funds for construction. As a rule of thumb, banks will need the pre-sales to cover the construction equivalent to 70 per cent of the total development cost or 65 per cent of the end value of the project.

Stage 3: Develop a market-oriented strategy

With these targets in mind, the developer will begin by determining what activities will be required to achieve these goals and find out who are the best parties that can assist. When choosing marketing activities, the developer should choose those that suit the project and the potential buyers. For example, if the project is targeting people within a certain market radius and class, it is pointless advertising on national television.

It is also a good idea to choose multiple activities that complement one another to get the marketing message across. For example, a developer trying to establish a new product in the market may choose to advertise on local radio, set up a social media account and introduce a low-cost pricing strategy for first home buyers. When used together, these complementary strategies will help you reach a broader market.

If the project is in a market where there is plenty of competition, the developer may need to think of alternative strategies. The following possibilities are worth considering.

Developer finance

The developer and the financier can offer finance packages to prospective purchasers. These packages can include an interest rate fixed lower than other finance competitors for the first few years.

Instalment sales

Although not common, sellers of property may use instalment sales either for realising gain over a number of years or when the market dictates that the deposit be divided into a number of payments over a few years. This recognised gain is spread over the life of the debt in the proportion in which the payments are received.

Stage 4: Create a marketing budget

Budgets will vary according to the type and size of the development project. As the project plans mature, so will the marketing budget. It will be constantly refined based on the design concept and the marketing program. Marketing is expensive, but no matter how good your development is you still need to put some money into marketing it. Remember that money spent on marketing is an investment—what you put into it determines what you get out of it.

The marketing budget should include the potential uses of funds together with the timing of these funds. The budget should be updated every week, month or quarter, depending on the type and size of development. The marketing funds may be spent to draw people to the development. If visitors are not being attracted, the marketing agent should try another option and adjust costs within the budget. The following is a sample list of broad categories that can be included in the marketing budget:

- advertising agency fees and expenses
- public relations fees and expenses
- marketing and sales office set-up cost, rent, furniture
- architectural model, renderings/plans/elevations
- brochures and printing
- signage
- displays
- media advertisements
- sales brokerage fees.

Stage 5: Appoint the marketing team

When selecting a team to assist in the marketing strategy, the developer must look for the very best available. The developer may decide to establish an in-house team or employ other professionals whose primary business is marketing and selling real estate. If the latter course is decided on, references and the track record of the company selected should be checked. Professionals who have a good understanding of the area and the community in which the project is located are better placed for marketing the project. The following is a list of potential members of a marketing team. Their selection will depend on the scale and type of project to be marketed.

Advertising agencies

An advertising agency can provide all or part of the overall marketing concept. They will prepare all your marketing material, such as brochures, fliers, business cards, letterheads and media advertising. Fees charged by these agencies can be based on a flat rate for time spent on production as well as a placement fee for arranging media advertising.

Public relations agencies

The function of public relations is to manage the public image of the developer's project. It involves media relations, organising, writing, production, speaking and training in order to build the public profile of the developer or the project. These individuals usually work on a fee per assignment or on a monthly retainer.

Real estate agents

If it is decided to contract the sales and marketing to a real estate agency the developer should make a list of companies, check their references and interview them before making the appointment. Generally, real estate agents will work on a percentage fee of each sale. This fee is negotiable but some agents may request that you pay for the advertising cost.

Project marketing consultants

These are real estate agents who specialise in pre-sales or selling off plan. They will work for a flat fee or a percentage of the gross sales. They will also consult with the developer or advertising agency to position the development for marketing.

Stage 6: Execute the marketing and sales activities

The objective in marketing is to maximise your advertising, and minimise wasted money, by making it response-driven and measurable. The developer's marketing team should advise on the type of medium to be used for marketing. Following are the various mediums that are available to the developer, along with their benefits.

Newspapers

These comprise national and local newspapers, including daily and weekend papers; weekly, community and organisation newsletters; and, of course, industry periodicals. The benefit of advertising in any newspaper is that the distribution rate is usually high. You may want to keep sales within a certain geographic area. In that case, you may want to look at a campaign that is more focused. You will find the appropriate medium as you read on.

Magazines

Magazines offer a high distribution rate. The benefit to advertising in a magazine is that the shelf life is a little longer, and magazines are often more market focused than a newspaper. In choosing which to use, ask the publisher for their statistics. These will include distribution figures and reader demographics that tell you their age group, income, industry and often much more. Find the magazine that targets your specific market.

Television

Television advertising is exciting but expensive. It is also one of the most effective forms of advertising available. The benefits are a wide audience, timing, focus and audience. If television is not an area of your marketing plan, then you should not try it without the assistance of a professional. These consultants will also be able to assist you with viewer demographics, channel comparisons, tone, times and much more.

Radio

Australia has an enormous audience for radio. In some communities radio has become an object of pride, almost a status symbol. Particular radio stations will have their own listeners based on demographics such as age, income and geography. Select the station that will best suit the target market you are aiming for.

Posters and billboards

Poster and billboard advertising in this country is a rather limited medium, unlike areas in America and Europe where such advertising is extremely common. The benefits of poster advertising are full colour, control over coverage and choice of location. Posters are generally a good medium for awareness campaigns and, of course, if you have a captive market, for example on bus shelters, you can increase copy and include telephone numbers and contact addresses.

Internet

Recently we have seen an upsurge in property marketing through the internet. With more households and businesses coming online every day it is essential to use this form of marketing. With new technology available you will be able create virtual walk-throughs and 3D models of your development before physical construction starts. This form of marketing will help those developers who would like to sell a percentage of their development 'off plan' before they fully commit to the project. This is an inexpensive way of getting your message across to the public when compared with the large capital costs involved in your development.

Exhibitions

This category includes trade fairs and even seminars. The benefits of these are enormous. Firstly, it is the only arena where a large percentage of your target market will travel to and present themselves at your stand or premises to find out more about your project. Exhibition organisers often create databases of the attendees and exhibitors, which means your follow-up can be quite painless and your communication ongoing. The time spent at seminars, trade shows or exhibitions is focused on your product and prospective clients only. Again, before you rent your space, make sure that the demographics of the visitors match those of your target market. Find out the attendance figures of the last exhibition, trade fair or seminar.

Social media

Like other industries, real estate social media marketing has become more important than ever. Under Chapter 8, Utilising Modern Technology, social media was explained in more detail. It is a cost-effective form of marketing, and it appeals to the younger generation. With so many social media platforms such as Facebook, Twitter, Instagram, Telegram, YouTube and many more, it is confusing which platform is best suited to your project. Therefore, it is wise to employ a social media expert.

Stage 7: Check and evaluate progress

You will know what you get out of it only if you measure and analyse the return. If the marketing plan is not working go back to the drawing board and review your strategy. Update your budget every week, month or quarter depending on the type and size of your development. Take remedial action as necessary.

Developers often find it hard to know whether their marketing plan is working. This can be difficult when a combination of marketing activities is used simultaneously. Following are a few ways to evaluate the progress of a marketing plan.

Monitor the sales

They should be steadily going up. Be careful about what is being measured as some markets have a longer sales cycle than others. To get an accurate picture, you should also measure the number of new leads being generated or the number of appointments being made.

Ask your buyers

Find out where they heard of the project. This will give you valuable insights into how buyers chose your project instead of the competitors.

Check the advertising results

If they are not working, action should be taken to improve response rates. Make sure that the right media are used and choose media to suit your selected audience. Be as specific as possible. Change the copy or redo the look of the advertisement. Use a strong headline that asks a pertinent question or gives a solution-oriented statement.

Check your sales conversion rate

The best approach here is to look at your historical records and determine whether your conversion rate has improved. 'Selling' is an important part of the marketing function, so make sure you assess your success in closing the sale, rather than just focus on generating new leads.

Selling off plan strategy

Pre-sales or selling a development 'off plan' can be at the best of times extremely difficult. Unfortunately, pre-selling is at times a condition of the development financier. These institutions will provide development finance only if they can be shown that there is a market for the project. They will also predetermine a specified percentage of the development that must have bona fide sale commitments prior to funding.

Pre-selling of residential units will depend on the economy and the number of buyers in the market. During the pre-selling stage, the marketing agent will try to secure signed agreements for reservations for buyers to purchase. These offers may include a reduced price or extra concessions to induce the purchaser to commit prior to seeing the completed project. An effective pre-sale marketing campaign will include various public relations events and articles about the progress of the development, along with mailings to interested parties concerning the construction and sales/leasing progress. Following are some pre-selling marketing strategies.

Pre-launch promotion parties

A pre-launch promotion party helps to spread word of the development. Invitees are not necessarily all buyers—they can include well-known personalities, councillors, real estate agents, journalists, anyone who will talk about the project. This would be their first presentation and the impressions of the development and feedback from the invitees would help to iron out any potential marketing issues.

Run a registrations-of-interest (ROI) campaign

This campaign can be promoted very early, before the official project launch. It will provide a good guide as to the public's interest in the project. With most ROI there is no formal commitment from the buyer and they will be more relaxed in signing up. This will also provide a potential buyer list when the project is officially launched.

Offer a special pre-sale price

Buyers love discounts. Offer a special pre-sale price to potential buyers at the official launch of the project. This could be limited to the first five buyers, for example. Instead of a special discounted pre-sale price, other promotions could be offered such as a furniture package.

Display unit

A completed display unit is a proven effective marketing tool for a number of reasons. It is a full-scale model for prospective users to experience prior to buying. The prospective purchaser will have a complete picture of the standard finishes, and more importantly they can see the possibilities of furniture layout and understand how their own furniture would fit.

Database marketing

Many of the major financial services networks, including financial planning dealer groups, mortgage aggregators and accounting firms in Australia and overseas, have a database of potential buyers and investors. These entities include financial planners, mortgage brokers, accountants and solicitors. On an international level there are international marketing agencies and overseas professional networks. Other groups that keep databases of buyers include property investment clubs and investor database specialists. The latter group's commission could be relatively high, so make sure to factor this into the marketing budget.

Summary

Most developers I have come across are not market oriented. They believe that if they build it the buyers will come. Nothing could be further from the truth. I have explained the importance of marketing and outlined how to implement it in your development business. Marketing should not be undertaken by you and your marketing team alone. You should also develop a strong and supportive infrastructure across your staff and development team so they are constantly marketing the project and feel part of the team.

CHAPTER 14
Residential land development

The benefit of developing vacant land lies in the potential to add value to it and the fact that it is a limited resource once built on. Vacant land can be subdivided or rezoned and the resulting portions of land can be sold for a higher price than the original purchase price and associated cost.

Buying raw land can be viewed from two perspectives: (a) as pure land speculation, known as land banking, or (b) to develop and sell. In the case of land speculation, the investor hopes to hold the land until there is a change in land use or a demand is created as a result of urban expansion. The land developer, on the other hand, plans to perform entrepreneurial activities on the land such as applying for a rezoning of land use and subdivision, installing infrastructure, such as roads, water, sewerage, gas and electricity, and then to sell the various subdivided portions for profit.

Land prices are sensitive to supply and demand. Where supply is limited and demand is heavy, the price of developable land rises rapidly. Perceptive residential land developers are aware of such demands and purchase land along future growth paths five to ten years before the urban crawl catches up. However, such developers require significant capital to sustain the holding of such land as during this period the land is not producing any income.

Benefits in land development

Land development can be rewarding for the following reasons.

Potential high returns

If the property is well located it can become a valuable asset, especially when natural forces such as an increase in population and migration create a demand for new subdivisions. For example, when rural land is rezoned to urban the land, which may have been bought at rural land prices, it is revalued at a significantly higher rate per square metre.

Rewards for entrepreneurial effort

Developers with vision can be rewarded for their entrepreneurial effort. For example, some developers have become millionaires overnight by analysing a city's growth patterns and buying large tracts of unused government land, rezoning it and selling the subdivision as residential lots.

Availability of finance

If the timing, location and feasibility study suggest a good return, most financiers would be in favour of lending money for residential land subdivision. Sometimes this finance is conditional on the rezoning and planning approval of various authorities.

Fewer contractual problems

Dealing with a natural resource that only needs roads and basic utilities to make it usable presents fewer headaches and less capital commitment than are normally associated with new building. In addition, land can be sold a lot earlier compared with a new building, where the developer will see cash only after the completion of the structure.

Risks in land development

The risks involved in this type of development depend mainly on timing, plus the following:

High holding cost

If the land is bought on a long-term speculative basis, the holding cost can be fairly high, especially if it cannot be rented out for any specific use or before any sale transactions take place. Delays in rezoning or subdivision approvals can be costly to the developer, who would be paying interest, land taxes and professional fees without any cash flow or return from the land.

Extensive government procedures

Any rezoning or subdivision of land attracts a number of government procedures and can involve both local and state departments. Depending on the size and location of the land, some government procedures may require the developer to conduct certain studies such as an environmental impact study, a traffic impact analysis and a social impact study.

Community approval

In addition to the normal government approvals, local active communities and action groups may raise concerns about the impact the rezoning could have on the local inhabitants and environment. These concerns, if not satisfied, can cause significant delays in development procedures.

Development strategies

To be successful in land development, a developer must constantly be aware of any changes in government planning policies and keep eye on where urban expansion is taking place. Visiting the state planning authority and obtaining the latest planning documentation of both present and future policies can achieve this. By having this information the developer has the following options in approaching a development:

Speculate

This can involve long-term or short-term speculation. Long-term speculation might mean, for example, purchasing a large tract of rural land, waiting for the urban expansion to encroach and then selling. With short-term speculation you would have to be aware of any imminent planning revisions, buy land that will be affected by the changes and sell at the increased value.

Rezone and sell

This would involve buying the land as an outright purchase or on an option with certain conditions. Time and effort would be spent in ensuring that the rezoning is successful and then in selling the land to another developer who is prepared to erect the buildings.

Rezone, subdivide and sell

This applies mainly to residential or large industrial land lots where the developer completes an overall township plan in conjunction with government planning policy and the long-term structure plans. The application will follow normal government procedures before being sold to various individuals as separate lots.

Role of the land developer

In a land development project, developers can play one of three roles:

- equity provider or co-developer
- fee developer
- sole developer.

Equity provider or co-developer

This arrangement requires the least hands-on participation by the developer. It leaves most of the development work to another organisation. The developer will receive a profit in proportion to their shareholding or a fee for their specialised expertise or efforts. The role and contributions of the developer in this situation can include:

- cash and upfront development money
- equity for land purchases
- a strong financial balance sheet
- working with governments and other authorities

- handling a specific job, such as marketing
- extensive land development experience and experienced staff.

Fee developer

In this development model, the developer fulfils the following roles and contributions for a fee:

- development and project management experience
- finding well-located development land
- strong ongoing relationships with architects, engineers and contractors that ensure a quality development
- selecting all professionals for the project
- handling all financing and cash flow needs.

Sole developer

In this model, the developer must have strong technical knowledge and experience in tax, financing, legal and construction activities. This model also requires a commitment to ongoing subdivision development to justify the high overhead costs associated with learning the business. In areas where the developer and team are confident of their skills and roles, they may consider taking on certain aspects of the project such as marketing, pre-purchase analysis, financing or community land planning.

Land development process

Developing and subdividing residential land involves matching raw land with potential buyers. The process includes nine stages, from strategic and program planning to eight execution steps, site control and feasibility, master planning, financing, obtaining approvals, specifications and contractor award, marketing and sales, construction, and transfer and settlement.

Stage 1: Strategic and program planning

During this stage, the developer and team evaluate the neighbourhood, the expected demand for homes, the availability of finance, and the strength and range of possible partners or investors, before deciding to embark on developing a new land subdivision. The developer needs to base the decision on facts and independent studies and not on the desire of a few professional team members, the local community or business associates who would just like to see some new houses in the neighbourhood.

Stage 2: Site control and feasibility

After locating a potential site, the developer obtains control over the site through a legal contract that gives the developer the sole right to purchase the land parcel at a given price within a specified time, which allows the developer to further test feasibility, secure finance and purchase the land. In testing the viability of the development, the developer and team work on several estimations, including the number of lots and projected sales, the price of land, construction and other expenses, and the costs of financing. The feasibility will be recalculated a number of times during the development process as new information replaces earlier estimates. Initial feasibility calculations will indicate the size of a possible subdivision. If the subdivision is too small the planners, contractors and marketers will not achieve economies of scale; if it is too large there may be too many lots to sell, which will make lenders apprehensive. The land must be close to existing roads and utility services so the costs of extending these services are not excessive.

During the feasibility stage:

- *A town planner is appointed to execute a preliminary design:* A planner's strength is in design, not cost estimating, so their estimate on construction costs requires verification.

- *A civil engineer is engaged to provide a reasonably accurate estimate of costs:* The engineer should also complete soil tests to determine if the site can support the homes to be built. The construction schedule should be thoroughly analysed with the engineer as it can significantly affect the financial viability of the project.

- *A lawyer should be retained if there are questions regarding zoning, planning issues or community concerns*

- *An inexperienced developer should consider hiring a development manager or consultant:* They would complete initial financial projections and map out an appropriate development strategy.

Stage 3: Master planning

Surveyors will undertake the task of providing detailed topographical maps that show the exact configuration of the site with all rises, falls, vegetation, trees, streams and so on. With this information, as well as the developer's research of the market, planners will start producing a master plan, which indicates and describes the locations of streets, sidewalks, service lines, driveways and houses. The subdivision master plan should consider a mix of site layout and building configurations that adds appreciably to the character and marketability of the development. As outlined in 'Planning considerations' later in this chapter, the planner will take into account detailed design aspects such as access and egress to the subdivision, street layout options, streetscape, buffer zones and community amenities. From this master plan, engineers will be able to determine a cost estimate for the planned subdivision.

Stage 4: Securing finance

With a site secured and a budget in place, the developer will be able to apply for financing. It helps to think of financing needs in phases: pre-development, acquisition and construction. Some funding sources may meet more than one need, but others will limit their support to one phase only. Some land developers will look to equity partners during the early, riskier stages; as the project progresses they are able to secure commitments from conventional lenders and further equity investors. Further details can be found under 'Sources of finance' later in this chapter.

Stage 5: Obtaining approvals

Depending on the size and complexity of the land subdivision the approval process could take several months or a few years. The approval process will be easier if the site is within an approved Town Planning

Structure Plan. However, with larger tracts of land changing zoning from rural to urban the approval process could take much longer. In most approvals the initial process will require development approval from the local council and in most cases approval from the state planning commission. The developer's planners can advise on the approval process, its timing and which authorities require submissions. They will also coordinate the relevant documents for approval and will monitor the process. The approval process is further explained later in the chapter.

Stage 6: Construction tenders and contractor award

During this phase, the developer's engineer finalises the working drawings together with specifications for selected civil contractors to tender to undertake the construction. The developer or engineer would have investigated potential tenderers, checking their reliability and quality of work and their track record in land subdivisions. The developer's engineer will then prepare and issue tender documents to the potential contractors. The documents should detail exactly what is expected of the contractor, based on specifications drawn from the engineering drawings. Any construction concerns particular to the developer, such as phasing of construction to match marketing strategies, must be part of the tender documents.

After the tenders are submitted, the developer will select one of the contractors and negotiate a final contract. The contract results must be realistic in terms of costs and time frames. The developer should not always accept the lowest tender, especially if it is unrealistic, as they may find that the contractor requests additional money or time midway through construction. The construction contract will have to be approved by construction finance lenders to the project.

Stage 7: Marketing

In this stage, marketing of the subdivision begins. Some lenders will require that a specific percentage of the subdivision lots are pre-sold prior to the beginning of construction. In such cases the marketing should begin at the end of the approval stage. The developer or a selected marketing agent will undertake the marketing and sales and plan a marketing strategy. For example, in most larger development estates the subdivisions are released in phases, with the first phase price at breakeven level. As demand grows the later phases are released at increased profit margins.

Stage 8: Construction

During the construction stage, the developer or appointed team should monitor and oversee the contractor, keeping the marketing and lenders informed of progress. The developer needs an experienced project manager to oversee the quality of construction. The project manager tours the site frequently, always inspecting the work done when the contractor requests a draw of funds. Construction is carried out according to a specified schedule created by the contractor and approved by the developer prior to the start of construction. The contractor will receive draws based on its progress. The developer or supervising team need to have weekly or fortnightly construction meetings to confirm that everything is moving according to schedule. When progress is not on schedule or costs are off budget, the developer's team must immediately find out the reasons and get the contractor back on track. Problems caught early are easier to resolve than those that get out of hand.

Stage 9: Settlement and transfer

When construction is completed, the lots pegged and individual titles approved by the various authorities, purchasers are in the position to take transfer and possession of the land they purchased. Possession and transfer will happen only when the full purchase price has been settled with the developer. The developer will receive their profit share only after outstanding amounts to the lender have been paid.

Market demand

In previous chapters the demand of various forms of new residential property developments was described. Land development is no different and is subject to the same principal market forces.

Successful land development depends on the land's ultimate use, so when analysing the market demand the developer should take into consideration the variables associated with specific real estate use. The following list summarises the main variables to be analysed:

- *Transformation in population:* The growth patterns and movement of the general population on a macro level should be analysed.

- *Transformation in the economy:* The national, state, regional and local economies as they affect the demand for land should be studied.

- *Transformation in government policies:* Changes in government policies at any level could affect the demand for land. New zoning policies could affect the viability of a land development.

- *The availability of land:* Well-located, developable land can increase the demand for and pricing of a subdivision.

- *New social services:* Provision of new services in a new area will influence the demand for new subdivisions.

Analysing the location

In order to find the best locality for a land development the developer will have to spend time researching and keeping up to date with the future planning policies of the state and regional planning authorities. Research should also take into account the long-term planning of road and rail transport systems adopted by the Main Roads Department and the movement of people closer to employment opportunities.

If possible, environmentally sensitive areas should be avoided as this could cause undue delay in rezoning and subdivision applications. Land that should be avoided includes low-lying or natural wetlands, landfill sites such as former rubbish tips, areas with large overhead power lines and land near airports or heavy industrial zones. Land that contains steep rises and falls should also be avoided as this will increase servicing and road access costs, unless the land has spectacular views that would justify the increased costs.

When seeking the right location, a study should be undertaken that takes into account all potential uses for the land, which may include a mix of residential, office or retail usage. A residential subdivision that provides good access to shopping, schools and community services will add value to the development.

Analysing the market

In analysing the possible buyers of the subdivided lots, market research should be undertaken covering the following areas:

- demographics
- consumer profile
- historic sales evidence
- planned infrastructure
- competitors
- sales forecasting
- future profits.

Using real estate agents, property valuers or professional market researchers can help with the research. The market study must answer the following questions.

- How big is the total market in the local area and what percentage can the project capture?
- What are the demographic and lifestyle characteristics of the chosen target market?
- What is the household income range?
- What housing lifestyle preferences, such as types of developments, location, amenities and services, does your target group demand?
- Based on local development cost, the competition and the economic factors shaping the target market's buying power, what is the project's absorption rate within a given period?

The development team

The team of consultants may vary according to the size of the development but besides the developer or project manager, the three other consultants who will play a pivotal part in rezoning or subdivision of land are the town planner, the civil engineer and the land surveyor.

It is typical to work with many consultants in developing subdivisions. Besides the professionals named here, others required could be lawyers, accountants, quantity surveyors, architects, and specialists in financing and structuring a deal. The work involved in putting together a subdivision is very detailed, and even the most experienced developers use professional advice. The following list of consultants is typical.

Lawyer

The lawyer must be skilled in partnership negotiations and knowledgeable about land development issues. It helps if the attorney is also experienced in property, town planning legislation and construction law. The developer should look for an attorney with a reputation for cost-effective service and consider establishing a fixed-price contract.

Town planner

A town planner's services may be used from inception to completion, but this will depend on the scale of the project. Their expertise is required mainly in the initial stages, when they will be required to conduct a number of investigations and consultations with various authorities to provide a conceptual sketch layout plan with a proposed subdivision and zoning. With input from other consultants, the planner will be able to provide a detailed master plan, which will become the framework for the subdivision that will be lodged with various authorities for approval. If rezoning is required a town planner will be able to prepare application and motivation documents for council approval.

Civil engineer

A civil engineer will be required in the initial stages to investigate servicing opportunities and restrictions with relevant authorities. These will include water, electricity and gas authorities, the local authority for development standards of roads and stormwater management, telecommunication service providers, and the Departments of Transport and Environmental Protection. The engineer will inspect the land and investigate the soil and vegetation types, ground water, existing services, terrain and any other factors that may affect development costs and planning by the town planner. In consultation with other team members such as electrical and hydraulics engineers, the civil engineer will prepare detailed drawings and specifications, which will be issued for tendering to civil contractors. It is important to retain the services of the engineer to supervise the works during construction.

Land surveyor

The surveyor will be used in two stages of the development—at the start and at completion. In the initial stage of the project, the surveyor will prepare a complete topographical survey of the land to be developed, which will include all existing elements such as trees, water features and services. After completion of the project and approval by various authorities the surveyor will formalise the subdivision by preparing diagrams and pegging out the subdivided land so that titles can be issued.

Quantity surveyor

Depending on the scale of the project, a quantity surveyor with a strong knowledge of issues involving land development may be appointed. The developer should make sure the appointed person can serve as an adviser on financial management issues. The quantity surveyor will help in setting up a sound financial management system that gives the development a clean audit and clear, timely reports on:

- the budget, showing actual income and expenses, providing line-item analysis and explaining any substantive variations
- steps to bring expenses into line with the budget
- cash flow, including a comparison of projections and actual performance
- sources of funding and the performance of each source.

Other consultants

Additional consultants that could be required but might play a lesser role are:

- *Structural engineer:* for retaining walls, bridges and so on.
- *Electrical engineer:* for the provision of electrical supply to the projects and subdivided lots

- *Hydraulics engineer:* for water supply and drainage

- *Environmental scientist:* for any environmental studies that may be required by various authorities

- *Geotechnical engineer:* for any soil analysis that may be required by the civil or structural engineer

- *Anthropologist:* used mainly on larger scale projects, where they may assist and advise the town planner on the social aspects of the community

- *Architect:* may be required to provide conceptual buildings to show prospective buyers or authorities what the completed product would look like

- *Landscape architect:* may be required to advise on planting of trees and other vegetation to make the land more attractive

- *Property valuer:* to assess the value of the land and subdivision when completed

- *Real estate agent:* to assist with selling the subdivided land

- *Advertising and marketing professional:* to assist with the overall marketing campaign and marketing concepts.

Planning considerations

The number of dwelling units per hectare is the primary development standard that influences the lifestyle, economics and environmental considerations of a residential land development. As net density increases, lot sizes become smaller and land needed for roads per housing unit decreases. While these constraints may limit the planner's ideal design, a good planner will incorporate such economic restrictions while still creating a vibrant community with well-planned amenities and open spaces. The following design elements should be considered.

Entrance to development

The entrance could be formal or informal depending on the prestige of the development. Carefully designed walls and signage to announce a strong presence with formal landscaping will give the estate a defined identity, while a low-key development would have minimal walls and signage for understated presence.

Lot size and orientation

The size and orientation of lots varies widely across different states in Australia. In the past the standard lot ranged from around 500 to 800 square metres for detached houses. In order to achieve cost efficiency, a number of local authorities now encourage lot sizes of 400 to 450 square metres or less. Australian households are getting smaller and lifestyles are changing, with more time spent on leisure activities away from home, so homeowners do not have as much time to maintain big gardens. When designing for smaller lots the planning team should, where relevant, take into account the following factors:

- the natural contours and orientation of the land and soil conditions

- the need to retain special features such as trees and views

- the efficient cost of providing new and existing services

- the need to avoid unnecessary repetition

- the ability to facilitate energy conservation through correct solar orientation.

Built form

The final design and planning of homes on each lot is not part of a land developer's financial feasibility, but it will be beneficial to the marketing strategy to consider the following design factors:

- the scale, height and density of the homes

- the overall housing theme or character

- the provision of privacy, daylight and energy conservation

- the building lines and various setbacks

- the provision of private open space.

Transport networks

During the preparation of the overall conceptual site layout the design team should start with the most sensitive areas of transportation, which are the needs of pedestrians and cyclists. The major routes should follow easy gradients and should link residential areas with schools, open spaces and community activity centres. The layout of possible bus routes and the development of the street network should subsequently be considered. As a general rule, traffic volumes and speeds should be minimised on streets within the residential zone for reasons of safety and to mitigate the impact of traffic movement and noise.

Street design

Besides the overall transport network the design team should take special care with the detail and design of the street layout by considering factors such as:

- street reserve width and pavement width
- sightlines and distances
- street and pavement markings and design
- turning circles to accommodate refuse trucks and fire engines
- provision for buses and public transport
- street furniture, including street lighting.

Consideration should also be given to whether the streets are developed in a straight line with a focal point at the end, with a grid layout or in a curvilinear loop as a cul-de-sac.

Streetscape

The design and character of the streetscape in a residential land subdivision is important in determining the value and image of the properties and contributes significantly to neighbourhood identity. The factors that contribute to the value of a streetscape are:

- the quality of formal and informal landscaping
- the retaining of natural vegetation and existing trees

- the use of natural features and terrain
- the design of street paving and verge widths
- the control and design of street furniture such as poles and signs
- the control of architectural styles
- the design and control of the height and material of fences.

Pedestrians and cyclists

The provision of facilities for pedestrians and cyclists must be an integral part of the design of the total transportation network. All residents should have the opportunity to walk or cycle to community facilities. Designing for the safety of children, disabled people and aged persons is particularly important, especially where they have to cross a busy street.

Services

Servicing of residential subdivision developments includes water supply, sewerage, electricity, gas, telephone and stormwater, which are usually provided through a series of underground ducts either within the road reserve or at the rear of a lot. These utilities are controlled by separate authorities and in the past no attempt was made to combine installation other than an agreed location for each service. More recently attempts have been made to share trenches, which has the following advantages:

- cost-effectiveness, with fewer trenches and less construction
- accurate location of services for maintenance and repairs
- reduced verge width and disturbance, and earlier settlement and reinstatement.

Amenities

Natural amenities found on the site such as lakes, creeks, meadows, marshes and mature vegetation should be incorporated into the design. In addition, constructed amenities such as day-care centres, convenience stores, community centres, playgrounds, recreation centres and gymnasiums should be considered and located within easy access to the future homeowners.

Public open space

Local authorities will normally stipulate the minimum open space required to ensure that sufficient space is planned at the design stage. In recent times the ongoing maintenance of these spaces has become a concern for local authorities so when planning open areas it is important to balance the actual and future use against ongoing maintenance requirements.

Development cost

Development cost can be broken down into 'hard costs' and 'soft costs'. Hard costs are land acquisition and construction costs, while soft costs account for valuation, marketing, application fees and so on. Table 14.1 shows a typical breakdown of costs for a land development project. While most items are listed they will vary in different localities, and the developer should always check with local conditions and laws that may affect the final cost.

Table 14.1: typical development costs

Item	Total cost	Average cost per lot
LAND PURCHASE		
Option fee (if applicable)		
Purchase price		
Settlement fees		
Stamp duty		
Survey		
Prepaid rates and taxes		
Subtotal land acquisition cost		
CONSTRUCTION COST		
Engineering		
Road construction		
Services		
Stormwater		
Landscaping		

Item	Total cost	Average cost per lot
Contingency		
Contractor's fee		
Subtotal construction cost		
PROFESSIONAL FEES		
Project manager		
Land surveyor		
Town planner		
Engineer		
Architect		
Other		
Subtotal professional fees		
FINANCING COST		
Bank charges and fees		
Interest on land acquisition loan		
Interest on pre-development loan		
Interest on construction loan		
Subtotal financing cost		
FEES AND COMMISSIONS		
Planning application fees		
Service connection fees		
Valuation fees		
Land title fees		
Marketing fees and commissions		
Subtotal fees and commissions		
DEVELOPER'S FEE		
5% of development cost		
Total development cost		
Total development cost per lot		

Sourcing finance

The approval of finance for a subdivision land development will depend largely on the feasibility study and the developer's own equity, but more importantly on the cash flow of the project in line with the planned stages or phases. The developer should approach financial institutions in the early stages of the project so they can get a feel for and understanding of the project as the development concept progresses. Before seeking finance, the developer should have at least the following information to present:

■ historical background of the land and surrounding areas

■ description of the project and any distinctive qualities

■ valuation report of the property

■ details of the market research conducted

■ details of the developer or development company and shareholders

■ details of the borrower's financial position.

Developers generally encounter three different capital needs when developing a successful subdivision land development project (see table 14.2).

Table 14.2: stages of financing

Phase	Uses	Sources
Pre-development	Planning, engineering and consultant costs	Developer's funds, equity partners, seed capital
Land purchase	Land costs, title and legal fees	Banks, equity partners, shareholders
Construction	Construction and engineering costs	Banks, equity partners, shareholders

Pre-development finance

The pre-development period lasts until the developer settles on the land purchase or the start of construction. The major costs in this period involve market analysis, planning, feasibilities and consulting fees. If applicable, land option costs are included as a pre-development expense. Alternatively, the developer can secure the site through a normal sale contract with a small deposit. This involves very little outlay of cash or interest payments prior to the initial settlement. Funding for this phase may come from the developer or equity partners, or they may decide to develop in partnership with a company that has in-house expertise and the capacity to pay some or all pre-development costs.

Land purchase and construction loans

The land purchase and construction loans could be separate loans or one, depending on development strategy. Some developers would buy the land with their own cash, as land typically does not produce any income and any borrowed funds with interest could eat away potential profit. If the developer has only one loan, the development process should progress efficiently and without delays. The loans are usually borrowed from banks once there is a guarantee of a permanent mortgage. These short-term loans are drawn down after the work is completed, less a retention amount based on the bank inspector's approval of the work completed.

Working capital

Inadequate cash flow is a major problem during most developments. It is imperative that the developer prepare a conservative project cash flow. Many cash payments are made prior to obtaining construction financing, including for environmental studies, preliminary plans, market studies and attorney's fees. In addition, cash flow during construction should be carefully estimated to ensure that financing sources keep pace with the demands of your contractor. Cash flow needs should be calculated on a month-to-month basis. If money is coming from other lending sources it is helpful to obtain a bank overdraft to meet short-term cash flow shortages.

Authorities and approvals

Most new residential land developments take place in the outer ring of a city. Land that was once agricultural may be rezoned or may fall under a new structure plan as a suburban housing estate. If the land falls under a new structure plan the process will be a lot quicker. If rezoning or higher density is required, a developer must spend months and sometimes years collecting the appropriate approvals. Even in cases where the desired zoning is in place, the new subdivision will be subject to a review process. Representatives of various governmental authorities will review, approve and modify the plan for the layout of the streets, amenities and the general master plan. In many cases, this scrutiny will require the services of a specialised lawyer, town planner and civil engineer, who will help to prepare the necessary documentation and complete the necessary applications.

In most applications, whether for rezoning or development, the local community's interests have to be addressed. It would be advantageous if the developer addressed the community's concerns early so as to have their support for, rather than opposition to, the development. Developers should analyse community issues and address the following questions.

- Will a proposed project meet community opposition?

- What are the plans in place to deal with potential conflicts?

- Have any potential problems been addressed with key supporters?

The developer should meet with key individuals, politicians and appointed officials to build or maintain positive support for the proposed development.

The process for land subdivision approval is different from that for a building development approval, as different state and local authorities will be involved. Each state in Australia has its own development process for approvals and a local town planner or state planning authority would be able to assist. Figure 14.1 outlines a land development approval process in Western Australia.

Figure 14.1: a typical land development approval process in WA

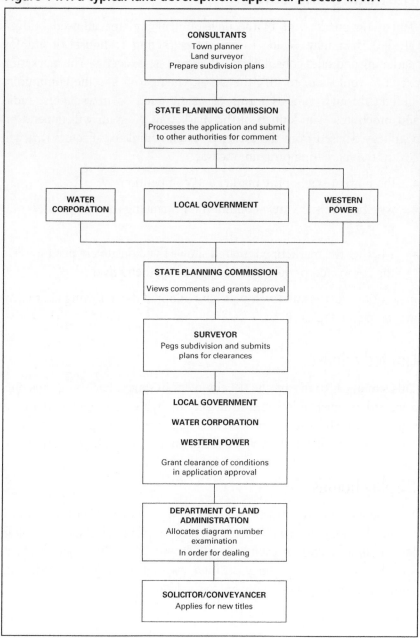

Marketing and sales

Depending on the size of the development and the allowed budget, the developer may decide to handle marketing 'in-house' or employ marketing and sales consultants such as real estate agents. The marketing exercise would aim to link the development to a specific community lifestyle through various forms of media such as newspapers, radio and brochures. The launch of the marketing program will depend on a strategy devised from the earlier research completed. Factors that will govern the marketing program include:

- the present state of the market and competition
- whether pre-sales are a condition for financing the start of the project
- whether the marketing research shows that consumers need to see the completed project before committing themselves.

In addition, successful developers have adopted the following alternative marketing strategies.

Limited release

This strategy is to release the development in stages. Each stage has only a limited number of lots and invariably there are more buyers than lots available, which creates a 'must buy' mentality before the price increases at the next stage. This strategy will depend on prevailing market conditions.

Display homes

Most new land developments will have a number of lots at the entrance to the development available to project builders. This has a twofold benefit as it creates an established look and generally project builders spend a great deal of money on their own advertising, thus attracting large numbers of potential buyers to the land.

Developer finance

Having the developer's own financier offer finance to potential buyers will assist the developer, the buyer and the financier, who would already have valued the land and would possibly offer better terms and conditions to purchasers.

Incentives

A number of incentives can be offered, such as free fencing, an allowance for free landscaping or a cash discount on early completion of a buyer's new home.

Marketing materials

A well-produced brochure that highlights the development's features is recommended. A complete marketing packet is useful and should contain the project name, the developer and a number to call for more information, along with a colour site plan, drawings of multiple views of the completed estate and a description of the estate. A site sales office with professionally trained staff is essential for successful sales.

Summary

Some developers specialise in developing land and have made substantial returns. Residential land development is less risky than the built form, where there are a multitude of areas where things can go wrong. The downside of land development is that the approval process can be very protracted and it can take a long time to realise a return on the money you have tied up. Should you decide that this type of development is for you, ensure that you have sufficient money to sustain you through a period of negative income and that you have the patience to wait for the anticipated windfall.

Case study

About six years ago a developer purchased a property on the outskirts of Perth with a view to creating a land subdivision. The developer appointed a professional team of consultants to undertake the relevant tasks to secure approval to subdivide the land, construct the infrastructure and then sell the lots for housing.

The site is part of a precinct that is broken up into sub-precincts. There was an acknowledgement for the subject site to be rezoned from rural to urban. The following planning milestones had to be achieved in order to realise urban subdivision:

1   lifting of 'Urban Deferred' zoning under the Metropolitan Region Scheme

2   preparation and adoption of an Outline Development Plan (ODP) for a sub-precinct

3   preparation of an application for approval of a subdivision.

In order to establish the yield that might result from the current ODP process, a concept subdivision was prepared for the subject site. In summary, the concept subdivision plan (see figure 14.2) defines the following:

- 18 R30 lots

- 48 R40 lots

- 1366 square metres of public open space.

Figure 14.2: subdivision plan

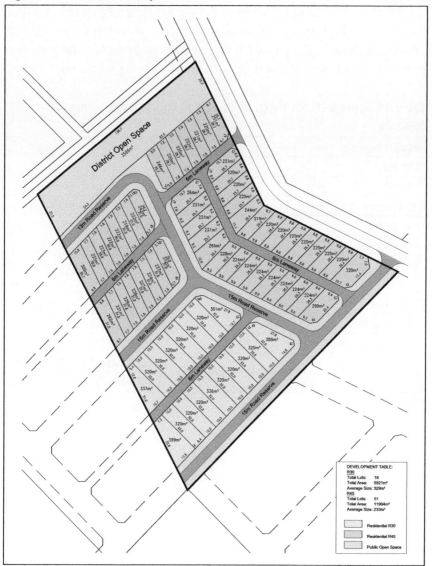

Figure reproduced courtesy of Dynamic Planning.

An income analysis and a prefeasibility study (see tables 14.3 and 14.4) was undertaken that took into consideration the current lot prices within the area, and both the professional and civil costs were provided by the professional team. The study has found that the project is viable subject to market conditions at the time of the project being launched.

Table 14.3: project: southern river — land subdivision — income analysis

Income analysis	Rate	Amount
R30 Lots		
Total lots	18	$4 140 000.00
Total area m²	5921	$4 144 700.00
Average size m²	329	$230 000.00
Recommended sale m²	$700.00	
R40 Lots		
Total lots	48	$10 080 000.00
Total area m²	12441	$9 952 800.00
Average size lots	259	$210 000.00
Recommended sale m²	$800.00	
	Total sales	**$14 097 500.00**
	Total lots	**66**

Table 14.4: project: southern river—land subdivision—prefeasibility study

Income	Amount	Sub-total	Total
Total sales	$ 14 097 500.00		
Less GST	$ 1 281 462.75		
Less commission	$ 352 437.50	$ 12 463 599.75	$ 12 463 599.75
Development cost	**Amount**	**Sub-total**	**Total**
Land purchase cost			
Purchase	$ 2 100 000.00		
Stamp duty	$ 107 000.00		
Conveyancing fees (purchase)	$ 6 300.00	$ 2 213 300.00	
Consultants			
Civil and electrical engineer 7%	$ 296 344.65		
Principal's surveyor 2%	$ 84 669.90		
Geotechnical engineer 1%	$ 42 334.95		
Planning 2.5%	$ 105 837.38		
Environmental 1%	$ 42 334.95		
Landscaping 0.5%	$ 21 167.48	$ 592 689.30	
Council and government			
Water Corporation Fees	$ 353 562.00		
City of Gosnells Supervision	$ 49 250.00		
City of Gosnells Bond	$ 164 200.00		
Western Power	$ 475 000.00		
Developer's contribution	$ 693 100.00	$ 1 735 112.00	
Management fees			
Project manager	$ 107 434.93	$ 107 434.93	

(continued)

Table 14.4: project: southern river—land subdivision—prefeasibility study *(cont'd)*

Development cost	Amount	Sub-total	Total
Construction works			
Preliminaries	$ 226 200.00		
Earthworks	$ 1 563 900.00		
Sewer	$ 502 800.00		
Stormwater and drainage	$ 568 200.00		
Water	$ 88 500.00		
Power, gas, telecommunications	$ 347 800.00		
Road works	$ 419 800.00		
Retaining walls and fencing	$ 314 700.00		
Contingency 5%	$ 201 595.00	$ 4 233 495.00	
Legal and capital			
Legal	$ 6 600.00	$ 6 600.00	$ 8 888 631.23
Less GST			$ 807 976.58
Development cost			$ 8 080 654.65
Borrowing interest			$ 223 113.15
Total development cost			$ 8 303 767.79
Profit margin			**$ 4 159 831.96**
Total development cost			$ 8 303 767.79
Margin on development cost %			50.10%

CHAPTER 15

Villas and townhouses

Townhouses and villa units have been common housing in Australian cities and towns for a number of years. These developments have occurred as a result of a number of factors, including affordability, higher density rezoning, the changing demographic distribution of our population and changing household structures, which have created a demand for more diversified housing types. This demand has occurred in older suburbs, such as land infill sites and near transport nodes.

Unlike flats and high-rise apartment buildings, where it is often difficult to tell where one unit starts and another ends, townhouses and villas still retain some recognisable individuality. Usually they do not contain lifts. Often they have wide balconies, decks, small gardens and dividing walls. The design and layout of these buildings are well suited to communal living, theme housing developments, holiday resorts and retirement villages.

Definitions

The definition of these developments varies from state to state and even from city to city. Generally they fall under the category of 'Grouped Dwellings' and can be further defined as townhouses, villas and retirement villages. A group dwelling is normally one of a group of two or more homes constructed at the same time, with each dwelling having its own private garden area attached. Further definitions of grouped dwellings are as follows.

Units

This is a broadly used word to define higher density residential developments, whether townhouses or apartment buildings. Smaller unit developments can be further categorised as duplex, triplex or quadruplex. These smaller developments appeal to apprentice developers who do not want to invest a great deal of capital in their early developments.

Villas

Villas are units in a development consisting of five or more dwellings, built with a certain theme and generally individualised with their own name. These dwellings can be of one or two storeys, are generally independent of each other (that is, without a common wall), and have their own front and rear gardens. Villas tend to be smaller than suburban houses. This usually arises from the developer's desire to take maximum advantage of the number of units the council's planning regulations allows on the site. Some council regulations set minimum sizes for one-, two- and three-bedroom units, and developers try to keep the size down to the regulation limits to increase the number of units on the site.

Townhouses

Like villas, townhouses are dwellings that are normally found closer to city centres and are built on sites with a higher density. They generally are built on two levels, have common walls and may have a communal parking garage. Each unit will have access to a private garden on the ground floor. A typical example is the Paddington-style development, a style similar to the terrace housing that originated from Sydney between the 1850s and 1890s. With increased densities in suburban areas, townhouses are being developed in larger complexes with security fencing and resort facilities such as swimming pools, gyms and playground equipment.

Benefits and risks

The developer contemplating getting involved in these types of developments should evaluate the benefits and risks in relation to their expertise and financial resources. The following benefits may be considered.

Competent use of land

With the increase in coverage and plot ratios, land in higher density residential areas normally utilises the developable land to its greatest extent. Generally, land with a higher density zoning is at a premium in terms of property prices and is located in prime positions, forcing developers to build the maximum allowable units on the site in order to capitalise on their investment. Concern does arise from a design perspective, however, as increased densities tend to have a negative impact on privacy and solar orientation.

Range of sizes and prices

Experienced developers do not build and sell only one typical floor plan. They try to incorporate as many flexible designs as possible to cater for the broader taste of the market. They offer choices such as two- to three-bedroom units and single or double garages. By using a standard format they are able to vary the room combinations and floor areas.

Less sophistication required

As the units are standardised and at times the elevations are not seen from all sides, less elaborate detailing is required to both the internal and external parts of the buildings. Depending on the market niche, standard finishes can be used in all the units unless the buyer requests changes. This increases the developer's profit, as they are able to negotiate better prices for both volume and repetitive finishes. In addition, any variation requested by prospective purchasers will have a surcharge and higher mark-up for the developer.

Broader market

Depending on their location, higher density residential developments can cater for a broader market, including singles, young couples without children, young families or empty nesters, and even retirees. Not only can they cater for most people looking for a home with convenient facilities in close proximity, they can also attract investors looking for a long-term investment in a good location and a building requiring very little maintenance.

Better control

Unlike several single-home developments or renovations where the developer is building in different locations, villa and townhouse developments, being on one site, can be better controlled. For instance, preliminary costs (such as set-up costs) are reduced and there is continuity and flow of work for subcontractors, allowing management to control the flow of materials on site. Materials and finishes are repetitive and therefore there is less margin for error.

The following risks should be taken into account.

Volatile market

The 'boom and bust' periods in the housing market are very relevant. Whenever there is a boom, building resources are pushed to the limits, causing a shortage of materials and labour and increased prices. The opposite occurs in recessive periods. Developers entering this market should keep ahead of these cycles.

Exposure to overbuilding

As these developments are greater in number and therefore take longer to build, the developer may be midway through the project and be caught at the tail end of the boom cycle, leaving a number of units unsold. This could have a severe effect on the developer's profit and cash flow, especially if borrowed money is used to finance the buildings. In addition, at the peak of a construction boom interest rates tend to rise, forcing the developer to look for other forms of financing or cut their losses and sell the units at cost.

Higher demands for management

The greater amount of building activity together with a larger number of clients to deal with will require a greater number of staff and therefore more management expertise. A developer's failure to manage the development and the people involved in the various stages of the development will cause delays, poor construction and therefore a loss in sales.

Higher demands for finance

These projects require larger budgets and therefore more personal equity in the development. By using debt finance the developer is exposed to fluctuations in interest rates. To give you peace of mind you should sell as many units off plan before you start building as possible. Regrettably, this is easier said than done, as buyers are becoming more astute when buying through this method.

Shifts in consumer taste

To attract buyers and renters, developers and their designers are constantly creating new concepts, which invariably set new trends. Other developers have to keep in touch with these new ideas so their own proposed development is in line with the latest consumer tastes.

Demand for unit-type living

The demand for villas and townhouses is driven by the same population growth and migration factors affecting single family homes in suburban areas, but there are certain differences between the demands for this housing type and for higher density housing.

Travelling distances

With the increase in population, new suburbs are expanding at a rapid rate in areas away from the central business district (CBD) and major leisure and recreational activities, making travelling times to these locations longer and travel more expensive. Most higher density residential developments have become more attractive because they are closer to these activities. With the rising cost of fuel and motor vehicle expenses, a near-city residence looks more attractive to people working in the office towers of the city centre area.

Change in lifestyle

Economic changes, improved facilities, new technology and better health mean many people have changed their lifestyles. We now find both marriage partners working and more women following a career path before starting a family. Even empty-nester couples are looking for a 'lock-up-and-go', maintenance-free residence that will give them more leisure time to spend in their holiday home. This increases the demand for more compact, easy-care and convenient styles of living.

Aging population

With Australia's aging population there will be a growing demand for retirement and compact, unit-style living. This is the inevitable result of a long trend towards smaller families and increasing life expectancy. Australia's population is projected to rise to around 38 million by 2060. The proportion of the population aged 65 years or more will increase from around 1:7 in 2013 to 1:4 by 2060, and close to 1:3.5 at the turn of the next century (see figure 15.1). People in this category will be looking for smaller, more compact homes with less maintenance and a high level of security in locations that provide easy access to public amenities. In addition, the homes should preferably be on a single level within a community of people of similar age and interests.

Figure 15.1: Projected population age structure, Australia, 1999–2051

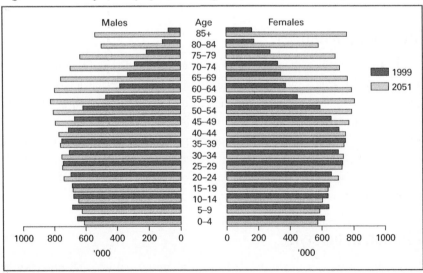

Source: Australian Bureau of Statistics 2014.

Development strategies

Most developers in this category, especially builders, sell the units in their development so they can plan and start their next new project. Such builder developers often have a large workforce and are looking for ongoing work to keep their staff employed.

Sell and hold

Investor developers, on the other hand, will sell part of the development and retain a number of units for rental as part of their long-term investment strategy. Investor developers are normally businesspeople running their own business other than building and use the services of a number of professional consultants. The profit margin is not as high as for the builder developer as a number of fees and charges have to be paid out.

Develop in phases

Developers tackling a larger project of 20 or more units should consider building in phases. This strategy has the benefit that should there be a lull in housing demand the developer is not exposed with unsold units, and should there be an increase in housing demand the developer can increase prices, producing a better profit margin.

House and land package

Another possible strategy is to design the project as a strata lot development and sell the villas as 'house and land packages'. Townhouses can be marketed on this basis as well, except they will not be attached by a common wall. The overall project will share a similar theme and design with plans already approved by the council before they are marketed. With this strategy, the developer is effectively a land developer as the buyer signs two contracts simultaneously, a land sales contract with the developer and a building contract with the nominated builder. The benefit to the developer is that they do not have to borrow for the building construction and therefore do not take on the construction risks. However, the developer will still have to finance and construct the roads and provide the services to the strata lots. It must be noted that not all sites can be developed in this format so it is best to check with your local council.

Location

When searching for the ideal location for a townhouse or villa development, apply the following principles:

- Shopping facilities should be within walking distance, especially for elderly people.

- Restaurants and recreation facilities should be close at hand, especially for young, career-minded residents.

- Access to public transport is a priority.

- Public open space should be close by.

- The site should be within a certain radius of the CBD or major business area.

- Access to and availability of recreational and cultural amenities should be of a good standard.

- The quality and prestige of the community should suit your target market.

In addition, weigh up the following factors:

- the quality of and access to schools

- the population density and the homogeneity of the population

- the quality of community facilities and council services

- the level of crime in the area

- the availability of medical facilities.

Site analysis

The principles of site selection discussed in chapter 4 also apply to a group dwelling development, but three specific aspects should always be considered:

- *Avoid steep sites:* To reduce the cost of expensive retaining walls, build on land that is relatively flat but with a reasonable gradient for stormwater runoff, and ensure that all the essential services, such as water, electricity, gas and sewerage, are located near the development site.

- *Look for a regularly shaped site:* For economies of scale it is always better that the plans of the units are similar, and this requires a site of regular shape. Be cautious with an irregularly shaped site as you may need a number of different designs to accommodate the maximum number of units.

- *Analyse the site regulations:* Always check the zoning, the allowable density, height restrictions and building setbacks. It is imperative to analyse these regulations by preparing a quick schematic layout. A site may be zoned for 10 units, but the reality may be that only 9 units can be comfortably accommodated on the site because of building setbacks and height restrictions.

If you are uncertain about any conditions or irregularities about a site it is advisable to consult your architect or designer before making any commitment.

Market profile

The market profile of potential buyers or renters for villa or townhouse development is varied so it can appeal to various age groups. People buy into these developments either for personal use or as a long-term investment. The four key buyer groups that can be identified are:

- *Matures:* Born between 1925 and 1945

- *Baby Boomers:* Born between 1946 and 1964

- *Generation X:* Born between 1965 and 1978

- *Generation Y:* Born between 1980 and 1994.

Two more powerful groups in this market who will live in a unit development are the *mature generation* and *new generation* (Generations X and Y), while baby boomers are the more likely investors. Summarised in the next section are the characteristics of each generation. There is another generation that will be coming into the housing market soon, and that is Generation Z. This newest generation are people born between 1997 and 2012. Research shows that most of this generation will be looking at apartment style living.

Mature generation

This group is more likely to look for a retirement village but will consider moving into a villa.

- Their priorities are comfort, lifestyle, security, companionship and a sense of community.

- They are sensitive to value, ongoing costs and paying only for what they need.

- They are sensitive to body corporate fees.

- They want to live close to family and friends.

- They want newer styles of compact residences.

- They want health and convenience services on site.

- They want to live out their last years in the one place.

Baby boomers

This generation can be broken into two groups: (a) independent and (b) independently wealthy. The first group will sell their home to buy a smaller one and are the most likely group to consider moving into a villa or townhouse as owner-occupiers.

- They are increasingly amenable to having someone maintain the property on their behalf.

- They prefer single-level living and are moving from the suburbs closer to town.

- They regard personal security as a priority.

- They welcome the opportunity to live in communities with large gates at the front.

- They appreciate luxury fittings and quality, seeing them as rewards for a lifetime of hard work.

- They want to live downstairs. This includes the master bedroom, although they are happy for other bedrooms for younger visitors to be upstairs.

- They want to see the finished product before they will buy and are very sceptical of any promises from developers and marketers.

The independently wealthy group is generally too independent to live in a medium-density development that has a body corporate.

- They are happy to buy an investment property managed by a body corporate.

- A high proportion are divorcees, which doubles the number of homes demanded but halves their purchasing power.

- They prefer zero-lot homes (homes built close to the side boundary without any building setback) and sophisticated forms of townhouses on the waterfront, golf course or other high-profile sites.

- They purchase homes for lifestyle, exclusivity and status.

- They are style and brand conscious.

- They rate residential and personal security very high.

- They need space for their diverse interests and their toys, which range from motorcycles to home entertainment systems and sports cars.

- They are late savers but enthusiastic investors. They want it now.

New Generation X and Y

These two groups are more likely to rent a villa or townhouse, as 70 per cent of them rent and are happy to continue doing so.

- They tend to rent investment homes owned by baby boomers.

- They respond to style, design and locations close to cafés and other meeting places as well as employment.

- They are well educated, are less competitive than their parents and have endless patience, rarely rushing into important decisions such as buying a house.

- They are the 'options' generation—more inclined to rent to keep their options open.

- The buyers in this age group want to be close to work, cafés and meeting places.

Market analysis

Unless the developer is building in a greenfield area or the development is larger than the norm, a market research company may play an important role. If the development is in an established area there is enough statistical data from previous sales and established trends to assist with the market research.

In order to achieve a better understanding of the targeted market, the developer and team would have to conduct research in the following areas so the correct development brief can be formulated.

Demographics

This study is to analyse the breakdown and profile of the possible buyers. The study can be broken down into age, sex, marital status, income and occupation. The research should generally be conducted within 20 kilometres of the development site.

Consumer taste

Consumer taste will vary from area to area and research into present and future consumer trends and tastes needs to be conducted. These trends can be analysed in terms of architecture, accommodation and planning. Be careful not to create an architectural masterpiece or anything outlandish as it will only appeal to a certain sector of the market and may date over time.

Consumer demand

Analysis of growth patterns in terms of population and immigration (both current and future) will have to be evaluated to justify the construction of the development. This information can be gathered from property valuers, real estate agents and the local planning commission.

Local competition

A study should be conducted to establish the details of present and future competitors in the area to evaluate if there is room for your proposed development. In addition, it should be established whether there is an adequate development margin with the pricing structure among current competitors.

Current and possible future rental

This is an important aspect when establishing the financial gearing of a project. Will current and future rentals cover the development mortgage should the market fall into a recession? The types of tenants currently occupying properties, the occupancy rate and the fees charged by local property managers should also be evaluated.

Current and possible prices of units

Current prices paid for similar developments in similar locations will indicate to the developer if there will be a profit after development costs have been deducted. An analysis of the price increases over the past few years will also give the developer some confidence, especially if the trend is upward. For developments that are new in concept it may be more difficult to establish the correct market price, which generally relies on past sales and a number of assumptions.

Development team

Creating an effective development team is not merely a case of briefing a number of consultants. Experience has shown that the team must be led and coordinated by an experienced and motivated developer or development/project manager. If the developer has in-house staff available it is in their best interest to keep strict control of the project. If not, then they should be careful in the selection and appointment of the consultants, as they may not have the same objectives. For villa or townhouse developments, the developer should appoint consultants only when necessary. If the project is small the developer can approach a project builder who specialises in building this type of unit. For a larger project, the developer may consider selecting the following consultants.

Architect or building designer

Experience is the key factor when employing an individual to design this type of project. Good designers will know the tricks of designing tight but functional residential spaces and at the same time understand the necessity of superior, cost-saving design and planning.

Quantity surveyor or estimator

The need for a quantity surveyor will depend largely on the size and complexity of the development. A building estimator may be used where a development is based on a subcontracting system and the developer does their own feasibility. In smaller developments of up to 10 units, these consultants would not necessarily be employed, especially if the project is tendered to several builders.

Civil engineer

With larger group dwellings such as a theme village of villas or townhouses, and where the site conditions are difficult, the services of a civil engineer will be required. With some local councils, the civil work has to be signed off by a qualified civil engineer.

Structural engineer

Double-storey group dwellings and designs that incorporate retaining walls will require a structural engineer to design and document all the structural elements.

Land surveyor

As most villa and townhouse developments are sold on a strata-title basis, a good land surveyor who has a good understanding of the various regulations, especially the strata title acts, is essential.

Conveyancer

The transfer and settlement of sales are paramount to your cash flow, especially in this type of development, so an inexperienced or inefficient conveyancer could cost the project a great deal of money.

Solicitor

A legal expert has an important role in drafting the purchase agreements, especially if the units in the project are to be sold off the plan.

Design considerations

Because of the need to maximise the number of units on a site, townhouses and villas can be difficult to design well. Often the council planning codes complicate rather than help the matter. The need for solar- and energy-efficient design often conflicts with the need for cost-efficient design. The margin for error is not as great as with the design of suburban houses, where, if it is not quite right, the owner can adjust a feature later or grow a tree to hide it. Townhouses are more intricate structures, and because of the fire safety requirements of building regulations as well as the limitations of body corporate organisations, it is rare that individual owners can do much about built-in design faults.

As noted earlier, the key to successful group housing or multiple dwelling developments is the appointment of an experienced architect or building designer who understands the needs of the consumer and has the skills to handle cost-effective design. More importantly, they should have a good knowledge of the building codes and council regulations and have the ability to come up with a good design within these restrictions. A good architect or building designer should take the following design requirements into account.

Theme

If a special character or theme is adopted it should follow through to all design elements of the buildings. Creating a unique theme would give the development a unique identity and a marketing edge.

Scale

The scale, height and density should suit the characteristics of the surrounding area. Ensure that the buildings do not appear overbearing or claustrophobic. Create an ambience with both good vistas and a domestic feel.

Privacy

Planning for privacy can be a problem when density requirements are high, especially with townhouses. Designers should use their skills to plan for visual privacy and a minimum of noise penetration between units.

Daylight

The internal planning should incorporate as much daylight as possible. This can be achieved by larger windows, which will provide better ventilation as well as a greater sense of space. Be careful to avoid having large windows facing the hot westerly sun.

Energy conservation

With our extreme climatic conditions, architects and designers should plan units with the correct orientation in order to reduce the need for air-conditioning and artificial heating.

Security

With the crime rate on the increase, security in higher density developments has become an important design factor. Incorporating good fencing and security systems will boost the sale of the units.

Maintenance free

Ongoing long-term external maintenance can become a burden to a body corporate that has to increase levies to unit owners. More buyers and investors are aware of these problems and are attracted to developments with less maintenance.

Communal facilities

Depending on the size of the development and to make the project more marketable, the developer should consider incorporating communal facilities such as a swimming pool, gymnasium and workshop.

Cost factors

Compared with a renovation or a single residential development, a higher density project will require a more detailed feasibility study and should take into account a number of cost factors. These include:

- land cost
- rezoning cost (if necessary)

- connection and headwork fees (includes all essential services such as water, electricity, gas and sewerage)

- bulk services—if they are not adjacent to the property the cost of providing such services could have a major impact on the feasibility of the project

- development approval and building plan fees

- developer's contribution—mainly in built-up suburban areas where densities have increased and councils require developers to contribute to additional infrastructure requirements to the area

- site cost—is there a gentle fall across the site and are there any large trees to be removed?

- construction cost—what type of construction and building contract will be used?

- holding cost—plan your phases to suit your cash flow

- escalation costs—have these been taken into account in establishing the sale price of the units?

- development manager's or project manager's fees

- professional fees

- insurance—employ a competent broker and read all the fine print

- rates and taxes

- transportation levy and any other government levies or fees

- external development cost (such as road widening)

- bank charges and fees

- marketing—brochures, site billboards and displays

- sales commissions

- contingency—set aside an amount of money for unforeseen expenses.

Finance

Since the global financial crisis (GFC) lenders' requirements have become more stringent. Financiers look for developers with experience and a good track record. Apprentice developers should include an experienced person in their development team, such as a project or development manager.

Every financier will study the developer's feasibility carefully but, more importantly, will look at market evidence in terms of sales within the development area. This evidence is critical, as most financiers will base their lending decisions on this factor and whether there is still a demand for such a development. In some instances, pre-sales or sales-off-plan are critical to gain project finance. In some instances the pre-sales requirement will be up to 100 per cent of the amount being borrowed. In general, financiers will lend up to 70 per cent of the total development cost (TDC) or 65 per cent of end value (EV). For example, if a project has a TDC of $5 million and the EV is $6 million then they will lend either $3.5 million or $3.9 million.

If the development is large — say, 30 units — it would be wise to develop it in three phases, as besides mitigating development risks it makes financing easier. For example, the total development cost (TDC) is $7.5 million, made up of land of $1.5 million, which is fully paid up, and building plus consultant costs of $6 million. If the first-phase building and consultants cost is $2 million, the developer will be borrowing 57 per cent ($2 million/$3.5 million) of the TDC. If the whole project is being developed, then the leverage position will be 80 per cent ($6 million/$7.5 million) of TDC, which will be too high for most financiers, and the developer would have to look for more equity.

Contracts

If you are not a builder developer, the type of contract to be signed will depend on the size of the project and possibly the phasing of the overall development. Your architect or development manager would be able to advise which contract would be most applicable. Whichever contract you use, ensure that you have rates for variations confirmed before formalising, as invariably your purchasers will request alterations to your standard plans or specifications. Most importantly, always negotiate a fixed-price contract even if the development is in phases.

Another contract that can be considered is a design and construct contract. A developer can approach project builders who specialise in this type of construction and have in-house designers who will undertake all the planning issues. The downside of this approach is that the developer is locked in with the specific builder without knowing if the price could be lower, as the plans have not been competitively tendered. Alternatively, it may be worthwhile for the developer to appoint their own architect or designer, complete a set of estimating drawings (partial working drawings) together with a specification, and then tender these to several builders. The architect or designer will be novated to the selected builder, who will then pay the architect or designer the balance of their fees for the working drawings. Another positive with this approach is that should the project be over budget, the developer can work with the builder to analyse cost savings before the final working drawings are completed.

Marketing

Consider the following aspects when marketing a villa or townhouse development.

In-house marketing

If your development is a reasonable size and will take a number of months to complete, it may be preferable to create your own marketing division. Not only will you have better control over the marketing, but you will also have sales consultants who are dedicated to and focused on selling your project. If you follow this route make sure you employ experienced salespeople who understand the scheme and construction principles.

External marketing

If you have to use an external agent make sure that they keep their promises and keep them on their toes.

Selling off the plan (pre-sales)

Using this system in marketing will require some excellent presentation drawings and advertising material. With modern CAD software, virtual walk-through of various interiors can be created, which will assist buyers in visualising the finished product.

Display unit

Some purchasers do not buy homes and units off plan, so a completed display unit would assist in marketing. The display unit should never be the larger and better unit as purchasers would expect the same and this could lead to disappointments and possible disputes.

Strata title

All home units, villa units and townhouses are sold under strata or company titles. For the prospective buyer this means legal relations with all other titleholders in the development. The titleholders may be residents, absentee landlord investors renting the unit, the developer holding unsold units, and mortgagees with first mortgagee's rights.

Developers at the early stage of the project should consider engaging a strata-title management company to handle all the body corporate affairs. Alternatively, they can undertake the management of the building's affairs by forming a body corporate together with the new purchasers. Of course, the latter approach would save the management fee normally paid to another company. It is advisable, however, to use the services of an independent management company, as they would act as an independent party whereas members drawn from among the titleholders might have their own private agendas that could lead to conflict. In addition, should the administrator of the body corporate sell their unit there would be no continuity of the administrative work.

The legal relations are described in the title, the by-laws, and the minutes of the body corporate or the board of directors meetings. These, along with the minutes and accounts of the body corporate or the company, the insurance policies, the Strata Plan and Unit Entitlement, property maintenance contracts, and performance of the managing agent, if one has been appointed, have to be kept up to date and in a retrievable format.

Property maintenance requires careful attention by the body corporate. Villas and townhouses and retirement villages are more complex buildings than private homes. The property maintenance involves the grounds and gardens, as well as the buildings and their electrical, water, drainage, ventilation, security and lift services. Repairs can sometimes involve tens or hundreds of thousands of dollars.

Summary

With increases in immigration, baby boomers reaching retirement age, natural population growth and the scarcity of land close to the city, a golden opportunity has been created for housing developers. Most developers tend to sell their product to the public but this is not the way to get rich, especially after tax issues have been taken into account. Some astute developers have accumulated great wealth by selling a few units and renting out the rest, providing themselves with a wonderful cash flow in their retirement years.

Instead of waiting for a government pension or for your superannuation to payout (which will eventually dry up), start building a portfolio of housing units. If you are concerned about over-gearing then sell one part of the development, but definitely retain the other portion for rental or get an equity partner involved with your project.

Case study

The development site was made up of four individual lots located on land with an R17.5/R40 zoning. The development proposal (see figure 15.2, overleaf) included developing the site into 16 affordable villa units on surveyed strata lots. The four lots can be developed in two phases of eight villa units each, or two lots can be developed separately as an eight-villa unit development.

Figure 15.2: Queens Park site plan

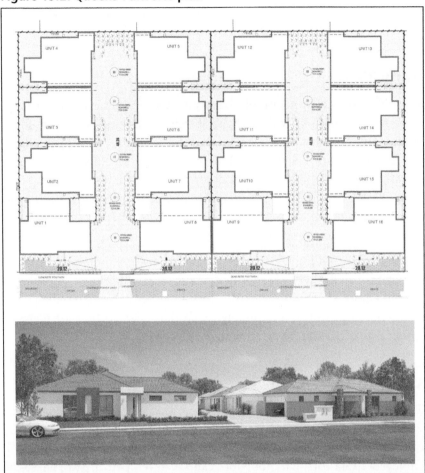

Figure reproduced courtesy of Urban Villages Pty Ltd.

The development fitted perfectly into a survey strata lot model. This development model aimed to limit the risk to the developer by pre-selling the units through its marketing network and contracting a builder to build the units on behalf of the buyers. Table 15.1 shows the prefeasibility study for this project.

Table 15.1: villa development—Queens Park 16—prefeasibility study

Income	Amount	Sub-total	Total
Projected Sales			
16 units @ $405 000 each	$6 480 000.00		
less Contracted Unit @ $150 000	$2 400 001.60	$4 079 998.40	
Less: GST		$ 370 871.85	**$3 709 126.55**
Less development cost	**Amount**	**Sub-total**	**Total**
Land purchase cost			
Purchase	$1 800 000.00		
Stamp duty	$ 96 000.00		
Conveyancing fees (purchase)	$ 2 487.00	$1 898 487.00	
Consultants			
Development/Project Manager	$ 137 557.56		
Town/Urban Planner	$ 5 200.00		
Engineers / Civil / Electrical	$ 31 200.00		
Surveyor	$ 9 600.00		
Geotechnical Engineer	$ 4 000.00		
Architect (DA Drawings)	$ 12 000.00	$ 199 557.56	
Council and government			
Statutory fees	$ 6 880.00		
Western Power design fees	$ 16 000.00		
Valuation / Unit Entitlement	$ 5 920.00		
Developer's Contribution	$ 72 000.00	$ 100 800.00	
Construction works			
Construction ($25 000 pu + GST)	$ 400 001.60		
Demolition	$ 28 801.60		
Headwork's ($6000 pu + GST)	$ 96 001.60		
Contingency 10%	$ 41 984.38	$ 566 789.18	

(continued)

Table 15.1: villa development—Queens Park 16—prefeasibility study *(cont'd)*

Less development cost	Amount	Sub-total	Total
Real estate and legal			
Legal fees	$ 4000.00		
Selling fees (2.0%)	$ 129600.00		
Conveyancing fees (sale)		$133600.00	
Less: GST input tax credits		$ 90967.88	$2808265.87
Margin before Interest			$ 900860.68
Less Borrowing Interest			$ 144000.00
Profit margin			$ 756860.68
Total development cost			$3853126.55
Margin on development cost			20%
Margin on equity (assume 50%)	$1504132.93		50%

CHAPTER 16

Apartment developments

Before the 1970s very few Australians lived in high-rise flats or apartments, and, if they did, they were either tenants of various state housing commissions, or lived in such unusual residential areas as Kings Cross and Potts Point in Sydney. High-rise living was almost 'un-Australian'.

Over the past decade we have seen a surge in new apartment blocks in most capital cities of Australia. One of the motivating factors is the drive by town planners to bring more life to the city after normal business hours. In addition, with increasing workloads in the 1990s and the demand for convenience, older style inner-city suburbs have increased in popularity. Land values closer to the central business district are increasing and inner-city housing is becoming more and more expensive. These high land values in turn have forced densities to increase so developers can use this expensive land more efficiently by constructing well-planned apartments.

While urban-style apartments have recently become popular, a substantial number of holiday apartments were developed in the building boom of the 1970s in Queensland and significantly on the Gold Coast, which now has a fair sprinkling of 15-, 20- and even 30-storey high-rise apartment buildings located close to recreation facilities, or taking advantage of spectacular beaches and views.

The demand and development principles of apartment buildings are similar in many respects to medium-density housing described in the previous chapter. This includes the benefits and risks, the development process, team selection and finance. However, this chapter highlights some of the distinct differences between these two types of developments.

One of the major differences from a risk point of view is that villas and townhouses can be built in phases and according to demand, whereas with an apartment building the developer's risk is higher as there is a commitment to develop a single building with many units that cannot be phased or staged.

Types of apartments

Basically there are two types of apartment developments: urban and holiday. The accommodation and size of these apartments will to a greater degree depend on the targeted market but are similar in planning concepts. An apartment development can be defined as a building that incorporates five or more housing units on different floor levels and can be further categorised in the following way:

- *Low-rise*: Two to three storeys without elevators
- *Mid-rise*: Three to eight storeys with elevators
- *High-rise*: More than eight storeys with elevators.

Low-rise

Low-rise apartment complexes are usually located in the outer suburbs where the density zoning is lower than those closer to the CBD. With no lifts they are also known as *three-storey walk-ups*. The structural system discipline of a low-rise is not as strict as for a mid- or high-rise building, which means they offer more flexibility in design. In addition, the building codes are far more liberal, particularly in regard to fireproofing. Parking is generally 'on grade' at ground level, which is less costly than basement parking.

Mid-rise

Mid-rise apartments are buildings up to eight storeys high. This height is defined by the accessibility of a fire-engine ladder, which is 24 metres in length. In terms of the Building Code of Australia (BCA) any building above this height requires a sprinkler system, which from a developer's viewpoint is an additional cost. These buildings, which average between five and eight storeys in height, are developed in suburbs adjacent to the CBD or within Transport Oriented Development (TOD) sites. The structural system of a mid-rise apartment is not as flexible as a low-rise because of the additional loading of the floors above. Underground parking serving mid-rises is not uncommon, with the number of units absorbing the cost of parking.

High-rise

The design of high-rise apartment buildings is limited by the structural system, which is mainly concrete or steel frame, and the vertical lift core plays a major role. The vertical repetitiveness of the high-rise demands considerable design discipline, which means, with some exceptions, that all apartment floors are similar. With higher plot ratios offered and less parking requirements these high-rise developments are found mainly in the CBD. High-rise apartments generally offer a variety of accommodation, from studio apartments to penthouses on the top floors. A high-rise can also be part of mixed-use development, with retail, commercial or restaurants on the ground level and the first floor.

Types of apartment units

Depending on locality and market requirements, apartment units can be categorised or designed into the following segments:

- *Penthouses*: Usually located on the top floor of an apartment block and generally occupying the whole floor

- *Luxury*: Spacious and lavishly decorated to appeal to the executive, with at least two bedrooms, two bathrooms plus a study, and in excess of 150m^2

- *Three-bedroom apartments*: Mainly for a growing family, with an internal floor area ranging from 100m^2 to 150m^2

- *Two-bedroom apartments*: For singles and married couples, with one or two bathrooms and with an internal area between 70m^2 to 90m^2

- *One-bedroom apartment*: Predominantly for singles but also for young couples, with an internal area ranging from 50m^2 to 65m^2

- *Studio apartments*: Also known as a bedsitter and mainly for singles with an independent lifestyle, with a minimum area of 40m^2.

The provision of parking facilities for these varying types of apartments will depend firstly on local council requirements and secondly on market considerations. If the location of the apartment development does not have access to good public transport, a minimum of one parking bay per apartment may be required. If the location is within a transport hub then less parking will be required.

The mix of apartments will depend on the market and demographic research undertaken by the developer and team. Some local council regulations stipulate that at least 20 per cent of units in new apartment developments should be single-bedrooms.

Demand for apartment living

Over the past decade a number of factors have influenced the types of dwellings being added to Australia's housing stock. The demand for more variety in dwelling types has been influenced by changes in the age structure of the population, and household and family composition and size, as well as demand for lower priced accommodation and housing closer to employment centres.

Government planning policies

During this period government and urban planners have supported and promoted increased housing choice, essentially increasing the availability of various types of higher density housing. Other factors influenced this policy push towards higher density housing, including the increased price of land close to city centres, the infrastructure costs of developing non-urban land and environmental concerns relating to the spread of urban development. The creation of urban sprawl requires additional road infrastructure and public transport at a cost to the government and taxpayers, making it untenable.

Increased cost in suburban land

Besides the cost of raw land, the cost to subdivide land is now averaging between $60 000 and $100 000 per lot. Developers experience greater difficulties in absorbing unforeseen costs because of barriers such as government planning system complexity, uncertain time frames and unpredictable costs. A lack of process transparency, inconsistent planning requirements across local government areas and a lack of trust between local councils have also emerged as significant barriers to negotiating the planning system and have impacted significantly on the development costs, which have been passed on to the homebuyer.

Change in lifestyle

Today Australians live quite differently from how their parents did. The size of households is shrinking and they are working longer, starting families later, and have less time for other activities. This means proximity to cafés, shops, transport and lifestyle amenities is becoming more important than owning a piece of land with a big backyard for the dog and extra bedrooms for the kids. In addition, baby boomers who were previously content with living in their family home after the kids had moved out are increasingly seeking to sell their big, high-maintenance four-bedroom homes so they can live in smaller, lower maintenance, lock-and-leave apartments near amenities, shops and café strips.

Family composition

Research undertaken by property analyst Michael Matusik clearly shows that single- or two-person households are on the rise, comprising more than 60 per cent of the housing market. The Australian Bureau of Statistics (ABS) suggests there will be an additional 1.7 million single-person households over the next two decades. They also predict that couples without children will eventually outnumber the typical 'nuclear family', and sooner rather than later, with the takeover due to happen around 2031. This means that not only will we require more housing to satisfy the needs of our growing population, but they will also need to be smaller dwellings, in keeping with demand.

Affordability

According to a 2014 IMF report, the Australian housing market is among the most expensive in the world. The IMF's Global Housing Watch has Australia ranked as the third least affordable place in the world to buy a house, behind only Belgium and Canada. In addition, Australia's housing debt to disposable income ratio is at a record level, which means many do not qualify for a housing loan, forcing them to rent. Therefore apartment developers are creating smaller units in an attempt to keep prices lower.

Investors

Due to the increase in the rental market, investors are buying into apartments close to amenities. Generous incentives, including negative gearing and concessions on capital gains tax, encourage investment in housing, to the extent that around one in seven Australian taxpayers now owns one or more investment properties. Overseas investors are adding to that demand. The Foreign Investment Review Board enables global investors to buy new housing in Australia. Along with Canada, Australia has emerged from the 2008 global financial crisis as a stable economy and good investment prospect with one of the strongest property markets in the world.

Advantages, disadvantages and challenges

Apartment developments have the following advantages over other types of developments:

- efficient use of land due to higher plot ratios, meaning more building to land value
- rewards for entrepreneurial efforts with high profit margins
- less sophistication required due to repetitiveness of construction
- variety of sizes and prices, from one to three bedrooms, to suit a variety of purchasers
- broad rental market due to location and amenities
- good resale market if well located and well designed
- relatively stable cash flows for long-term investment
- rapid depreciation write-off and high tax-shelter potential.

Developments in large apartment complexes may have additional advantages over developments in smaller apartment buildings because of decreases in per-unit operating costs (due to scale economics) and ease of renting due to the additional amenities (pools, tennis courts) that large apartment buildings may provide. However, apartment development may involve some or all of the following disadvantages:

- incomplete market assessment, such as of consumers' needs
- consumers' inability to pay projected sales price or rents
- competition from other projects, either existing or in development promotion
- inappropriate site or location
- politics of community opposition to apartment development
- project funding difficulties because developer lacks a track record or experience
- higher demands for management time, skill and money
- greater exposure to government regulations
- transient tenants and no key tenants to bank the development
- exposure to overbuilding and swings in residential construction cycles.

To be successful in apartment developments, the developer has to overcome the following challenges:

- securing sufficient operating capital
- planning for long-term responsibilities
- building or contracting for specialised skills in finance and asset management
- understanding the broader housing market, both short and long term
- managing a large development team of both staff and contractors
- facing political and community opposition
- the availability of suitable and affordable development sites
- understanding and handling complex laws and regulations.

Selecting the project type and site

The selection of an apartment development project involves consideration of both size and location. The size desired will depend on available capital, market demand, lender attitudes, site limitations, and the developer's own willingness to accept risk and handle operations at various project sizes.

The location may be a question of opportunity or individual judgement. Quite often experienced developers will seize upon an available option if the terms are right and the location appears viable. Where there is an opportunity to choose it pays to consider the alternatives before selecting a site. The preferred site should be large enough to accommodate a project of the right size, located in an area or neighbourhood that will attract potential buyers able to pay the price. In addition, the site should have:

- high visibility

- adequate soil conditions

- good drainage

- availability of all services

- pleasant environment and surroundings

- appropriate access and egress

- distinguishing amenities such as a good view

- access to public transport and shopping

- access to restaurants and entertainment facilities

- access to public parks and other communal facilities.

The required zoning should be in place or available within a reasonable period of time. Environmental or other constraints limiting development must not be unduly restrictive, and the site should be available on terms that give the developer maximum freedom to investigate the site before committing large amounts of money, if possible under an option agreement that can be extended if necessary.

Role of the developer

The fledgling developer looking at developing apartments as an ongoing business should give thought to their long-term goals and what resources they have available. They have to be aware of the two main external limitations to their goals—that is, the availability of good development sites and the limits to their financial resources. As most apartment developments require greater capital commitment and time when compared with smaller villa developments, depending on their financial position developers can play one of the following three roles.

Co-developer

This structure requires the least amount of personal time and participation. It is an ideal starting place for a novice developer who would like to learn about apartment development from an experienced developer with a good track record. It leaves most of the daily development activities to the experienced developer. Joining forces as a co-developer, the fledging developer can bring one or more of the following resources to the development effort:

- cash and upfront development money
- equity for land purchases
- a strong financial balance sheet
- extensive business experience and network
- strong ongoing relationships with other potential investors
- back-office support to ensure compliance with all rules and deadlines.

Sole developer with track record

In this development model, the experienced developer with a track record generally works on their own but is surrounded by independent and knowledgeable consultants they have worked with in the past. This developer handles the following tasks:

- finding land and analysing the viability of the project

- working closely with a team of trusted consultants

- structuring all financial aspects

- working with silent investors and other potential investors

- handling all financing and cash flow needs

- managing the project on behalf of the investors.

Developer with in-house expertise

In this model, the developer must have strong technical knowledge and experience in tax, financing, legal and construction activities. The model also requires an organisational commitment to ongoing apartment development to justify the high overhead costs associated with the business. This developer is either a private or a public corporate entity that has made apartment development a long-term business. This developer:

- procures potential development projects

- has an in-house design and estimating team

- has a construction division that undertakes all the construction work

- has a financial division that raises equity capital from investors through a fund or a syndicate.

Buyer profile

The following categories can be considered specific or niche markets in typical apartment developments around Australia. A particular apartment might fit more than one niche to a greater or lesser degree, but it is important it fits at least one.

Corporate market

A corporation or interstate company will generally be prepared to pay a significantly higher price or rent for the apartment they want as it will still be far less expensive than providing an employee with hotel accommodation. To appeal to the corporate market an apartment development should be a modern-style designed building, with full security, within a few minutes' walking distance of the occupants' workplace, and be capable of being fully serviced. This market's ideal location is in the CBD and within walking distance of their office.

City professionals

Professional people working in the city increasingly choose to live close to their office. These people want a city lifestyle, such as cafés, quality restaurants and night life, ahead of accommodation facilities. Quality finishes are more important than space, and the location is important as well. Smart developers will develop as close as possible to major office towers and the appropriate city lifestyle facilities.

Short-term rentals

Short-term rentals or short-stay accommodation for tourists and business visitors achieve significantly higher rental levels than longer term residential rents. In order to attract such tenants the building should be fully furnished and well managed. In developing such apartments the developer's strategy would be to hold the development as a long-term investment or to sell some apartments to offset some of their borrowing cost and hold the balance.

Lifestyle buyers

A wide range of young professionals, semi-retired couples or empty nesters prefer the concept of living in a building that offers an individual lifestyle. The lifestyle can be created by common area facilities, such as a gym, swimming pool, terraces with a view and concierge service.

Singles resident market

Unmarried or divorced people who prefer to live independently look for one-bedroom units, studio-style apartments, loft-style units or bedsitter-type apartments. The style of building is not a prerequisite, but price and rental should be affordable and restaurants and entertainment close by.

Investors

Investors buy an apartment for the short term or the long term. With the former, the investor normally buys off plan in the hope of selling the unit at an escalated price once completed. The long-term investor buys as part of their property portfolio or buys and rents for a period of time until they occupy the building in their later years.

Buyer demand for apartments is in many respects closely tied to the same economic, monetary and consumer variables affecting the demand for single-family homes. However, there are certain important differences between the characteristics of apartment buyers and homebuyers:

- Apartment buyers are more sensitive to commute distances.
- Apartment buyers are more sensitive to access to public transportation.
- Apartment buyers are more mobile and willing to move to more attractive, newer or popular apartments.
- Apartment buyers are more sensitive to distances to shopping facilities, and recreational and cultural amenities.
- Apartment buyers are more sensitive to amenities and building age.
- Apartment buyers' incomes are more vulnerable in periods of recession.
- Apartment buyers tend to be in the lower and upper age brackets.

Design and planning aspects

The developer's appointed architect should be briefed on the following design aspects in order to ensure that an apartment development is cost effective and appealing to the market being targeted.

Maximise usable plot ratio

The usable plot ratio is the habitable square metres relative to the site area. For example, if the site is 2000 square metres and the plot ratio is 1, then 2000 square metres of habitable area can be constructed. The habitable area does not include public corridors, stairways, lifts, mechanical and electrical rooms, storerooms, balconies and, depending on the council, bathroom areas. While it is preferable to maximise the available plot ratio, this may not always be the case, as some markets may require at least one parking bay for each apartment even if it is not a council requirement, which leads to an additional, costly multi-level parking area.

Exterior design

For a property to be competitive in the marketplace, its design should fit with or be better than other properties in the neighbourhood and not be considered dated by local standards. External façade treatments such as feature stone and glazed balustrades help create a point of difference to attract buyers, as long as the extra cost can be recouped in the sales price. The use of non-maintenance materials should be considered as maintenance on multi-level buildings can prove to be expensive over the long term.

Unit size and mix

The size of each unit in a residential property should be reviewed to make sure it conforms to the market demand. One-bedroom apartments with 100 square metres are not feasible in today's market. There is a trend away from three-bedroom apartments to two bedroom plus two bathrooms, two bedrooms plus one bathroom and one bedroom plus one bathroom apartments for reasons of affordability. Determine whether the mix of units in each size meets the current market demand. If the property has only two-bedroom units in a market that demands one-bedrooms, then there will be a potential marketing problem.

Energy conservation

Given the high cost of energy, developers will need to evaluate the utility system for the development and the conservation techniques being used to reduce energy costs. Consideration should be given to the solar orientation of the building, wall insulation, double glazing, solar panels and low voltage light fittings, for example. The energy efficiency of appliances should be checked before they are specified.

Security

People who move into apartment buildings are security conscious. As most apartments are well above ground, entry from outside through windows or balconies is less likely than in a two- or three-storey townhouse building. However, because public areas, such as basement car parks, lobbies, lifts and corridors, are anonymous environments, and with more people living in the building it is easier for intruders to go unnoticed. Consider security systems such as electronic keying systems with video or voice access and closed circuit television (CCTV) in public areas and parking areas. Depending on the security risks in the area and the size and cost of the development, security staff may also be engaged in patrolling or controlling access to the building.

Noise

Most apartment buildings are built in noisy locations such as on major transport routes. Traffic noise is part of their natural environment. While most occupants get used to this type of noise they would object to noise coming from adjacent neighbours. Design and material selection should aim to minimise noise penetration between units. Double glazing will help reduce external noise. An acoustic engineer will assist in providing solutions in areas with high noise levels.

Privacy

Occupants' privacy is paramount in apartment buildings. When planning the development, the architect should ensure each unit has its own privacy by locating windows or balconies of one unit so as not to allow views of neighbours' bedrooms, bathrooms, living areas or outside spaces. If this cannot be achieved because of tight planning conditions, then privacy screens or obscure glazing can be strategically placed.

Balconies

Apartment units above ground level deny the occupants at these levels access to the ground so a balcony becomes their only private outdoor living space. Balconies should be large enough to accommodate an outdoor setting such as a table and chairs. A balcony of 3.5 metres by 1.8 metres is the minimum that should be provided. Some local authorities have regulated that a minimum area of 10 square metres be provided for each apartment. In addition, units at a higher level will encounter windy conditions. The balustrade should give some protection while still allowing occupants to enjoy the view from a seated position in the living room.

Lobbies, corridors and passages

Public areas such as lift lobbies, corridors or passages to the various apartments create either a good or a bad impression of a new apartment development. These areas should be well lit, preferably by natural light, and well ventilated. Dark and dingy public areas are not only unsightly but also unhealthy.

Communal facilities

Provision of communal facilities in an apartment development will depend on the size and type of the building, and the lifestyle of the occupants. Facilities could include a swimming pool, gymnasium and spa. However, careful consideration should be given to the design of these facilities as they are costly items not only at installation but also in terms of long-term maintenance, which adds to the strata levies.

Exclusivity

Apartments being developed in a competitive location should offer buyers something that is exclusive in order to give the building a marketing edge. This could be a unique architectural style, better communal facilities, views or vistas, or the latest technical systems or appliances. While developers should aim to maximise the number of units in a new project, they should not sacrifice quality for quantity.

Window cleaning

Cleaning of exterior of windows in apartments at higher levels is difficult unless they face the balcony or a cleaning ledge is provided. How the windows will be cleaned should be considered during the planning stages. There are specially designed windows with openings that pivot, allowing the exterior section to be cleaned.

Air-conditioning

Given Australia's hot summers, most apartment dwellers will want air-conditioning units installed, unless they have not been provided for as part of the initial contract. Most air-conditioning units are very unsightly if not planned for and located in discreet locations. If units are not provided, make sure that there is a specified location and size of unit, where the unit does not look unsightly. Special ventilated screening will help to conceal these units from the public eye.

Clothes drying

According to the national building codes all new apartment developments should provide facilities for clothes drying. If an electric clothes dryer is not included in each apartment then an outdoor area with clotheslines should be provided. In larger apartment complexes a central laundry room can be provided.

Apartment development principles

Many of the relevant development principles have been described in earlier chapters of this book. However, it is worth noting and repeating those principles that relate specifically to apartment developments, as the risk and commitment to this type of development are higher compared with other residential developments.

Land purchase

Before purchasing a potential apartment development site, the developer should undertake a residual land analysis, starting with how many apartments the site can accommodate and the average sale price for an apartment in the area, then deducting risk profit, professional fees, construction cost, marketing, interest and so on, to arrive at a residual land value. For example, if a potential site of 2000m² has a plot ratio of 1 then 2000m² of habitable area can be built on, and if the average apartment is 65m² then 31 (2000/65) apartments can be accommodated. Using a selling price of $450 000 for an average unit, the analysis in table 16.1 can be considered.

Table 16.1: residual land analysis for apartments

Item	Amount
Selling price per apartment:	$ 450 000
Less marketing cost:	$ 20 000
Less targeted profit:	$ 85 000
Less consultant fees:	$ 40 000
Less construction cost:	$ 190 000
Less finance cost:	$ 35 000
Less miscellaneous cost:	$ 35 000
Residual land value/unit	$ 45 000
Total land value for 31 units	$1 395 000

The above analysis is described only in principle. A developer should undertake a more detailed analysis with further research related to the specific site.

Site analysis

When viewing the site, the developer should find out the following related to the site:

- Look at the vehicular access and egress and if it is safe. Consider how refuse collection will operate, as large refuse trucks need space for collection.

- Check the soil conditions, especially if the site had any previous industrial use. Environmental and remedial work may be required.

- Look at the gradient of the site. A sloping site can at times be of benefit for an apartment project as the lower levels can be used for parking below the building.

- Check headwork charges. Increases in density and numbers of people using utility services will impact on the cost, especially if the site is some distance away from existing utilities.

The above list briefly outlines some potential areas to consider. The developer should visit the site with key consultants to pick up any other items of concern.

Team selection

In an apartment development project it is typical to work with a larger team of consultants, including lawyers, accountants, architects and specialists in financing and structuring a deal. The developer will require the coordinated activities of design, building, legal, property management and financing experts. Capable individuals who work well as a team will increase the likelihood of long-term success. The work involved in putting together this type of residential development is very detailed and even the most experienced developers know that there are no short cuts and would use professional advice from the best advisors. Good consultants are:

- respected in their community or have regional or national reputations

- well capitalised and very experienced

- successful in their previous development efforts.

Apartment developments have four general phases.

Prefeasibility analysis

All of the previous discussion concerning the calculation and analysis of feasibility studies and cash flow applies to an apartment development. The prefeasibility analysis for apartments should include consideration of other costs that may be unique to the area where the apartment project is located. These costs can relate to:

- compliance with local health, zoning, building and environmental regulations

- developer's contribution required for improvement to the existing infrastructure

- waste and refuse disposal restrictions

- elevator maintenance requirements

- sprinkler systems and additional firefighting equipment

- building compliance and occupancy certificates

- business licences and taxes

- additional liability insurance cost

- in-house management requirements due to local landlord-tenant laws.

In addition, carefully estimate cash flows for the development process. These should be calculated on a month by month basis from the start to settlement of sales, evaluating the largest cash drain during the project. Long-term financial risk can be reduced by budgeting sufficient reserves. Banks and investors often require operating reserves of six months' debt service and operating costs. Therefore this reserve or contingency should be allowed for in the cash flow analysis.

Finance

Development and construction funding has been fully explained in earlier chapters. For apartment development the same finance principles apply. Banks and lenders would finance 75 to 80 per cent of the TDC (total development cost) or 60 to 65 per cent of the end value with a prerequisite of pre-sales to the value of the debt. With more developers entering the apartment market and the increasing need for creative funding, there are now finance products available that assist a developer in keeping most of the profits or that speed up the pre-sales process.

Developers who are confident in their project and do not wish to take on investor partners or dilute their shareholding can look at *mezzanine funding*. Mezzanine funding is generally placed after the senior debt as a second mortgage. However, mezzanine funding requires higher interest rates and upfront costs. The developer who intends using mezzanine funding should undertake a comparative analysis between this funding and investor equity.

On the pre-sale there are finance and insurance companies willing to underwrite the resale requirement from a bank. The fee for this undertaking is relatively high but it will help to speed up the development process. Sometimes this underwriting is worth considering, especially if construction prices look set to rise in the near future.

Building contractors

Besides securing a fixed-price contract, quality control for apartment construction is another vital development issue. Buyers can see the difference between good and poor quality. The initial buyers can be the developers' greatest marketing tool. Therefore selecting the cheapest builder or the builder without a reputation for quality workmanship could spell disaster for the development and the developer's future career.

Finishes are the most important item in terms of quality control for apartments, because these are what the buyers see first and most. Attention to detail is a priority. Throughout the construction process the developer's team should carry out regular quality-control inspections and should increase this emphasis throughout the finishing process.

Project marketing

If a condition of construction finance is for the developer to secure a certain percentage of pre-sales before a bank will allow their funds to be committed to the project, the developer has to choose the best project marketing team and have an adequate marketing budget. The developer has to find a successful project marketer with full knowledge of the market who can provide a marketing strategy and team that can pre-sell the development off plan. Most project marketers would want an exclusive mandate or contract. This is fine for a smaller development but for a large-scale development the developer should look to at least two groups, creating a competitive environment.

When selecting a project marketer, it is wise to find out about their track record, their investors or buyer database and whether they are using all the modern marketing technology tools such as Facebook and blogs, as many apartment buyers are younger people.

Renting

If the aim is to hold onto all or some of the apartment units as an investment then a minimum of rent increases can be expected during the life of the lease. Most apartment rents rise in line with CPI increases, but do not expect annual rent increases of more than 3 per cent. A low rent with a good tenant is far better than a higher rent with a bad tenant. The lower you can set your rents, the broader the market you can reach. Depending on your rental property portfolio, it is best to have a good property manager managing your rentals and to stay at arm's length from tenants should problems arise.

Summary

Apartment development is demanding and difficult, but when the timing and market variables are in place it can also be rewarding. Current market conditions that affect apartment development favourably include attractive interest rates, an aging baby boomer market seeking less upkeep but more luxury, and a growing Australian economy. Waterfront views and good access to amenities are examples of key elements for successful apartment developments.

Although demand for suburban houses will continue strongly in the future, there is definitely a shift towards apartment living in our cities. Some people will still be keen to move to the outer suburbs in order to buy a house with a backyard, but more Australians are choosing to live close to work, and that usually means living in an apartment. This solid and increasing demand means apartments make great investments, offering stronger capital and rental growth than houses in the outer suburbs, and this trend is likely to increase in the future.

Case study

The site is made up of two blocks with a total area of 1214.14 square metres. An existing warehouse houses a motor panel business and there is an existing car park. As this is a brownfield site, there are utilities such as power, water and drainage, but they have to be upgraded to allow for the increase in occupants of the site. The site is surrounded by a number of older buildings and recently completed apartments. The street has been upgraded to keep in line with the new developments. This project was contracted on a design and construct basis. The development is summarised in table 16.2, with an artist's rendition in figure 16.1. Table 16.3 shows a prefeasibility study for the project.

Table 16.2: development summary

Proposal	55 strata-titled apartment units
Site details	Existing building to be demolished Area: 1214.14 square metres
Building	Basement plus 6 levels above ground
Types of units	12 × 1 bedroom units 41 × 1 bedroom plus study units (some 2 bedroom) 2 × 3 bedroom units
Price of units	From $350000.00 to $675000.00
Achievable rents	1 bedroom — $430 to $460 per week (unfurnished) 1 bedroom plus study — $440 to 470 per week (unfurnished) 3 bedroom — $620 to $660 per week (unfurnished)
Financials	Total development cost — $15.56 million (without interest) Total sales after commission — $20.50 million (net after GST and commission)

Figure 16.1: artist's rendition of development

Figure reproduced courtesy of Archiplan Pty Ltd.

Table 16.3: brown street apartments — prefeasibility study

INCOME	Amount	Sub-total	Total
Total sales	$ 23 350 000.00		
Less GST	$ 2 122 515.00		
Less commission	$ 700 500.00	$ 20 526 985.00	$ 20 526 985.00
DEVELOPMENT COST	**Amount**	**Sub-total**	**Total**
Land purchase cost			
Purchase with DA	$ 3 800 000.00	$ 3 800 000.00	
Consultants			
Architect	$ 165 000.00		
Other consultants (incl. in Construction)	$ —	$ 165 000.00	
Council and government			
Application fees etc.	$ 127 600.00	$ 127 600.00	
Management fees			
Development manager	$ 198 000.00		
Project manager	$ 214 500.00	$ 412 500.00	
Construction works			
Design and construct quote			
Constructions (quote attached)			
Inclusive of consultants' fees and			
5% Contingency	$ 12 650 000.00	$ 12 650 000.00	

(continued)

Table 16.3: brown street apartments — prefeasibility study *(cont'd)*

DEVELOPMENT COST	Amount	Sub-total	Total
Legal and capital			
Legal	$ 20 000.00		
Capital raising	$ –	$ 20 000.00	$ 17 175 100.00
Less GST			$ 1 215 796.59
Development cost			$ 15 959 303.41
Borrowing interest			$ 1 031 848.00
Total development cost			**$ 16 991 151.41**
Profit margin			**$ 3 535 833.59**
Total development cost			**$ 16 991 151.41**
Margin on development cost			**20.81%**
Margin on Equity (assume 35%)	**$ 5 946 902.99**		**59.46%**

Conclusion

Whether you decide to be an investor or a developer of residential property you will face an associated risk and reward. The question you have to answer is whether the reward is commensurate with the risk. The choice you make will depend on a number of variables, such as your age, current career, financial position and taxation status. Each individual will have their own special financial and investment goals. For example, an older person nearing retirement may simply be looking for a steady income from renting a property and be not overly concerned with capital growth. A younger, more motivated person may look to capital growth in the shortest space of time and be prepared to take a bigger risk. If you are financially fairly conservative and are looking for a steady income and inflation-related growth, then investing in established buildings is the better option. On the other hand, if you have an entrepreneurial outlook and a goal to increase your net worth in a shorter period, and if you are willing to take risks to achieve this, then developing is the option to follow.

Advantages of investing

The primary goal of most investors is to maximise their total net worth, and the two options available are through income or through capital growth, or at best a combination of the two. Investing in property offers both, as it offers an income through rent and capital appreciation in line with inflation. By investing in an established building, the investor is not haunted by daily operational headaches. Once the purchase is complete, the investor can employ a property manager to attend to the maintenance and tenancy problems while the investor merely ensures that the rent is paid into their account.

Established value — budget blow-outs

When an established building is offered for sale there is usually a bottom-line price. For residential the price is normally determined by current values in the area, whereas for commercial property the current lease in operation is capitalised according to a market-acceptable net return on that specific property sector and location. The guaranteed net rental return gives a degree of comfort to the investor, who is also assured that the property's value will increase with inflation. Once the price is settled between the seller and the investor, the investor is liable only for additional costs such as stamp duty and conveyancing fees. In contrast, when building new, the developer generally knows the fixed price for the land but may find themselves in the situation where, because of unexpected conditions, the final cost of the building blows out beyond the targeted budget. These cost blow-outs could include, for example, additional foundation costs due to poor soil conditions or additional tenant requirements. Or the developer may get carried away and have the best looking building in the area, only to find that they have overcapitalised.

Tangible investing

For new buildings an initial idea or concept is developed into a set of working plans. To most people, reading and visualising the completed building from architectural drawings is a difficult task. With an established building, on the other hand, you can walk through and gain a full appreciation of the layout, spaces and room sizes.

Established tenants

When an established block of apartments is offered for sale, the sale generally recognises the tenants and leases in place. When you develop a new property, on the other hand, the rental return can be evaluated only when the building has been completed and fully leased, and this can take a number of months.

Immediate returns

With leases and tenants in place, an investor is assured an immediate return on the money invested once the property is settled and money transferred to the seller. With new developments there are also the costs of drawing up new leases, finding tenants and paying commissions to brokers for finding tenants, and on top of this some units may be left vacant for a period of time.

Risk with contractors

Disputes with builders can delay the completion of a development project, which increases a developer's holding cost, thus reducing their profit. The reports of unscrupulous builders we hear about from various media sources are enough to make many people shy away from tackling a new development, but not all builders are dishonest. Most often the worst that can happen with a new development is that the builder goes bankrupt halfway through the contract. This will cost the developer dearly in loss of rental and the added cost of finding a new contractor to complete the building, normally at a price higher than that of the liquidated contractor.

Ease of financing

Lenders financing either residential or commercial properties will look at established buildings more favourably than a new development. This is because existing buildings have a financial history so there are not so many unknown factors as with new developments. Some lenders will not consider any financing on new developments without significant pre-sales.

Established location

When buying a residential building an astute investor will choose to buy in an established area rather than newer locations. The reasons are simple. For example, an older residential building located in an established neighbourhood will have good access to shopping, schools, community centres and transport systems, which appeals to potential tenants. In contrast, new residential developments in younger suburbs need time for these required features to be developed.

Advantages of developing

Property development is all about adding value, whereas property investors are content to buy a property and wait until the market and economic forces provide them with capital growth. In today's economic climate of low inflation and relatively modest property growth rates in most areas, many investors have taken a more proactive approach and have become small-time developers, adding value to their properties by building, refurbishing, rezoning, extending or subdividing.

Free equity

Property developments offer a number of opportunities to build up your net worth in a short space of time. If you have done your research and you are a good negotiator, there is always an opportunity to purchase developable land at a good price and to negotiate a building contract at discounted rates. Experienced developers know how to save money, and a number will invest their own sweat to undertake certain aspects of the project themselves. They charge the project for these services but may choose not to withdraw the money from the project, instead leaving their fees as part of their equity. This can include development fees, marketing fees and leasing fees, for example. In this way they are creating 'free equity'.

Design to suit present market trends

With advances in digital technology and growing environmental concerns, developers and their architects constantly have to find new concepts incorporating these new elements into their buildings. Like the fashion industry, architectural trends and building materials are constantly changing to adapt to consumer taste and changes. Some older, established buildings look tired and may be outdated in terms of their function. Some investment properties may outlive the market needs in terms of function and architectural style, with the risk that they will lose their tenants to new and modern developments.

Stimulating

Successful developers are visionaries and entrepreneurs, always thinking about and creating new development ideas. Together with their development team they will select the best of these concepts and work on them until they come to fruition. Watching their plans unfold as the architect gives them form, selecting their own finishes and watching the various stages of construction, seeing their dream coming to life, is an exhilarating and stimulating experience. The same cannot be said of purchasing an established building. Here the excitement is more limited, focused mainly on renovating and improving the spaces and finishes to suit the present market.

Longer lifespan

All older buildings suffer wear and tear and will require maintenance. Before buying an older building, an investor may need to engage the services of a building consultant or architect to seek out any structural defects, electrical faults, roof leaks and so on. If purchasing existing buildings, the investor needs to set aside funds for long-term maintenance, for example for new paintwork or new air-conditioning plant. A younger building constructed to quality standards should require less maintenance over the short period.

Tax benefits

The Australian Taxation Office allows investors in buildings a depreciation allowance, which is the proportion of the cost, or the book value of a building, that may be deducted annually as a legitimate expense and is normally determined by the original cost of the building set against the life of the building. At the time of writing, the allowance is 2.5 per cent over 40 years. This allowance, like negative gearing, is offset against the investor's personal income but applies only if the property is registered in the investor's own name. These tax write-off benefits have a longer lifespan for new buildings than for older ones.

All new properties for sale are subject to the goods and services tax (GST). If, therefore, you embark on a new development project every year, or if your annual income on developments exceeds $100 000, you will be liable to register as a GST vendor and to add the GST amount onto the sale of your building(s). In addition, all goods or services with GST supplied to the development can be offset against the project. Therefore any GST applied to building materials, building contracts or professional fees can be claimed against the development, which can add up to close to the total development cost. With older, established buildings there is normally no

GST applied to the sale unless the seller is registered as a vendor, and the investor cannot claim the GST unless registered as a GST vendor.

Less upfront capital required

With most property transactions that are financed a deposit or similar equity is required, and this is generally around 20 per cent or more. With a new development the deposit is required mainly when purchasing the land, which is lower in price than an established building that includes both land and buildings. There are additional incidental costs such as stamp duty and conveyancing fees, which are usually higher in a completed development.

Social and community benefits

A property developer who contributes to the community by designing and building a project that complements the social and historical setting of the community will always be recognised for their efforts. Being sensitive to the surrounding neighbourhood, traffic patterns and environmental issues, and incorporating materials and designs that are sympathetic to the area, will raise the developer's profile and credibility, which will ensure that more opportunities will be offered to them.

The decision

The decision whether to invest in an established building or to develop your own will be a personal one and will depend on factors outlined above and throughout this book. If you are prepared to go through the processes of negotiating land deals, working out the design with your architect, selecting and negotiating with a builder, and experiencing a certain amount of stress during construction, there is nothing to beat the excitement and stimulation of creating a new development.

Whether you choose to be an investor or a developer, always look at all the options when offered a development property opportunity. Making the most of real estate opportunities seems to be part art, part science, combining intuitive and quantitative elements. Most investors and developers in this sector seem to follow the latter path in an effort to leave as little as possible to chance.

Index

Connect
with WILEY ▶▶▶

WILEY
Browse and purchase the full range of Wiley publications on our official website.

www.wiley.com

Check out the Wiley blog for news, articles and information from Wiley and our authors.

www.wileybizaus.com

Join the conversation on Twitter and keep up to date on the latest news and events in business.

@WileyBizAus

Sign up for Wiley newsletters to learn about our latest publications, upcoming events and conferences, and discounts available to our customers.

www.wiley.com/email

Wiley titles are also produced in e-book formats. Available from all good retailers.

WILEY

Learn more with practical advice from our experts

Wrightbooks

SMSF DIY Guide
Sam Henderson

The One-Page Financial Plan
Sam Henderson

The Real Deal
Brendan Kelly and Simon Buckingham

Your Property Success with Renovation
Jane Slack-Smith

Property and Taxation
Jimmy B. Prince

Find the Right Property, Buy at the Right Price
Melissa Opie

Property Rich
Melissa Opie and Stephen Zamykal

Property vs Shares
Peter Koulizos and Zac Zacharia

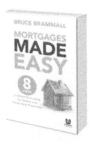

Mortgages Made Easy
Bruce Brammall

Available in print and e-book formats

Printed and bound by CPI Group (UK) Ltd, Croydon, CR0 4YY

07/03/2023

03198958-0003